THE HEALING
EXPERIENCE

Readings on the Social Context of Health Care

William Kornblum

City University of New York,
Graduate School and University Center

Carolyn D. Smith

PRENTICE HALL, *Englewood Cliffs, New Jersey 07632*

Library of Congress Cataloging-in-Publication Data

KORNBLUM, WILLIAM.
    The healing experience : readings on the social context of health
care / William Kornblum, Carolyn D. Smith.
        p.   cm.
    Includes index.
    ISBN 0–13–501040–3
    1. Social medicine.   I. Smith, Carolyn D.   II. Title.
RA418.K66   1994
    306.4' 61—dc20
                                                    93–29810
                                                       CIP

Acquisitions editor: Nancy Roberts
Editorial/production supervision: Janis Paris
Copy editor: Carole R. Crouse
Cover designer: Ray Lundgren Graphics, Ltd.
Production coordinator: Mary Ann Gloriande
Editorial assistant: Pat Naturale

 ©1994 by Prentice-Hall, Inc.
A Paramount Communications Company
Englewood Cliffs, New Jersey 07632

Printed in the United States of America

10   9   8   7   6   5   4   3   2   1

ISBN 0-13-501040-3

PRENTICE-HALL INTERNATIONAL (UK) LIMITED, *London*
PRENTICE-HALL OF AUSTRALIA PTY. LIMITED, *Sydney*
PRENTICE-HALL CANADA INC., *Toronto*
PRENTICE-HALL HISPANOAMERICANA, S.A., *Mexico*
PRENTICE-HALL OF INDIA PRIVATE LIMITED, *New Delhi*
PRENTICE-HALL OF JAPAN, INC., *Tokyo*
SIMON & SCHUSTER ASIA PTE. LTD., *Singapore*
EDITORA PRENTICE-HALL DO BRASIL, LTDA., *Rio de Janeiro*

To Drs. Richard Berkowitz and Sidney Wolfe
and the road not taken

CONTENTS

HEALERS AND PATIENTS

HEALING AND WOMEN

HEALING AND OUTSIDERS

RE-CREATING HEALING INSTITUTIONS

FOREWORD

Samuel W. Bloom, Ph.D.

The Healing Experience is notable not only for the quality and the wide variety of its papers but also because of the social context in which it appears. Medicine, its leaders argue, is going through a major revolution.[1] There is widespread agreement that the sciences basic to medicine are the impelling force behind this revolution. Molecular biology, genetics, communications science, and behavioral science, each separately but in combined force, are revolutionizing medicine in a way that has not occurred since the radical transformation of microbiology in the late nineteenth century. In the wake of that historical event, all aspects of medicine—education, practice, and scientific research—were dramatically changed, together with its major institutions, especially medical schools and hospitals. Now again, it appears that the same kind of revolution is occurring.

The danger of such transforming events is always greatest to the interpersonal relations involved. Thus, over the past 50 years, the developments that began a century ago grew into a degree of high technology and specialization that left both the professionals who serve and the people in need feeling often lost and alienated. As medicine became more and more technically proficient, its human side either deteriorated or could not keep up. Now the same kind of scientific revolution in biology is occurring, apparently with ever increasing speed and intensity. In its wake, the human side of medicine is at risk.

Yet, as *The Healing Experience* documents, there are voices that emerge with messages to balance the professional environment. Each of these readings, whether

Samuel W. Bloom is a professor of sociology and community medicine at Mount Sinai School of Medicine, City University of New York.

in the highly informed and historically grounded voice of Lewis Thomas, correcting myths and arrogances of the profession, or in the lyrical writing of Richard Selzer, brings our vision of the experience of illness and medical treatment into a vivid and human scale.

There is a long, distinguished history of participation by physicians in the arts and especially literature. Jack Peter Green recently chronicled this history, pointing out that "pleas for a more humane, compassionate, empathic medicine have been made for centuries, including pleas by such great clinicians and teachers as Oliver Wendell Holmes, Osler and Peabody."[2] Green cites Rolliston: "To their patients, what are the most scientific physicians if they know all things save the human heart?"[3] Green also reminds us of the versatility of the profession: St. Luke was a physician, as was the man who became Pope John XXI in 1276. Pioneers of science like Copernicus, Linnaeus, and von Helmholtz and a broad range of politicians such as Sun Yat Sen, the first president of the Chinese Republic in 1912, Georges Clemençeau, prime minister of France in 1917, François Duvalier of Haiti, Che Guevara of Cuba, and Salvador Allende of Chile—all were physicians.[4]

Some of the contributions of *The Healing Experience* are by individuals who are widely known, including physicians like Lewis Thomas, Richard Selzer, Robert Coles, and William Carlos Williams, as well as authors like James H. Jones, and sociologists like Renée C. Fox and Richard Titmuss. Others are less widely known but add here unusual and important contributions. All share a deep sympathy and respect for the human individual. Their stories offset the impersonal and sometimes cold impression of the reports of the medical sciences and even of the clinical sciences. Their value, however, should not be read simply as "humanizing." These are highly informative statements that contribute to knowledge no less than any other category of the literature of medicine.

The editors have chosen a strong representation of women who write about the healing experience. In addition to Renée C. Fox, Marcia Millman, Barbara Ehrenreich, Deirdre English, Barbara Katz Rothman, Susan Sheehan, Ruth Macklin, and others are included here. Through their writings, women's perspective on medicine and medical institutions is clearly portrayed.

Medical sociology has a long history. The name is new, but medicine as a social science dates back to the mid-nineteenth century. In 1948, for example, Rudolph Virchow, better known as the father of modern pathology, recognized the importance of both social factors and the social environment in understanding disease.[5] His colleague, Salomon Neumann, studying the influence of poverty and work on the state of health, wrote in 1847:

> Medical science is intrinsically and essentially a social science, and as long as this is not recognized in practice we shall not be able to enjoy its benefits and shall have to be satisfied with an empty shell and a sham."[6]

There followed a promising trend toward collaboration between medicine and social science. Unfortunately the bacteriological revolution of the latter part of the nineteenth century interrupted this shared interest in trying to solve the problems of health and illness. It was not until the end of World War II that a consistent and continuous development occurred in the intellectual activity that is widely known now as medical sociology. *The Healing Experience,* with its focused and highly personal view, adds in important terms to this field.

Virchow embodied that aspect of the history of medicine in which the physician, as physician, takes the role of public benefactor. In modern Western medicine today, all the various possible roles of the physician are assigned some place. Recruits to the profession have a choice to focus their activities in a primary role, as healer, physician-scientist, or public benefactor. At the same time, the society changes as one or more aspects of a profession press for emphasis by adding or subtracting the allocation of public resources. *The Healing Experience* is an expression of medicine in the role of public benefactor. It appears in a period of history when the society's emphasis has been on medicine as science, with the consequence that research and the highly developed technology of specialized clinical medicine have been elevated to primacy in the agenda of the profession. The contributors to *The Healing Experience* serve admirably to remind us that medicine is also a profession with human and social responsibility. But, as this book also reminds us, benefaction is not without risks. Medicine, even when motivated to contribute only benefit to individuals and society, is not always even-handed. McCord and Freeman tell us how being black and living in the urban ghetto involves health costs. Being a Native American is no better, as Kane and Kane document in assessing medical care on the Indian reservation.

The role of the physician has always been plagued by the dualism of matter and spirit. Too often, when physicians venture into the realm of benefaction, they are looked upon as worthy but "soft." Although Hippocrates, the so-called father of modern Western medicine, was himself an early (third century B.C.) model of the physician as public benefactor, it was not until the mid-nineteenth century that this side of the role of the physician was to find its full expression. Only then did a genuine public health movement occur, but when it did, it emerged as secondary rather than a specialization of the first rank. I am not speaking here about the importance of the contributions of public health and community medicine to modern medicine, but rather about the reputation and support that prevails within the profession itself. From antiquity, Western European societies have been dominated by a search for both knowledge and healing skills that focused on human biology. In the prevailing dualism of the body and the soul, the body was the domain of the physician and the remainder of the human experience the province of the philosopher or the priest. *The Healing Experience* attempts to show how this dualism can be avoided, but its pages also testify to its persistence.

Finally, I must speak about my joy in seeing Richard Titmuss included here. I will not try to summarize his superb statement, except to recommend it as an example of his humanity and intelligence. But I feel compelled to say that this man, who is clearly a pioneer and an inspirational figure in modern medical sociology, is neglected and often unknown to Americans. This is not true in his native Britain, where both during his lifetime and after, he was recognized and honored. This book would not be complete without his work being included.

The final section of *The Healing Experience* brings the discussion full circle to issues of policy. Above all, this book is a pleasure to read as a sample of how a variety of physicians, writers, and social scientists perceive and experience problems of health and illness. It is also a valuable source book for those who seek a humanized view of medicine and its world.

NOTES

1. See the final report of The Robert Wood Johnson Commission on Medical Education: The Sciences of Medical Practice, ed. Robert Q. Marston and Roseann M. Jones. 1992. *Medical Education in Transition*. Princeton N.J.: The Robert Wood Johnson Foundation. Also the W. K. Kellogg Foundation, "Community Partnerships with Health Professions Education"; The Charles E. Culpepper Foundation, with the Association of American Medical Schools, "Assessing Change in Medical Education: The Road to Implementation," *Academic Medicine,* Vol. 68, No. 6, Supplement; and The Pew Health Professions Commission, "Healthy America: Practitioners for 2005."

2. Jack Peter Green, "Physicians Practicing Other Occupations, Especially Literature," *The Mount Sinai Journal of Medicine,* Vol. 60, No. 2, 2 March 1993.

3. H. Rolliston, "Some Worthies of the Cambridge Medical School," *Annals of Medical History,* 1926; 8: 331–346.

4. Green, "Physicians Practicing Other Occupations," p. 132.

5. See Samuel W. Bloom and Edward J. Speedling. 1989. "The Education of Physicians: Training for What?" in P. Saladin, H. J. Schaufelberger, and P. Schlappi, editors. *"Medizin" für die Medizin.* Basel: Helbing & Lichtenhahn, p. 108.

6. George Rosen, 1974. *From Medical Police to Social Medicine: Essays on the History of Health Care.* New York: Science History Publications, p. 63.

PREFACE

This book is about the experience of healing and being healed, for better and worse, in modern medical institutions. Some of the selections included here also deal with the improvement or, in a sense, the healing of those institutions themselves. Most of the essays were written by authorities in the fields of medicine, medical sociology, and medical ethics. They are, for the most part, well-known contributions to contemporary discussions of medical practice and medical sociology. A few, however, are being published for the first time in this volume.

Our aim in selecting these essays from the rich literature about medical practice was to provide students of medical sociology and related fields with a sample of writing about the first-hand experiences of people working and being cared for in healing institutions. By bringing the reader closer to those experiences, these essays give a human face to many of the issues facing medical institutions today. The challenges involved in improving healing institutions become clearer when the statistics of success and failure, cost and benefit, are accompanied by insights into the daily struggles of real people. The picture of modern medicine offered here is not always favorable, but the strengths and limitations of the people involved are evident.

We have attempted to include a range of selections that represent several perspectives on the healing experience. The first set of readings takes a long view of healing institutions and introduces the book's phenomenological theme through the essays by Freidson and Baron. These are followed by several selections that vividly portray the thoughts and feelings of medical practitioners and patients. Issues related to health care for women are the focus of selections by Ehrenreich and English, Stockton, and Katz Rothman; these are followed by several essays presenting the perspective of minority groups and other "outsiders." The selections in the final section present a variety of views on medical ethics and the reform of healing institutions.

Throughout this project we benefited greatly from the advice and counsel of colleagues in the Medical Sociology Program of the City University of New York Graduate School. Professors Judith Lorber, Barbara Katz Rothman, and Samuel Bloom suggested readings for review and graciously shared their knowledge of the medical sociological literature (in the broadest definition of that exciting field). Two of the entries in this book—those by Ayala and Deierlein—are based on medical-sociological research carried out at the CUNY Graduate Center. Original inspirations for the project came from the writing of William Carlos Williams, Robert Coles, Lewis Thomas, and Richard Titmuss. Reviewers Paul Brezina, County College of Morris, and Daniel J. Klenow, North Dakota State University, offered helpful suggestions.

The project was made possible in large part by Nancy Roberts, sociology editor at Prentice Hall. Over many years of working with Nancy we have learned to greatly value her ability to steer book projects past the many obstacles they inevitably face. We also wish to thank Joan Stone, production coordinator, and Janis Paris for their careful and thoughtful editorial assistance, and Michael McSpedon for his research efforts.

William Kornblum
Carolyn D. Smith

1

MEDICAL LESSONS
FROM HISTORY

Lewis Thomas

Lewis Thomas, former chancellor of Sloan Kettering Memorial Hospital, is among the nation's foremost medical essayists. In this selection he shows that medicine's ability to actually heal the patient dates from relatively recent times. Many people alive today can remember a time when medicine was incapable of curing the most common illnesses. Millions of people died of pneumonia, infections of the respiratory system, and the infectious diseases of childhood. The germ theory of disease, which established the role of single-celled parasites, bacteria, and eventually viruses in the spread of many diseases, brought about a medical revolution, which Thomas describes as both a witness and a participant.

The optimism voiced by Thomas regarding continuing advances in medical science dates from before the AIDS epidemic, which has humbled contemporary medical researchers and doctors. But despite the frustration of efforts to find a cure for AIDS, medicine will never return to the dark period of superstition described here. Nor does the AIDS epidemic give reason to reject the belief that science will continue to unlock the secrets that can relieve human suffering. Still, the complexity of AIDS and other serious illnesses makes it even more important to learn about what medicine was like before doctors could actually heal most infections.

More than most doctors alive today, Thomas knows how young the science of medicine actually is. In this essay he uses this knowledge to gently remind doctors and patients alike that the source of much healing has always been the human body itself.

It is customary to place the date for the beginnings of modern medicine somewhere in the mid-1930s, with the entry of sulfonamides and penicillin into the pharmacopoeia, and it is usual to ascribe to these events the force of a revolution in medical practice. This is what things seemed like at the time. Medicine was upheaved, revolutionized indeed. Therapy had been discovered for great numbers of patients whose illnesses had previously been untreatable. Cures were now available. As we saw it then, it seemed a totally new world. Doctors could now *cure* disease, and this was astonishing, most of all to the doctors themselves.

It was, no doubt about it, a major occurrence in medicine, and a triumph for biological science applied to medicine but perhaps not a revolution after all, looking back from this distance. For the real revolution in medicine, which set the stage for antibiotics and whatever else we have in the way of effective therapy today, had already occurred one hundred years before penicillin. It did not begin with the introduction of science into medicine. That came years later. Like a good many revolutions, this one began with the destruction of dogma. It was discovered, sometime in the 1830s, that the greater part of medicine was nonsense.

The history of medicine has never been a particularly attractive subject in medical education, and one reason for this is that it is so unrelievedly deplorable a story. For century after century, all the way into the remote millennia of its origins, medicine got along by sheer guesswork and the crudest sort of empiricism. It is hard to conceive of a less scientific enterprise among human endeavors. Virtually anything that could be thought up for the treatment of disease was tried out at one time or another, and, once tried, lasted decades or even centuries before being given up. It was, in retrospect, the most frivolous and irresponsible kind of human experimentation, based on nothing but trial and error, and usually resulting in precisely that sequence. Bleeding, purging, cupping, the administration of infusions of every known plant, solutions of every known metal, every conceivable diet including total fasting, most of these based on the weirdest imaginings about the cause of disease, concocted out of nothing but thin air—this was the heritage of medicine up until a little over a century ago. It is astounding that the profession survived so long, and got away with so much with so little outcry. Almost everyone seems to have been taken in. Evidently one had to be a born skeptic, like Montaigne, to see through the old nonsense; but even Montaigne, who wrote scathingly about the illness caused by doctoring centuries before Ivan Illich, had little effect. Most people were convinced of the magical powers of medicine and put up with it.

Then, sometime in the early nineteenth century, it was realized by a few of the leading figures in medicine that almost all of the complicated treatments then available for disease did not really work, and the suggestion was made by several courageous physicians, here and abroad, that most of them actually did more harm than good. Simultaneously, the surprising discovery was made that certain diseases were self-limited, got better by themselves, possessed, so to speak, a "natural history." It

Lewis Thomas, "Medical Lessons from History," reprinted by permission of *Daedalus,* Journal of the American Academy of Arts and Sciences, from the issue entitled "Discoveries and Interpretations: Studies in Contemporary Scholarship, Volume I," Summer 1977, Vol. 106, No. 3.

is hard for us now to imagine the magnitude of this discovery and its effect on the practice of medicine. The long habit of medicine, extending back into the distant past, had been to treat everything with something, and it was taken for granted that every disease demanded treatment and might in fact end fatally if not treated. In a sober essay written on this topic in 1876, Professor Edward H. Clarke of Harvard reviewed what he regarded as the major scientific accomplishment of medicine in the preceding fifty years, which consisted of studies proving that patients with typhoid and typhus fever could recover all by themselves, without medical intervention, and often did better for being untreated than when they received the bizarre herbs, heavy metals, and fomentations that were popular at that time. Delirium tremens, a disorder long believed to be fatal in all cases unless subjected to constant and aggressive medical intervention, was observed to subside by itself more readily in patients left untreated, with a substantially improved rate of survival.

Gradually, over the succeeding decades, the traditional therapeutic ritual of medicine was given up, and what came to be called the "art of medicine" emerged to take its place. In retrospect, this art was really the beginning of the science of medicine. It was based on meticulous, objective, even cool observations of sick people. From this endeavor we learned the details of the natural history of illness, so that, for example, it came to be understood that typhoid and typhus were really two entirely separate, unrelated disorders, with quite different causes. Accurate diagnosis became the central purpose and justification for medicine, and as the methods for diagnosis improved, accurate prognosis also became possible, so that patients and their families could be told not only the name of the illness but also, with some reliability, how it was most likely to turn out. By the time this century had begun, these were becoming generally accepted as the principal responsibilities of the physician. In addition, a new kind of much less ambitious and flamboyant therapy began to emerge, termed "supportive treatment" and consisting in large part of plain common sense: good nursing care, appropriate bed rest, a sensible diet, avoidance of traditional nostrums and patent medicine, and a measured degree of trust that nature, in taking its course, would very often bring things to a satisfactory conclusion.

The doctor became a considerably more useful and respected professional. For all his limitations, and despite his inability to do much in the way of preventing or terminating illness, he could be depended on to explain things, to relieve anxieties, and to be on hand. He was trusted as an adviser and guide in difficult times, including the time of dying.

Meanwhile, starting in the last decade of the nineteenth century, the basic science needed for a future science of medicine got under way. The role of bacteria and viruses in illness was discerned, and research on the details of this connection began in earnest. The major pathogenic organisms, most notably the tubercle bacillus and the syphilis spirochete, were recognized for what they were and did. By the late 1930s this research had already paid off; the techniques of active and passive immunization had been worked out for diphtheria, tetanus, lobar pneumonia, and a few other bacterial infections; the taxonomy of infectious disease had become an orderly discipline; and the time was ready for sulfanilamide, penicillin, streptomycin, and all the rest. But it needs emphasizing that it took about fifty years of concentrated effort in basic research to reach this level; if this research had not been done we could not have guessed that streptococci and pneumococci exist, and the search for antibiotics would have made no sense at all. Without the long, painstaking research on the tubercle bacillus, we would still be thinking that tuberculosis was due to night air and we would still be trying to cure it by sunlight.

At that time, after almost a century of modified skepticism about therapy amounting finally to near nihilism, we abruptly entered a new era in which, almost overnight, it became possible with antibiotics to cure outright some of the most common and lethal illnesses of human beings—lobar pneumonia, meningitis, typhoid, typhus, tuberculosis, septicemias of various types. Only the virus diseases lay beyond reach, and even some of these were shortly to come under control—as in poliomyelitis and measles—by new techniques for making vaccines.

These events were simply overwhelming when they occurred. I was a medical student at the time of sulfanilamide and penicillin, and I remember the earliest reaction of flat disbelief concerning such things. We had given up on therapy, a century earlier. With a few exceptions which we regarded as anomalies, such as vitamin B for pellagra, liver extract for pernicious anemia, and insulin for diabetes, we were educated to be skeptical about the treatment of disease. Miliary tuberculosis and subacute bacterial endocarditis were fatal in 100 percent of cases, and we were convinced that the course of master diseases like these could never be changed, not in our lifetime or in any other.

Overnight, we became optimists, enthusiasts. The realization that disease could be turned around by treatment, provided that one knew enough about the underlying mechanism, was a totally new idea just forty years ago.

Most people have forgotten about that time, or are too young to remember it, and tend now to take such things for granted. They were born knowing about antibiotics, or the drugs simply fell by luck into their laps. We need reminding, now more than ever, that the capacity of medicine to deal with infectious disease was not a lucky fluke, nor was it something that happened simply as the result of the passage of time. It was the direct outcome of many years of hard work, done by imaginative and skilled scientists, none of whom had the faintest idea that penicillin and streptomycin lay somewhere in the decades ahead. It was basic science of a very high order, storing up a great mass of interesting knowledge for its own sake, creating, so to speak, a bank of information, ready for drawing on when the time for intelligent use arrived.

For example, it took a great deal of time, and work, before it could be understood that there were such things as hemolytic streptococci, that there were more than forty different serological types of the principal streptococcal species responsible for human disease, and that some of these were responsible for rheumatic fever and valvular heart disease. The bacteriology and immunology had to be done first, over decades, and by the early 1930s the work had progressed just far enough so that the connection between streptococcal infection and rheumatic fever could be perceived.

Not until this information was at hand did it become a certainty that rheumatic fever could be prevented, and with it a large amount of the chief heart disease affecting young people, if only a way could be found to prevent streptococcal infection. Similarly, the identification of the role of pneumococci in lobar pneumonia, of brucellae in undulant fever, typhoid bacilli in typhoid fever, the meningococci in epidemic meningitis, required the sorting out and analysis of what seemed at the time an immensely complicated body of information. Most of the labor in infectious-disease laboratories went into work of this kind in the first third of this century. When it was finished, the scene was ready for antibiotics.

What was not realized then and is not fully realized even now was how difficult it would be to accomplish the same end for the other diseases of man. We still have heart disease, cancer, stroke, schizophrenia, arthritis, kidney failure, cirrhosis, and the degenerative diseases associated with aging. All told, there is a list of around twenty-five major afflictions of man in this country, and a still more formidable list of parasitic, viral, and nutritional diseases in the less developed countries of the world, which make up the unfinished agenda of modern biomedical science.

How does one make plans for science policy with such a list? The quick and easy way is to conclude that these diseases, not yet mastered, are simply beyond our grasp. The thing to do is to settle down with today's versions of science and technology, and make sure that our health-care system is equipped to do the best it can in an imperfect world. The trouble with this approach is that we cannot afford it. The costs are already too high, and they escalate higher each year. Moreover, the measures available are simply not good enough. We cannot go on indefinitely trying to cope with heart disease by open-heart surgery, carried out at formidable expense after the disease has run its destructive course. Nor can we postpone such issues by oversimplifying the problems, which is what we do, in my opinion, by attributing so much of today's chronic and disabling disease to the environment, or to wrong ways of living. The plain fact of the matter is that we do not know enough about the facts of the matter, and we should be more open about our ignorance.

At the same time, and this will have a paradoxical sound, there has never been a period in medicine when the future has looked so bright. There is within medicine, somewhere beneath the pessimism and discouragement resulting from the disarray of the health-care system and its stupendous cost, an undercurrent of almost outrageous optimism about what may lie ahead for the treatment of human disease if we can only keep learning. The scientists who do research on the cardiovascular system are entirely confident that they will soon be working close to the center of things, and they no longer regard the mechanisms of heart disease as impenetrable mysteries. The cancer scientists, for all their public disagreements about how best to organize their research, are in possession of insights into the intimate functioning of normal and neoplastic cells that were unimaginable a few years back. The eukaryotic cell, the cell with a true nucleus, has itself become a laboratory instrument almost as neat and handy as the bacterial cell became in the early 1950s, ready now to be used for elucidating the mechanisms by which genes are switched on or off as developing cells differentiate or, as in the case of cancer cells, dedifferentiate. The ways in which carcinogenic substances, or viruses, or other factors still unrecognized intervene in the regulation of cell behavior represent problems still unsolved, but the problems themselves now appear to be approachable; with what has been learned in the past decade, they can now be worked on.

The neurobiologists can do all sorts of things in their investigation, and the brain is an organ different from what it seemed twenty-five years ago. Far from being an intricate but ultimately simplifiable mass of electronic circuitry governed by wiring diagrams, it now has the aspect of a fundamentally endocrine tissue, in which the essential reactions, the internal traffic of nerve impulses, are determined by biochemical activators and their suppressors. The technologies available for quantitative study of individual nerve cells are powerful and precise, and the work is now turning toward the functioning of collections of cells, the centers for visual and auditory perception and the like, because work at this level can now be done. It is difficult to think of problems that cannot be studied, ever. The matter of consciousness is argued over, naturally, as a candidate for perpetual unapproachability, but this has more the sound of a philosophical discussion. Nobody has the feeling any longer, as we used to believe, that we can never find out how the brain works.

The immunologists, the molecular biochemists, and the new generation of investigators obsessed with the structure and function of cell membranes have all discovered that they are really working together, along with the geneticists, on a common set of problems: how do cells and tissues become labeled for what they are, what are the forces that govern the orderly development and differentiation of tissues and organs, and how are errors in the process controlled?

There has never been a time like it, and I find it difficult to imagine that this tremendous surge of new information will terminate with nothing more than an understanding of how normal cells and tissues, and organisms, function. I regard it as a certainty that there will be uncovered, at the same time, detailed information concerning the mechanisms of disease.

The record of the past half century has established, I think, two general principles about human disease. First, it is necessary to know a great deal about underlying mechanisms before one can really act effectively; one had to know that the pneumococcus causes lobar pneumonia before one could begin thinking about antibiotics. One did not have to know all the details, not even how the pneumococcus does its damage to the lungs, but one had to know that it was there, and in charge.

Second, for every disease there is a single key mechanism that dominates all others. If one can find it, and then think one's way around it, one can control the disorder. This generalization is harder to prove, and arguable—it is more like a strong hunch than a scientific assertion—but I believe that the record thus far tends to support it. The most complicated, multicell, multitissue, and multiorgan diseases I know of are tertiary syphilis, chronic tuberculosis, and pernicious anemia. In each, there are at least five major organs and tissues involved, and each appears to be affected by a variety of environmental influences. Before they came under scientific appraisal each was thought to be what we now call a "multifactorial" disease, far too complex to allow for any single causative mechanism. And yet, when all the necessary facts were in, it was clear that by simply switching off one thing—the spirochete, the tubercle bacillus, or a single vitamin deficiency—the whole array of disordered and seemingly unrelated pathologic mechanisms could be switched off, at once.

I believe that a prospect something like this is the likelihood for the future of medicine. I have no doubt that there will turn out to be dozens of separate influences that can launch cancer, including all sorts of environmental carcinogens and very likely many sorts of virus, but I think there will turn out to be a single switch at the center of things, there for the finding. I think that schizophrenia will turn out to be a neurochemical disorder, with some central, single chemical event gone wrong. I think there is a single causative agent responsible for rheumatoid arthritis, which has not yet been found. I think that the central vascular abnormalities that launch coronary occlusion and stroke have not yet been glimpsed, but they are there, waiting to be switched on or off.

In short, I believe that the major diseases of human beings have become approachable biological puzzles, ultimately solvable. It follows from this that it is now possible to begin thinking about a human society relatively free of disease. This would surely have been an unthinkable notion a half century ago, and oddly enough it has a rather apocalyptic sound today. What will we do about dying, and about all that population, if such things were to come about? What can we die of, if not disease?

My response is that it would not make all that much difference. We would still age away and wear out, on about the same schedule as today, with the terminal event being more like the sudden disintegration and collapse all at once of Oliver Wendell Holmes's well-known one-hoss shay. The main effect, almost pure benefit it seems to me, would be that we would not be beset and raddled by disease in the last decades of life, as most of us are today. We could become a healthy species, not all that different from the healthy stocks of domestic plants and animals that we already take for granted. Strokes, and senile dementia, and cancer, and arthritis are not natural aspects of the human condition, and we ought to rid ourselves of such impediments as quickly as we can.

There is another argument against this view of the future which needs comment. It is said that we are fundamentally fallible as organisms, prone to failure, and if we succeed in getting rid of one set of ailments there will always be other new diseases, now waiting out in the forest, ready to take their places. I do not know why this is said, for I can see no evidence that such a thing has ever happened. To be sure, we have a higher incidence of chronic illness among older people than we had in the early years of this century, but that is because more of us have survived to become older people. No new disease, so far as I know, has come in to take the place of diptheria, or smallpox, or whooping cough, or poliomyelitis. Nature being inventive, we will probably always have the odd new illness turning up, but not in order to fill out some ordained, predestined quota of human maladies.

Indeed, the official public-health tables of morbidity and mortality seem to be telling us this sort of thing already, even though, in all our anxiety, we seem unwilling to accept the news. We have already become in the Western world, on the record, the healthiest society in the history of humankind. Compared with a century ago, when every family was obliged to count on losing members throughout the early years of life, we are in a new world. A death in a young family has become a rare and dreadful catastrophe, no longer a commonplace event. Our estimated life expectancy, collectively, is longer this year than ever before in history. Part of this general and gradual improvement in health and survival is thanks to sanitary engineering, better housing, and, probably, more affluence, but a substantial part is also attributable, in recent years, to biomedical science. We have not done badly at all, and having begun so well, I see no reason why we should not do even better in the future.

My argument about how to do this will come as no surprise. I say that we must continue doing biomedical research, on about the same scale and scope as in the past twenty years, with expansion and growth of the enterprise being dependent on where new leads seem to be taking us. It is an expensive undertaking, but still it is less than 3 percent of the total annual cost of today's health industry, which at last count was over $140 billion, and it is nothing like as expensive as trying to live with the halfway technologies we are obliged to depend on in medicine today; if we try to stay with these for the rest of the century the costs will go through the ionosphere.

But I should like to insert a qualification in this argument, which may be somewhat more of a surprise, coming from a doctor. I believe that the major research effort, and far and away the greatest investment for the future, must be in the broad area of basic biological science. Here and there, to be sure, there will be opportunities for productive applied science, comparable, say, to the making of polio vaccine or the devising of multidrug therapy for childhood leukemia, but these opportunities will not come often, nor can they be forced into existence before their time. The great need now, for the medicine of the future, is for more information at the most fundamental levels of the living process. We are nowhere near ready for large-scale programs of applied science in medicine, for we do not yet know enough.

Good applied science in medicine, as in physics, requires a high degree of certainty about the basic facts at hand, and especially about their meaning, and we have not yet reached this point for most of medicine. Nor can we predict at this stage, with much confidence, which particular items of new information, from which fields, are the likeliest to be relevant to particular disease problems. In this circumstance there has to be a certain amount of guessing, even gambling, and my own view is that the highest yield for the future will come from whatever fields are generating the most interesting, exciting, and surprising sorts of information, most of all, surprising.

It seems to me that the safest and most prudent of bets to lay money on is surprise. There is a very high probability that whatever astonishes us in biology today will turn out to be usable, and useful, tomorrow. This, I think, is the established record of science itself, over the past two hundred years, and we ought to have more confidence in the process. It worked this way for the beginnings of chemistry; we obtained electricity in this manner; using surprise as a guide, we progressed from Newtonian physics to electromagnetism, to quantum mechanics and contemporary geophysics and cosmology. In biology, evolution and genetics were the earliest big astonishments, but what has been going on in the past quarter century is simply flabbergasting. For medicine, the greatest surprises lie still ahead of us, but they are there, waiting to be discovered or stumbled over, sooner or later.

I am arguing this way from the most practical, down-to-earth, pragmatic point of view. This kind of science is most likely, in the real world, to lead to significant improvements in human health, and at low cost. This is a point worth further emphasis, by the way. When medicine has really succeeded brilliantly in technology, as in immunization, for example, or antibiotics, or nutrition, or endocrine-replacement therapy, so that the therapeutic measures can be directed straight at the underlying disease mechanism and are decisively effective, the cost is likely to be very low indeed. It is when our technologies have to be applied halfway along against the progress of disease, or must be brought in after the fact to shore up the loss of destroyed tissue, that health care becomes enormously expensive. The deeper our understanding of a disease mechanism, the greater are our chances of devising direct and decisive measures to prevent disease, or to turn it around before it is too late.

So much for the practical side of the argument. We need much more basic science for the future of human health, and I will leave the matter there.

But I have one last thing to say about biological science. Even if I should be wrong about some of these predictions, and it turns out that we can blunder our way into treating or preventing one disease or another without understanding the process (which I will not believe until it happens), and if we continue to invest in biological science anyway, we cannot lose. The Congress, in its wisdom, cannot lose. The public cannot lose.

Here is what I have in mind.

These ought to be the best of times for the human mind, but it is not so. All sorts of things seem to be turning out wrong, and the century seems to be slipping through our fingers here at the end, with almost all promises unfulfilled. I cannot begin to guess at all the causes of our cultural sadness, not even the most important ones, but I can think of one thing that is wrong with us and eats away at us: we do not know enough about ourselves. We are ignorant about how we work, about where we fit in, and most of all about the enormous, imponderable system of life in which we are embedded as working parts. We do not really understand nature, at all. We have come along way indeed, but just enough to become conscious of our ignorance. It is not so bad a thing to be totally ignorant; the hard thing is to be part-way along toward real knowledge, far enough to be aware of being ignorant. It is embarrassing and depressing, and it is one of our troubles today.

It is a new experience for all of us. Only two centuries ago we could explain everything about everything, out of pure reason, and now most of that elaborate and harmonious structure has come apart before our eyes. We are *dumb*.

This is, in a certain sense, a health problem after all. For as long as we are bewildered by the mystery of ourselves, and confused by the strangeness of our uncomfortable connection to all the rest of life, and dumbfounded by the inscrutability of our own minds, we cannot be said to be healthy animals in today's world.

We need to know more. To come to realize this is what this seemingly inconclusive century has been all about. We have discovered how to ask important questions, and now we really do need, as an urgent matter, for the sake of our civilization, to obtain some answers. We now know that we cannot do this any longer by searching our minds, for there is not enough there to search, nor can we find the truth by guessing at it or by making up stories for ourselves. We cannot stop where we are, stuck with today's level of understanding, nor can we go back. I do not see that we have a real choice in this, for I can see only the one way ahead. We need science, more and better science, not for its technology, not for leisure, not even for health or longevity, but for the hope of wisdom which our kind of culture must acquire for its survival.

2

DILEMMAS IN THE DOCTOR-PATIENT RELATIONSHIP

Eliot Freidson

Eliot Freidson is among the foremost American medical sociologists. He has done pioneering research on the way doctors and patients view their situation and how those differing perceptions affect the healing experience. In this essay he describes some common types of doctor-patient interactions.

Freidson sees conflict as inherent in "the very nature of professional practice." As the science of medicine continually changes, doctors are able to apply more sophisticated methods to their diagnoses. But in any particular period of medical history, there are areas of knowledge that remain incomplete. Doctors therefore often make decisions about diagnosis and treatment under conditions of uncertainty. Patients, on the other hand, have a strong desire to understand and trust their doctors. When errors occur, that trust is jeopardized, and the patient naturally feels angry and frustrated.

There are also problems arising from more routine aspects of diagnosis and care. Doctors need to recognize patients' symptoms as the signs of an illness. The discomfort or pain experienced by the patient is often less important in making a diagnosis than other symptoms. For the patient, on the other hand, discomfort is often the primary reason for seeking a doctor's care. This disparity between the patient's need for attention to pain and the doctor's need to examine other symptoms can lead to conflict.

Freidson also provides insight into the way differences in social status between doctors and patients can affect the healing relationship. When doctors and patients are similar in status, the doctor-patient relationship is likely to be more conflicted than when doctors have higher status than their patients.

The result of such conflicts, according to Freidson, is that the doctor-patient relationship is forever changing. Doctors seek to accommodate the needs of patients.

> Patients often seek out doctors or healers who can relate to their perceived needs—
> or turn to nonmedical forms of care. The challenge for medical personnel is to learn
> to accommodate the patient's social and physical needs while learning how to ad-
> minister more effective care.

Almost 2500 years ago, the Hippocratic corpus presented doctors' complaints about the nonprofessional criteria that people use to select their physicians (Jones, 1943: II, 67, 281, 311), criticism of patients for insisting on "out of the way and doubtful remedies" (Jones, 1943: I, 317) or on overconventional remedies like "barley water, wine and hydromel" (Jones, 1943: II, 67) and for disobeying the doctor's orders (Jones, 1943: II, 201, 297). The physicians who have left us historical documents largely treat the patient as an obstacle, a problem of "management." From their point of view the patient is very troublesome, full of anxiety, doubt, and fear, insisting upon using his own scanty knowledge to evaluate the practitioner.

The patients who have left us documents often treat the physician as a potential danger to which one must respond cautiously and whom one must always be ready to evade. Patients have circulated stories about the occasions on which they successfully cured themselves or continued to live for a long time in defiance of medical prognoses. This sort of literature may be represented by the Roman "epigram about a doctor Marcus who touched a statue of Zeus, and although Zeus was made of stone he nevertheless died" (Pondoev, 1959: 87), and by Benvenuto Cellini's mild little story:

> I put myself once more under doctor's orders, and attended to their directions, but
> grew always worse. When fever fell upon me, I resolved on having recourse again to the
> wood: but the doctors forbade it, saying that if I took it with the fever on me, I should
> not have a week to live. However, I made my mind up to disobey their orders, observed
> the same diet as I had formerly adopted, and after drinking the decoction four days,
> was wholly rid of fever. . . . After fifty days my health was reestablished. (Cellini, n.d.: 128)

The struggle between physician and patient has continued into modern times. The cases recorded in Paul's volume (Paul & Miller, 1955), in the work of Saunders (1954), Clark (1959), Koos (1954), and in my own study (Freidson, 1961) have indicated that on important occasions patients do not necessarily do what they are told by physicians. They persist in diagnosing and dosing themselves and in assigning heavy weight to lay advice and their own personal dispositions. It is difficult to get them to cooperate wholly with health programs that professionals believe are for their own good (e.g., Cobb et al., 1957).

That the problem continues today is somewhat paradoxical, for it seems unquestionable that the medical practitioner has reached an all-time peak of prestige and authority in the eyes of the public. The physician of today is an essentially new

Reprinted from Eliot Friedson, *Medical Work in America: Essays on Health Care* (New Haven: Yale University Press, 1989). © Yale University Press.

kind of professional whose scientific body of knowledge and occupational freedom are quite recent acquisitions. His knowledge is far more precise and effective than it has ever been, since for the first time in history it could be said that from "'about the year 1910 or 1912 . . . [in the United States] a random patient with a random disease consulting a doctor chosen at random stood better than a 50–50 chance of benefitting from the encounter'" (Gregg, 1956: 13). The physician has obtained unrivaled power to control his own practice and the affairs that impinge upon it, and the patient now has severely limited access to drugs for self-treatment and to nonmedical practitioners for alternative treatment. But the ancient problem continues.

THE CLASH OF PERSPECTIVES

It is my thesis that the separate worlds of experience and reference of the layman and the professional worker are always in potential conflict with each other (cf. Becker, 1953; Merton, 1957). This seems to be inherent in the very situation of professional practice. The practitioner, looking from his professional vantage point, preserves his detachment by seeing the patient as a case to which he applies the general rules and categories learned during his protracted professional training. The client, being personally involved in what happens, feels obliged to try to judge and control what is happening to him. Since he does not have the same perspective as the practitioner, he must judge what is being done to him from other than a professional point of view. While both professional worker and client are theoretically in accord with the end of their relationship—solving the client's problems—the means by which this solution is to be accomplished and the definitions of the problem itself are sources of potential difference.

The very nature of professional practice seems to stimulate the patient on occasion to be especially wary and questioning. Professional knowledge is never complete, and so diagnosis, made with the greatest of care and the best of contemporary skill, may turn out to be inappropriate for any particular case. These mistakes may occur in two basic ways (cf. Hughes, 1958: 88–101).

First of all, it is obvious that in every age, including our own, there are likely to be worthless diagnostic categories and associated treatments—sometimes merely harmless without contributing anything to cure, sometimes downright dangerous. As Shryock put it for an earlier time, "No one will ever know just what impact heroic practice [heavy bleeding and dosing with calomel] had on American vital statistics: therapy was never listed among the causes of death" (Shryock, 1960: 111). In addition, in every age, including our own, there are likely to be diseases unrecognized by contemporary diagnostic categories—as typhoid and typhus were not distinguished before 1820, as gonorrhea and syphilis were once confused, and as mental diseases are no doubt being confused today. Thus, the best, most well-intentioned contemporary knowledge may on occasion be misdirected or false and some of the patient's complaints wrongly ignored.

Second, however, is a considerably more complex source of error that flows not from knowledge so much as from the enterprise of applying knowledge to everyday life. Insofar as knowledge consists in general and objective diagnostic categories by which the physician sorts the concrete signs and complaints confronting him, it follows that work assumes a routine character. This is the routine of classifying the flow of reality into a limited number of categories so that the individual items of that flow become reduced to mere instances of a class, each individual instance being considered the same as every other in its class.

The routine of practice not only makes varied elements of experience equivalent—it also makes them *ordinary*. This seems to be the case particularly in general medical practice. In general medical practice, while the range of complaints may indeed be unusually wide, the number of complaints falling within a rather narrow range seems to be overwhelming. In our day, for example, complaints that are categorized as upper respiratory infections are exceedingly common. Like malaria in the nineteenth century, they are so common that they are considered ordinary. And insofar as they are considered ordinary it is not legitimate for the patient to make a great fuss about the suffering they involve. His subjectively real pain is given little attention or sympathy because it is too ordinary to worry about. His likely response to this may be gauged by reading Dr. Raffel's account of the reception of his complaint of acute sinusitis (Pinner & Miller, 1952: 236–41).

What also happens is that more of reality than proves to be appropriate tends to be subsumed under the ordinary and commonly used categories. This again seems to be in the very nature of professional practice—if *most* patients have upper respiratory infections when they complain of sneezing, sounds in the head, a running nose, and fatigue, then it is probable that it is an upper respiratory infection that is involved when *one* particular person makes the complaint. It may indeed be an allergy or even approaching deafness (Pinner & Miller, 1952: 62–72), but it is not probable—that is to say, it has not commonly been the case in the past. The physician cannot do otherwise than make such assumptions, but by the statistical nature of the case he cannot do otherwise than to be sometimes wrong.

THE PATIENT'S PROBLEM

These problems of diagnosis are not only problems for the doctor but also problems for the patient. All the patient knows is what he feels and what he has heard. He feels terrible, his doctor tells him that there's nothing to worry about, and a friend tells him about someone who felt the same way and dropped dead as he was leaving the consulting room with a clean bill of health. The problem for the patient is determining when the doctor is mistaken. When are subjective sensations so reliable that one should insist on special attention, and when can one reasonably allow them to be waved away as tangential, ordinary, and unimportant? The answer to this question is never definite for any individual case and indeed cannot be resolved decisively except by subsequent events. All of us know of events that have contradicted the judgment of the physician and of course many others that have contradicted the patient.

The situation of consultation thus proves to involve ambiguities that provide grounds for doubt by the patient. Furthermore, those ambiguities are objective. Most reasonable people will agree that the doctor is sometimes wrong, whether by virtue of overlooking the signs that convert an ordinary-appearing case into a special case or by virtue of the deficiencies of the knowledge of his time. He is less often wrong now than he was a hundred years ago, but frequency is not really the problem for the individual. Even if failure occurs once in ten thousand cases, the question for the patient is whether or not it is he who is to be that one case, a question that no one can answer in advance. If the evidence of his senses and the evidence of his knowledge and that of his intimate consultants are contradicted by the physician, the patient may feel it prudent to seek another physician or simply to evade the prescriptions he has already obtained.

THE ROLE OF CONFIDENCE

If it is true that the very practice of medicine, through the process of diagnosis, is permeated with objective uncertainty of which the patient may become aware, it is at least as important to understand why patients do cooperate with doctors as to understand why they do not. One reason seems to be the ignorance of the patient—he may not be aware of or be sensitive to the contingencies of practice. Another reason seems to be the kind of situation with which the patient is confronted—whether it is a crisis situation that motivates him to be sensitive to uncertainties or a routine situation that blunts his sensitivity and attention. There is still another possible reason, however, which, if true, is more strategic than the patient's ignorance or the variable context of consultation. I refer to the special status of the professional in society that (unlike the businessman with his motto, caveat emptor) supposedly entitles him to a priori trust and confidence (Gross, 1958: 78).

The usual conception of confidence seems to be shallow and parochial. It is indeed true that under ordinary circumstances one goes to a doctor assuming that the doctor knows his business and that his judgment may be trusted, but it is no less true of the ordinary use of other services. It is a mistake to assume that the title "profession" confers a kind of expert authority on the practitioner that is greatly different from the authority of any fairly esoteric craftsman. Simmel pointed out some time ago that "our modern life is based to a much larger extent than is usually realized upon the faith in the honesty of the other. . . . We base our gravest decisions on a complex system of conceptions, most of which presuppose the confidence that we will not be betrayed" (Wolff, 1950: 313). Under normal circumstances we have confidence in a mechanic's ability to grease our car properly just as we have confidence in a physician's ability to prescribe the right drug for us and a pharmacist's ability to fill the prescription accurately. In the same fashion we have confidence in a variety of other service workers—appliance repairmen, bank clerks, carpenters, fitting-room tailors, and so on. Faith in the honest applications of specialized ability by a consultant seems to be connected not only with the use of those who are called professionals but also with the use of any kind of consultant whose work is fairly esoteric. Such confidence must exist if life is to function smoothly, routinely.

However, there seems to be a generic distinction in the way the definition of the situation of consultation varies. On the one hand, there is an unthinking and fundamentally superficial sort of confidence that is automatically attached to any routine consultation. It is manifested in uncritical cooperation with the consultant. This sort of confidence sustains the doctor-patient relationship in about the same way it sustains any consultant-client relationship. It appears to waver when the client's expectations are not fulfilled by the consultant and when the problem of consultation comes to be seen as critical (that is, nonroutine) to the patient. Questions arise when the consultant does not act as he is expected to, when the diagnosis seems implausible, when the prescription seems intolerable and unnecessary, and when "cure" is slow or imperceptible. They become pressing when the problem of consultation assumes what seem to be serious proportions. Under such circumstances what is needed to sustain the relationship is at least a different quantity if not a different quality of confidence.

It may be that it is this latter sort of confidence that is in the minds of those who make a special connection between professions and client confidence. Certainly it is true that three of the old, established professions deal with some of the most anxiety-laden topics of existence—the body, the soul, and human relations and property. Plumbing, internal combustion engines, and clothing are not likely to occasion as much anxiety. In this sense doctors, clergymen, and lawyers are more likely to require for their practice a special kind of confidence than are plumbers, mechanics, and fitting-room tailors. But, we may observe, it is precisely this special sort of confidence that is problematic for professions in general and medicine in particular; it is precisely this sort of confidence that does *not* flow automatically from professional status. Routine confidence is automatic but grants no special advantage to the professions. Confidence in crises, however, is demanded but not necessarily obtained by consultants with professional standing.

THE ROLE OF CULTURE

One of the things that breaks routine and thereby suspends routine confidence is an occasion in which the patient's expectations are not met. Instead of prescribing what seems to the patient to be a good sensible remedy like barley water, wine and hydromel, or penicillin, the physician suggests that the patient go on a dietary regimen or simply take aspirin. Obviously, we have in essence a clash of culture or education. The patient's culture leads him to expect what the doctor's culture does not suggest.

Cultural differences between patient and doctor have received a great deal of attention. The tenor of contemporary writings suggests that much patient-doctor conflict can be eliminated by reducing the differences between the two.

Some—particularly those writing about fairly exotic patients who cannot be expected to become "educated" quickly (Mead, 1955)—suggest that the physician should be able to get patients in to see him and to reduce conflict during consultation by adjusting himself to the patient's expectations. If, for example, his prospective patients interpret the professional attitude of detachment and impersonality to be hostile, the doctor should be prepared to behave in a less "professional" and more sociable way (Clark, 1959: 215). On the whole, the recent movement to bring social science into American medical schools seems to share this perspective: by teaching the prospective physician more about "the patient as a person," it is presumed that when he starts to practice he will be better equipped to understand, tolerate, and adjust himself to those expectations of the patient that contradict his own.

But how far can we expect the physician to adjust himself to the patient's lay (and sometimes bizarre) expectations without ceasing to practice modern medicine? There is of course a great practical difference between automatic and rigid compliance to a set of scholastic propositions and a more flexible kind of behavior, and certainly professionals would agree that the latter is likely to produce the better practitioner. But flexibility must remain within limits or it becomes irresponsible. The physician can listen closely to the patient and adjust to him only so far. If his adjustment is too great, the physician must deny the heritage of special knowledge that marks him off as a professional—in effect, he ceases to be a professional. Thus, we may say that some conflict in the physician-patient relationship may indeed be forestalled by educating physicians to be somewhat more understanding and flexible with patients, but that there is a line beyond which the physician cannot go and remain a physician. Some patients' expectations cannot be met.

It might be suggested that at the point where the physician must stop adjusting, the patient must begin. After the physician has accommodated himself to the patient as far as he can, the patient should make all further accommodation if conflict is to be forestalled without destroying medical authority. With the proper health education it is believed that the patient will understand and believe sufficiently in modern medicine to be able to approach his illness from the same perspective as the physician. Thus, *patients* are to be changed so as to conform to the expectations of the doctor.

The relation of health education to the reduction of conflict is, however, by no means clear. As one way of assessing it we might contrast the consequences of two extremes. First, we may ask, what sort of conflict exists when the patient has no health education at all—that is to say, no culturally determined expectations of the doctor. Situations like this are often found in veterinary and pediatric medicine—at least when the parent or owner of the patient does not take a surrogate sick role. Patients in both cases lack any health education. As such, they lack any of the knowledge that would lead them, when ill, to seek a physician. Unassisted, they are likely either to seek a familiar sympathetic person or, like the lion in the fable, lie helpless somewhere waiting for the chance and professionally unqualified kindness of an Androcles. If they should happen to strike upon a treatment situation, they prove incapable of indicating by any but the crudest and largely involuntary means—like a swollen paw and roars of distress—what is wrong with them. Nor can they themselves be counted upon to follow or even to submit to the treatment prescribed; indeed, it often happens that they must be physically restrained to be treated.

It is patent that there are shortcomings in working with patients with no health education at all, but are there any virtues? One is that while the patient may be incapable of illuminating his complaint due to his lack of education, he is also incapable of obscuring it by irrelevancies and misinformation or compounding it by imaginative anticipation. Another is that he has no expectations about treatment, so that once the consultant establishes control there is no contradiction of his authority. Another is that simply by reason of the fact that the patient cannot cooperate it is permissible to use physical restraint, a very convenient device for practice that cannot be used on people who theoretically can but will not cooperate. And finally, apocryphal but worth citing nonetheless, the ignorant client, once won over, may, like Androcles' lion, show undying gratitude and devotion to his healer. If this is true, it is no mean virtue.

However, the virtues of the completely ignorant patient may seem small in the face of the shortcomings. After all, patients who are educated in health affairs will have the knowledge to allow them to recognize symptoms so as to come in to see the doctor in time, to give a useful history, and to cooperate intelligently with treatment. Surely people with the most health education will be more cooperative and will not struggle with the doctor.

It does not seem to be so simple. The physician is the one with the greatest possible health education, but there are good grounds for believing that he is not a very cooperative patient at all. The physician is reputed to be given to a great deal of self-diagnosis and treatment. This follows in part from his advanced health education, which makes him feel competent to diagnose himself "scientifically," and in part, like his susceptibility to drug addiction, from his privileged access to the medication that his self-diagnosis calls for. And when, after the long delay caused by self-diagnosis and treatment, the physician does seek the aid of another, he is reputed to be an argumentative and uncooperative patient incapable of repressing his own opinions in favor of those of his consultant. This too seems to follow from his very health education, for it gives him a "scientific" position in which to stand and counter that of his consultant, and it gives him a clear insight into the uncertainties of practice such that he may feel strongly justified in holding to his own opinion.

This view of physicians as patients is supported only by the plausibility of what is essentially gossip. It is made substantially more credible, however, when we look at the behavior of well-educated middle-class patients. Fairly well versed in modern medicine, they can on occasion cooperate beautifully with the physician, but on occasion they are also quite active in evaluating the physician on the basis of their own knowledge and shopping around for diagnoses or prescriptions consonant with their knowledge. They are more confident and cooperative on a routine basis, perhaps, but they are also more confident of their own ability to judge the physician and dispose themselves accordingly.

Whether health education resolves or encourages conflict in the doctor-patient relationship, then, seems to depend upon the situation. Where the well-educated, acculturated patient's expectations are being met (and they are more likely to be met by a physician than are those of worse-educated patients), his cooperation can be full and intelligent by virtue of the correspondence between his conceptions and those of the doctor. But by the nature of the case, so much of diagnosis and particularly treatment being a matter of opinion even within the profession itself, the patient's expectations will on occasion be violated: here his education is more likely to encourage conflict than to resolve it, for it allows the conflict to be justified by the same authoritative norms as those of the physician himself. A worse-educated patient may be far more manageable.

THE ROLE OF LATENT STATUS

Thus far, the only clear way by which professional authority seems able to sustain itself consistently appears to lie in an at least partial compromise of the *content* of the authority—by taking patients' expectations into account and adjusting practice to them. At the point of adjustment to the patient beyond which professional authority must be sacrificed, however, an additional nonmedical element may work to control the patient without compromise. In political affairs we would call it power; in professional affairs we lack an adequate term but might call it ability to intimidate. This mode of resolving conflict flows not from the expert status of the physician but from the relation of his status in the community to that of his patient.

In the consulting room the physician may be said to have the manifest status of expert consultant and the latent status (cf. Gouldner, 1957) of his prestige in the lay community. His latent status has no necessary relationship to his technical qualification to be an expert but obviously impinges upon his relation to his patients. Indeed, latent status seems crucial for sustaining the force of manifest or professional status, for while many occupations possess expert knowledge, few have been able to control the terms of their work. The established professions, however, have obtained both the political power requisite for controlling the sociolegal framework of practice and the social prestige for controlling the client in consultation. Both the power of the profession and the prestige of the practitioner are quite separate from the "authority" inherent in technical expertness. They seem to be critical conditions for reducing doctor-patient conflict *without* compromising expert knowledge. However, even when professional power and technical expertness are high, the relative prestige of the practitioner varies. It is not a constant. It has varied through history; within any particular society it varies from one practitioner to another; within any particular practice it can vary from one patient to another. What are the consequences of variation in relative latent status for the doctor-patient relationship?

When the physician has had a lower standing than his patient, "more on a footing with the servants" (Eliot, n.d.: 91), he is likely to have to be either complaisant or nimble or both to preserve the relationship. This necessity is clearest in instances in which social standing is accompanied by absolute power and in which the severest result could ensue from failure. For example: "Astragasilde, Queen of France, on her death bed had begged her husband, Gontrano, to throw her doctor out the window immediately after her death, which was done with the greatest punctuality. . . . In the fifteenth century, John XXII burned an unsuccessful physician at Florence and, on this Pope's death, his friends flayed the surgeon who had failed to keep him alive" (Riesman, 1935: 365). Under such circumstances the difficulties of practice according to strictly professional standards must be very great indeed—beyond fear of severe punishment for failure, considerable frustration could be caused by the way a patient of relatively high standing could effectively refuse to cooperate, as the difficulties of Dr. Henry Atkins, physician to Charles, duke of Albany, indicated (Keevil, 1954).

Even today it seems plausible to think that physicians of eminent and powerful men have a trying practice and that their behavior in the presence of superordinate patients will differ considerably from their behavior in the presence of "charity" patients in a hospital outpatient clinic (cf. Turner, 1959: 211). Indeed, Hollingshead and Redlich observed that upper-class

> patients and their families make more demands of psychiatrists than other patients. . . . These patients and their families usually view the physician as middle class. In such relationships the psychiatrist is not in a position to exert social power; he is lucky if he is able to rely on professional techniques successfully. All too often he has to carry out complicated maneuvers vis-à-vis a critical, demanding, sometimes informed, and sometimes very uninformed "VIP." Some VIP's push the physician into the role of lackey or comforter, and some psychiatrists fall into such a role. (Hollingshead & Redlich, 1958: 353)

Obviously, where the relative latent status of the physician is below that of the patient, he is not in a very good position to obtain cooperation. Overt or covert conflict seems likely to ensue.

On the other side we have a situation in which the physician has considerably higher standing than his patient. The most extreme example illustrating this is found in the case of James IV, king of Scotland, who practiced on his subjects. Here, while the physician's behavior might be qualified by his sense of paternalistic or professional responsibility, we should expect that his standing is sufficiently intimidating to the patient that, while the patient is in his hands, he will be in a position to impose the full weight of his professional knowledge. However, in response to his lack of control over his own fate, the patient seems to be inclined to adopt the defense of evasiveness. He may avoid coming in to see the physician in the first place—King James, as a matter of fact, paid his patients a fee to get them into his consulting room—or he may play dumb, listen politely while in the consulting room, and, once outside, ignore the physician's advice. Evasive techniques seem to be very common in instances where the physician is in a position to intimidate his patients. As Simmons has observed: "The deference doctors receive as upper-status persons can easily be mistaken for voluntary respect and confidence. This error could prevent perception of substantial resentments and resistances of patients" (Simmons, 1958: 22).

I have argued that objective differences in perspective between physician and patient and uncertainties inherent in the routine application of knowledge to human affairs make for incipient conflict between patient and physician. Conflict occurs especially when the patient, on the basis of his own lay perspective, tries in some way to control what the physician does to him. It is more likely to occur when the patient defines his illness as potentially critical than when he sees it as minor and ordinary.

There seem to be three ways by which conflict may be forestalled, but each is problematic. The doctor may accommodate to the demands of the patient, but if he should do so extensively he ceases to be the doctor. The patient may be educated in health affairs so as to be more in agreement with the doctor, but education also equips him to be more self-confident and self-assertive in evaluating the doctor's work and seeking to control it. Finally, the physician may attain such relatively high social standing as to gain an extraprofessional source of leverage for controlling the patient, but the patient tends to answer by only superficial cooperation and covert evasiveness.

In the light of these dilemmas it might be asked how it is that medical practice can even persist, let alone grow as much as it has over the past fifty years. Pain and desire for its relief are the basic motives of the patient, and they are not diminished by any of the elements of contradiction in the doctor-patient relationship. The prospective patient will not stop seeking help, but the way these dilemmas are managed will figure in what he seeks help for, when he seeks help, the way in which he seeks help, whom he seeks help from, and how he will behave in consultation. How some of the dilemmas are managed, of course, also involves the physician—his willingness and ability to accommodate to the patient, and the presence of situations in which he must accommodate if he is to keep his practice. They are reflected in the way he tries to deal with the patient. Thus, the doctor-patient relationship is not a constant, as Parsons (1951) seems to imply, but obviously a variable. As I have tried to show elsewhere, systematic differences in the doctor-patient relationship such as Szasz and Hollander (1956) discuss may be seen to flow from historical and situational variability in the strength and content of struggling lay and professional systems.

REFERENCES

BECKER, H. S. 1953. Some contingencies of the professional dance musician's career. *Human Organization* 12:22–26.

CELLINI, B. N.d. *The autobiography of Benvenuto Cellini.* Trans. John A. Symonds. New York: Modern Library.

CLARK, M. 1959. *Health in the Mexican-American community.* Berkeley: University of California Press.

COBB, S., S. KING, and E. CHEN. 1957. Differences between respondents and nonrespondents in a morbidity survey involving clinical examination. *Journal of Chronic Diseases* 6:95–108.

COHEN, J. M., trans. 1957. *The life of Saint Theresa.* Harmondsworth: Penguin Books.

ELIOT, G. N.d. *Middlemarch: A study of provincial life.* New York: A. L. Burt.

FREIDSON, E. 1961. *Patients' views of medical practice.* New York: Russell Sage Foundation.

GOULDNER, A. W. 1957. Cosmopolitans and locals: Toward an analysis of latent social roles—I. *Administrative Science Quarterly* 2:281–86.

GREGG, A. 1956. *Challenges to contemporary medicine.* New York: Columbia University Press.

GROSS, E. 1958. *Work and society.* New York: Thomas Y. Crowell.

HOLLINGSHEAD, A. B., and F. C. REDLICH. 1958. *Social class and mental illness.* New York: John Wiley & Sons.

HUGHES, E. C. 1958. *Men and their work.* New York: Free Press.

JONES, W. H. S., trans. 1943. *Hippocrates.* London: William Heinemann.

KEEVIL, J. J. 1954. The illness of Charles, duke of Albany (Charles I), from 1600 to 1612: An historical case of rickets. *Journal of the History of Medicine and Allied Sciences* 9:410–14.

KOOS, E. L. 1954. *The health of Regionville.* New York: Columbia University Press.

MEAD, M., ed. 1955. *Cultural patterns and technical change.* New York: International Documents Service (UNESCO), Columbia University Press.

MERTON, R. K. 1957. The role-set: Problems in sociological theory. *British Journal of Sociology* 8:106–20.

PARSONS, T. 1951. *The social system.* Glencoe, Ill.: Free Press.

PAUL, B. D., and W. B. MILLER, eds. 1955. *Health, culture and community.* New York: Russell Sage Foundation.

PINNER, M., and B. F. MILLER, eds. 1952. *When doctors are patients.* New York: W. W. Norton.

PONDOEV, G. S. 1959. *Notes of a Soviet doctor.* New York: Consultants Bureau.

RIESMAN, D. 1935. *The story of medicine in the Middle Ages.* New York: Paul B. Hoeber.

SAUNDERS, L. W. 1954. *Cultural differences and medical care.* New York: Russell Sage Foundation.

SHRYOCK, R. H. 1960. *Medicine and society in America.* New York: New York University Press.

SIMMONS, O. G. 1958. Social status and public health. Social Science Research Council Pamphlets, no. 13. New York: Social Science Research Council.

SZASZ, T. S., and M. H. HOLLANDER. 1956. A contribution to the philosophy of medicine. *A.M.A. Archives of Internal Medicine* 97:585–92.

TURNER, E. S. 1959. *Call the doctor.* New York: St. Martin's Press.

WOLFF, K. H., ed. and trans. 1950. *The sociology of George Simmel.* Glencoe, Ill.: Free Press.

3

I CAN'T HEAR YOU WHILE I'M LISTENING

Richard Baron, M.D.

Richard Baron's apt phrase "I can't hear you when I'm listening" is an excellent way of introducing the phenomenological perspective that is central to the view of healing presented in this collection. The problematic aspects of medical practice, as experienced by healers and patients alike, support the central assumption of phenomenology: Situations that people define as real are real in their consequences. This postulate warns us that situations in which medical professionals experience reality in ways that are independent of the biological phenomena involved may have a significant bearing on the way the case is treated. For example, the doctor may be listening to the patient's heart through a stethoscope but is unable to listen simultaneously to the patient's account of the illness and the way it feels. At the same time, situations that patients define as real, such as pain felt in one part of the body that may be referred there by the nervous system from other areas of the body, are just as real to them as pain originating in the part of the body where lesions actually exist.

In the United States and other nations with highly scientific and technological systems for administering medical care, there is a frequent failure to understand what healing options may work for the individual patient. Baron alludes to this problem with respect to the treatment of peptic ulcer. Although invasive options like surgery may be suggested by a particular set of presenting symptoms, if the patient's ulcers are actually diminished by an over-the-counter antacid tablet taken regularly, that medical treatment is sufficient for that patient at that time. Similarly, if patients cannot medicate themselves consistently and doctors do not pay attention to this problem, the best diagnosis and treatment plan will have little effect on the actual course of the illness. These are only a few of the arguments Baron presents to show why the phenomenological viewpoint can be valuable in enhancing the efficacy of the healing experience.

A great gulf exists between the way we think about disease as physicians and the way we experience it as people. Much of this separation derives directly from our basic assumptions about what illness is. Our medical world view is rooted in an anatomicopathologic view of disease that precludes a rigorous understanding of the experience of illness. What we need to remedy this problem is not just the admonition to remember that our patients are people, but a radical restructuring of what we take disease to be. The philosophic discipline of phenomenology is used to present a vision of disease that begins with an understanding of illness as it is lived. "Nonmedical" descriptions of illness show how we can reorient our thinking to encompass both our traditional paradigm and one that takes human experience as seriously as it takes anatomy.

It happened the other morning on rounds, as it often does, that while I was carefully auscultating a patient's chest, he began to ask me a question. "Quiet," I said, "I can't hear you while I'm listening." This typical physician-patient encounter is emblematic of a deep confusion in clinical medicine today, a confusion that seems to arise from the roots of our medical conceptualization. It is as if physicians and patients have come to inhabit different universes, and medicine, rather than being a bridge between us, has become one of the major forces keeping us apart.

This article examines some of our intellectual presuppositions and their implications in a few paradoxes of everyday practice. It also defines and describes an emerging discipline, medical phenomenology, which offers a systematic approach to our dilemma and may provide us the tools we need to rediscover and realize the human goals of medicine. I cite some examples of successful phenomenologic work and indicate directions that I believe will be fruitful for future endeavors. This brief review is not a comprehensive survey of all work in the field. It is intended rather as an introduction, written by one who is engaged in fulltime practice, designed to stimulate thought among other practitioners and to open up for further consideration a literature and a way of thinking not generally considered to be medical, but believed by this author to be at the very center of our work.

THE INTELLECTUAL BASIS OF MEDICAL PRACTICE

In general, modern medicine takes disease to be an anatomicopathologic fact. We tend to see illness as an objective entity that is located somewhere anatomically or that perturbs a defined physiologic process. In a profound sense, we say that such an entity "is" the disease, thus taking illness from the universe of experience and moving it to a location in the physical world. We use object words to describe illness—lesion, tumor, infiltrate—and rely on pathologists reviewing disembodied

R. J. Baron, "An Introduction to Medical Phenomenology: I Can't Hear You While I'm Listening," Perspective, *Annals of Internal Medicine,* 103, no. 4 (1985):606–611.

tissue to define disease for us. We devote regular space in journals and great academic resources to the clinicopathologic conference, which postulates that a clinical puzzle is "solved" by a review of the anatomic facts. Clearly, much has been gained by this approach. It is our heritage and must not be frivolously denied. But has not something been lost? Having worked so hard to objectify illness, do we not have trouble confronting the fullness of the human context in which illness occurs? Have we not, in some consequential way, made disease our focus instead of sick people?

As an example of the limitations of our current vision and how blind we are in practice to these limitations, consider modern views of the disease category peptic ulcer. If one reviews comprehensive nosographies of the late 18th and early 19th centuries, one does not find gastric ulcer as a disease; instead one finds a variety of terms used to categorize a situation that we might call peptic ulcer disease. These include gastritis (which is defined in terms of pain and vomiting rather than pathologically), pyrosis, colica, gastrodynia, *dolorosi intrinseci gastrica,* dyspepsia, and even pain in the stomach. One nosology from 1823[1] even gives a thorough case description of a young woman with severe abdominal pain who was found at postmortem examination to have what we would call a perforated gastric ulcer. This case is classified as *gastritis adhaesiva,* defined as "inflammation of the stomach . . . pain very acute: fever violent." One can see that the disease was defined by its symptoms, not its anatomy. Not until the 1830s did the French physician Jean Cruveilhier publish his *Anatomie pathologique du corps humain*[2] and describe "simple chronic ulcer of the stomach," a finding that, he said, "does not appear to me to have attracted the attention of observers as a special disease." Peptic ulcer was thus born as a disease entity, an objective finding at postmortem that was thought to correlate with complaints made by patients.

The evolution of thought about peptic ulcer disease is characteristic of the general intellectual current of the mid-19th century. Under the influence of the German school of physiologic medicine (made up of Wunderlich, Virchow, Helmholtz, and others), anatomic pathology and pathologic physiology came to be seen as the focus of clinical medicine:[3]

> The ideal which we shall strive to realize, as far as it is in our power, is, that practical medicine shall become applied theoretical medicine, and that theoretical medicine shall become pathological physiology. Pathological anatomy and clinical medicine, the justness and independence of which we fully recognize, are essential to us as sources of new questions, the answering of which will fall to pathological physiology.

Clinical medicine is thus seen as a source of questions to be addressed by a higher discipline, pathologic physiology. Increasingly, the theoretical orientation of pathologic physiology became the ordering principle of clinical medicine. The history of our concept of peptic ulcer disease is exemplary of this process.

The anatomic reality of the ulcer was the engine for the development of a series of techniques, and the ulcer itself came to define the disease rather than the complaints made by patients. Various efforts were made to visualize the ulcer in living persons. Contrast radiography, rigid gastroscopy, and, in our own day, the flexible endoscope are all designed to "see" the disease of abdominal discomfort (or to categorize anatomically a family of diseases of discomfort).

Peptic ulcer disease has been the subject of intense clinical and basic science research, both as to pathophysiology (the perturbation of normal physiology that leads to the anatomic fact) and as to treatment (what interventions cause the anatomic fact to disappear). Yet a major study of ulcer treatment reported in *The New England Journal of Medicine*[4] revealed a surprising finding: the anatomic fact could not be correlated with the patient's complaint. When ulcer patients were asked to record symptom scores, these bore essentially no relationship to endoscopic findings: "Fifty-five percent of patients whose ulcers were unhealed after four weeks, regardless of treatment group, became asymptomatic during the course of treatment." Furthermore, 12 of 45 patients whose ulcer had healed endoscopically continued to have some ulcer symptoms. These findings led the authors to comment that "presence or absence of symptoms during the fourth treatment week was a poor predictor of presence or absence of an ulcer crater." This study is frequently cited as establishing the equal efficacy of antacids and cimetidine in the treatment of peptic ulcer disease. It has recently been cited in an article questioning the efficacy of medical treatment for ulcer.[5] Other investigators have duplicated these curious findings;[6] yet our commitment to the disease category peptic ulcer is undiminished.

The idea of the ulcer is so powerfully established in our medical consciousness that a recent review of the use of diagnostic procedures in gastrointestinal (GI) hemorrhage[7] has recommended "early endoscopy especially in upper GI bleeding, if the gastrointestinal lumen can be cleared of blood." This recommendation was made despite two prospective randomized controlled studies,[8,9] both cited in the article, that have shown no benefit to this approach. Our attachment to the anatomicopathologic fact of the ulcer persists despite solid clinical evidence that "seeing" the ulcer does not change the clinical outcome. Clearly, we are fascinated with disembodied anatomic realities, even when we have substantial reason to believe that they relate less and less to what bothers our patients or what ultimately happens to our patients.

The medical technology in which we take so much pride begins to take on a life and reality of its own. As Reiser[10] has argued so persuasively, a technologic capability in medicine becomes not just a better way to diagnose disease, it comes to define disease. Diseases become wedded to and are created by the technology that "diagnoses" them (for example, mitral valve prolapse and echocardiography; angina and coronary angiography; peptic ulcer and endoscopy). What occurs is a shift in focus from the human experience of illness to various technologic facts of disease. One can see this process in our current thinking about diabetes. Whereas the earliest descriptions of the illness dealt with experiential aspects, defining it as "a melting down of the flesh and limbs into urine,"[11] the modern definition focuses on the fact of elevated blood sugar levels. Our initial enthusiasm for insulin derived from the idea that because insulin controlled blood sugar levels, it therefore "cured" diabetes. Although we have learned diabetes is not quite that simple, we still regularly ask patients to alter dietary habits completely, stick their fingers four times a day, and inject themselves frequently with insulin, all to achieve a "tight" control, the value of which even experts debate.

What I wish to emphasize is not the correct management of gastrointestinal bleeding or diabetes. Rather, I wish to show that by taking disease to be an anatomic or technologic fact, we are led further away from any ability to understand disease in human terms. In the above instances, our understanding of disease derives not from anything intuitive or anything the patient tells us, but rather from a reification of our model of the disease. Our understanding of the nature of disease is limited by our model, and entire aspects of the phenomenon of illness remain inaccessible or incomprehensible to us. We seem to have a great deal of difficulty taking seriously any human suffering that cannot be directly related to an anatomic or pathophysiologic derangement. It is as if this suffering had a value inferior to that associated with "real disease." If anyone doubts this, let him consider our attitude towards such diagnostic entities as irritable bowel syndrome or fibromyalgia or hiatus hernia, each of which represents a disease in search of anatomicopathologic facts. In a sense, we seem obliged to remove ourselves from the world of our patients in order to categorize their diseases in a technologic manner. We cannot hear them while we are listening.

How can we as physicians re-enter the world of our patients? How can we train ourselves to listen and hear at the same time? Is there any intellectual system that allows us to take human experience as seriously as we take anatomic pathology?

MEDICAL PHENOMENOLOGY

The modern physician may wonder from time to time what kinship his or her medicine bears with that of an 18th century practitioner using leeches, or a 17th century practitioner using purgatives, or a Hippocratic physician using potions. We act as if such practitioners were but rudimentary versions of ourselves, struggling along as best they could in their ignorance. We believe we are simply better doctors and more knowledgeable, and we credit our superior knowledge to our commitment to scientific medicine. In a sense we are right; we have achieved great medical breakthroughs, such as the treatment of infectious diseases or the development of effective surgical techniques. But these accomplishments are not great in and of themselves. They derive their significance from what they mean for human beings and what effect they have on suffering and individual capability.

Our interest in the human consequences of illness unites us with our predecessors, not our commitment to any particular technologic system. Burton,[12] writing *The Anatomy of Melancholy* in the 17th century, and Kety,[13] writing about the biochemistry of depression in the 1970s, are studying the same human experience from two different poles. What legitimates them both as physicians is the human experience they study rather than the perspective from which they study it. Whereas Kety studies depression as an event taking place "out there" among the molecules, Burton sees melancholia as something that belongs to him, is somehow "in here" among other conscious experiences. Biochemical studies of depression may lead to a greater ability to manipulate depression, but they cannot enlighten us about the nature of our own experience.

As physicians, we need a descriptive structure that takes both poles of intellectual endeavor equally seriously. By believing that the real world is somehow "out there," we see ourselves as merely anatomic and physiologic entities, and we inevitably devalue the world of our experience, drastically limiting our ability to understand ourselves and others as people. We are unable to account for real human experiences such as suffering or pain. If we want to preserve the legitimacy of both approaches to the human dilemma, we need to examine other ways of thinking about our world.

In the early 20th century, a group of philosophers, led by Edmund Husserl and calling themselves phenomenologists, began questioning the philosophical completeness of natural science. They argued that the generally accepted concept of Cartesian dualism, which split the world into minds and bodies, a spiritual world and a physical world, was erroneous. They claimed that this division made it impossible to have a rational spiritual science and created a natural science that was impressive on the surface but that was precluded from helping people truly understand themselves and their world as it is given to them. Husserl[14] wrote of a major crisis in the European sciences that he attributed to the failure of positivist natural science to deal with fundamental human questions:

> The exclusiveness with which the total world view of modern man, in the second half of the nineteenth century, let itself be determined by the positive sciences and be blinded by the "prosperity" they produced, meant an indifferent turning away from the questions which are decisive for a genuine humanity. Merely fact-minded sciences make merely fact-minded people.... In our vital need—so we are told—this science has nothing to say to us. It excludes in principle precisely the questions which man, given over in our unhappy times to the most portentous upheavals, finds the most burning: questions of the meaning or meaninglessness of the whole of this human existence.

Husserl did not mean to gainsay the achievements of modern science; rather, he meant to put those achievements in a more fully human context. As such, phenomenology attempts to examine the ground on which natural science walks. By taking seriously questions about the world as experienced (rather than taking scientific description to be the world of all that is), phenomenologists seek to reunite science with life and to explore the relationship between the abstract world of the sciences and the concrete world of human experience.

Husserl proposed a method of radical questioning, or *epoche,* in which the questioner sets aside all preconceptions and attempts to understand the world as it is given in consciousness rather than as we think about it scientifically. The basic insight offered by phenomenologists is that even the "objective" world is always perceived in consciousness as objective. Instead of trying to study a world of real things in which human thinking and feeling are problematic, the phenomenologist tries to see man's consciousness as necessarily constituting this world. People and their experience are thus put squarely in the center of phenomenologic inquiry. The real world remains, but it loses its dominance over the total world of experience. It is seen as only one aspect of consciousness. The change in world view is analogous to what occurred with the development of relativity theory in physics. Classical physics remained intact, but only as a special case of a more general theory of the physical world. Medicine informed by phenomenology does not forget how to treat depression, but it can still talk seriously about melancholia.

Phenomenologists are acutely aware that words, especially everyday words, carry with them whole universes of philosophic presuppositions. Thus, though it sometimes involves great violence to language, phenomenologists try to be careful about the way that they use common words. So, for example, *body* in phenomenologic terms becomes *embodiment*. This serves to de-emphasize the physical body with its assumed subject-object split and instead to create an understanding of our bodies as they are given to us: agents of our consciousness that are capable of action on the plane of our experience that we have come to call the "physical" world. The difference is subtle yet significant: One view sees the body as a "real object" that is experienced; the other sees the experiencing as primary with "realness" being an aspect of that experience. To take this difference seriously is not to ignore or disparage gross anatomy; it is rather to recognize the limits of anatomic description and, knowing those limits, to continue our research for a more encompassing descriptive system of which gross anatomy would be only a part.

Of what use can all of this obscure language and metaphysics be to practicing physicians? It gives us a way to think about illness that allows us to take suffering as seriously as we take anatomy. It permits us to practice medicine in a way that remains faithful to the human needs that create medicine. As the examples in the preceding section show, our current technologic description of illness offers itself as complete (or, at least, potentially complete) and yet keeps us from being able to see the obvious. As doctors practicing what Pellegrino[15] has called "the most scientific of the humanities and the most humane of the sciences," we find ourselves acutely experiencing the crisis that Husserl described 50 years ago. If we can adopt a phenomenologic perspective, we can try to enter the world of illness as lived by patients rather than confining ourselves to the world of disease as described by physicians.

THE EXPERIENCE OF ILLNESS

Let us attempt, following Husserl's method, to put aside (or "bracket") the way we usually think about illness. For the moment, we will not use microscopes or x-ray machines. We will not think of the body as a machine. I remind you not to forget these skills we have developed so painfully, but to set them aside for the purpose of this discussion. The more we know about medicine in other cultures, or the history of our own medicine, the easier this will be. But imagination, self-knowledge, and the ability to listen to our patients carefully will suffice for this endeavor. We want to address ourselves to the question, What is it like to be ill? Several consistent features emerge.

The experience of illness seems to be intimately related to a sense of disorder, of loss of control, of things not being right with the world. In this sense, illness can be seen as a way of being in the world, as a loss of the familiar that pervades the way things are for someone. Illness is not (except when technologic description is used) necessarily localized to any one place. An obstructed bile duct may cause jaundice and vomiting, but nausea and malaise are ways of being that are not comprehended by knowing the anatomic lesion.

Illness obliges a loss of the taken-for-grantedness of things. Many definitions of health are structured in terms of the absence of disease; health is seen as a state of unselfconscious being that illness shatters. Illness can be described as a split between body and self[16] where the usual effortless, unselfconscious unity of the body and self is disrupted, making one pay explicit attention to the body as suddenly problematic. In this sense the concept of embodiment shows its value. Rather than trying to understand disease as a breakdown of the objectified body machine, a physician tries to approach illness as a disturbance in a person's ability to relate to and function in the world. It is one's embodiment, one's capability of interacting with the universe, that is damaged in the event of illness. Such an understanding permits a more rigorous approach to functional illness. Ultimately, all illness is functional, whether anatomically correlated or not, because illness is seen as a disruption of embodiment rather than as a structural change within the physical body. When the effortless experiencing of embodiment is compromised, one is obliged to deal with one's body as obstacle. Illness is then understood as a loss of the integrity of body and self.

People seek a variety of things when they experience illness: explanation, which reintegrates the experience and makes it feel less disorderly ("You have turned yellow because your bile duct is obstructed"); cure, which at heart is a perfect restoration to the ways things were before and in that sense is always unattainable; and prediction, which expresses the desire to reassert dominion over this fundamental experience of disorder by foretelling what will happen. These goals are ancient goals of medicine. We usually call these diagnosis, treatment, and prognosis, but we should remember that, as we usually use them, we are talking about derivative or secondary goals. Diagnosis for us is categorization (for example, acute promyelocytic leukemia or acute myelomonocytic leukemia), not explanation. Treatment virtually never results in cure, if only because treatment itself usually has an effect on people's lives, altering "the way things were before." Prognosis is always statistical and in that sense rarely tells a particular person what will happen to him or her. If one reminds oneself to take explanation, cure, and prediction seriously as primary goals (and refuses to accept the secondary goals that technologic description substitutes for them, for example, healing the ulcer), one can unite one's self with physicians in history and can help one's patients today—even (perhaps especially) those patients with incurable illness or those whose illnesses have no name, no anatomicopathologic reality.

IMPLICATIONS

A great gulf now exists between the way we think about disease as physicians and the way we experience it as patients.[17] In a sense this gap is unavoidable; research physicians need to objectify what they study, and they have a powerful and successful technologic system with which to work. But practicing physicians need to be aware of the gulf and need to know how to cross it. A phenomenologically informed view of medicine helps us do this, with definite implications for both teaching and practice.

An expanded role for the humanities in medical education is one consequence of such an orientation. The GPEP report, *Physicians for the Twenty-First Century*,[18] has called for this change, but meaningful teaching of the humanities in medical schools will only come from an appreciation of their significance in medicine. Medical phenomenology helps us articulate a major aspect of that significance: Humanities can teach us about the experience of illness in a way that our traditional paradigm does not. In this sense, many works of literature and art can be read as medical treatises that give physicians information absolutely essential to the practice of medicine.

Take, for example, the following account of a patient with a skin disease:[19]

> Oct. 31. I have long been a potter, a bachelor, and a leper. Leprosy is not exactly what I have, but what in the Bible is called leprosy (see Leviticus 13, Exodus 4:6, Luke 5: 12–13) was probably this thing, which has a twisty Greek name it pains me to write. The form of the disease is as follows: spots, plaques, and avalanches of excess skin, manufactured by the dermis through some trifling but persistent error in its metabolic instructions, expand and slowly migrate across the body like lichen on a tombstone. I am silvery, scaly. Puddles of flakes form wherever I rest my flesh. Each morning, I vacuum my bed. My torture is skin deep: there is no pain, not even itching; we lepers live a long time, and are ironically healthy in other respects. Lusty, though we are loathsome to love. Keen-sighted, though we hate to look upon ourselves. The name of the disease, spiritually speaking, is Humiliation.

If you read this and said, "Aha! I know what this man has: psoriasis!", you should ask yourself why you rejected the patient's own diagnosis, humiliation. The vivid contrast between the medical understanding of his disease ("some trifling but persistent error in its metabolic instructions") and the patient's understanding ("torture . . . ironically healthy . . . loathsome . . . Humiliation") is arresting. From the first paragraph of this story, we are confronted with the poverty of medical description. If a dermatologist were to read this story with the same seriousness and attention he devotes to this month's issue of *Cutis,* he would profoundly enrich his comprehension of the phenomenon of skin disease. There is a level on which it does not even matter whether the disease is psoriasis or leprosy; on such a level, one can talk seriously of "Humiliation," even as one decides whether to prescribe dapsone or psoralens with ultraviolet A.

Phenomenology gives a new dimension to the exhortation "Listen to your patients" by instructing us what to listen for. The work of Oliver Sacks illustrates this very well. In this book *Awakenings,*[20] he describes his experience with patients afflicted with postencephalitic parkinsonism when they were given L-dopa in the late 1960s and freed from decades of parkinsonian immobility. Instead of limiting his observations to the number of steps it takes for his patients to turn around, he asks them to use their new-found freedom to describe what it was like for them (and how it is for them now) being parkinsonian. Sacks is able to comprehend many aspects of the frightening and distorted world his patients live in. Consider, for example, his conversation with one patient before she was treated with L-dopa:

> "What are you thinking about Rosie?"
> "Nothing, just nothing."
> "But how can you possibly be thinking of nothing?"
> "It's dead easy, once you know how."
> "How exactly do you think about nothing?"
> "One way is to think about the same thing again and again. Like $2 = 2 = 2 = 2$; or, I am what I am what I am what I am. . . . It's the same thing with my posture. My posture continually leads to itself. Whatever I do or whatever I think leads deeper and deeper into itself. . . . "

Such a dialogue does not supplant our knowledge of alterations in neurotransmitters or in the substantia nigra that occur in parkinsonism, but it forces us to question the completeness of our medical understanding of Parkinson's disease. Because a practicing physician sees people with parkinsonism rather than seeing dopamine receptors or substantia nigras, it would seem that a phenomenologic understanding of this illness would be valuable and even necessary for one who would see patients.

It is striking that many physicians, when writing about their own illnesses, find themselves leaving their traditional medical orientation behind and adopting a distinctly phenomenologic approach. Dr. Max Pinner was a specialist in chest disease and the chief physician at the Montefiore Sanatorium before he was forced into retirement by his own heart disease. In his essay "Chronic Heart Disease,"[21] he talks about keeping his angina a secret from his friends and doctors. He uses words like defeat and shame to describe his experience of illness. It is difficult, after reading his essay, to see angina as a purely anatomic or pathophysiologic event. Though his description begins in an anatomic understanding of his disease, he moves on to encompass a wider, deeper, more human understanding of what illness is.

Finally, a phenomenologically informed view of medicine encourages us to trust our instincts and to be skeptical of technology. Too often we feel that we have to test[22] because we are pursuing a hard anatomic diagnosis. The calculus we use in making these decisions inevitably devalues such real human factors as pain and suffering. Whereas phenomenology will not tell us in any particular instance what is the right decision to make, it allows us to talk without shame or embarrassment about patients' feelings and to take such factors into account with a greater legitimacy.

If we want to practice a medicine that helps us bridge the distance between doctors and patients, we need to have a paradigm that incorporates a fuller understanding of the human predicament. Medical phenomenology can help us subject what we learn about disease as research physicians to the ordering principle of what we already know about illness as human beings. Phenomenologically informed medicine offers a discipline that serves patients, rather than one that they serve. It requires, as a central task of medical practice, that we reconcile scientific understanding with human understanding, using the one to guide the other. We must learn to hear our patients as well as their breath sounds; after all, what are we listening for?

REFERENCES

1. GOOD JM. *A Physiological System of Nosology.* Boston: Wells and Lilly; 1823:140–1.
2. CRUVEILHIER J. Anatomie pathologique du corps humain [1829:42]. In: MAJOR RH. *Classic Descriptions of Disease.* Springfield, Illinois: Charles C Thomas; 1932:594.
3. VIRCHOW R. Archiv I [1847]. In: FABER K. *Nosography in Modern Internal Medicine.* New York: Paul Hoeber; 1923: 67–8.
4. PETERSON WL, STURDEVANT RA, FRANKL HD, et al. Healing of duodenal ulcer with an antacid regimen. *N Engl J Med.*1977;297:141–5.
5. GOLDBERG MA. Medical treatment for peptic ulcer disease: is it truly efficacious? *Am J Med.* 1984;77:589–91.
6. LAURITSEN K, RUNE SJ, BYTZER P, et al. Effect of omparazole and cimetidine on duodenal ulcer: a double-blind comparative trial. *N Engl J Med.* 1985;312:958–61.
7. STEER ML, SILEN W. Diagnostic procedures in gastrointestinal hemorrhage. *N Engl J Med.* 1983;309:646–50.
8. DRONFIELD MW, MCILLMURRAY MB, FERGUSON R, et al. A prospective randomized trial of endoscopy and radiology in acute upper-gastrointestinal tract bleeding. *Lancet.* 1977;1:1167–9.
9. PETERSON WL, BARNETT, CC, SMITH HJ, et al. Routine early endoscopy in upper-gastrointestinal tract bleeding: a randomized controlled trial. *N Engl J Med.* 1981;304:925–9.
10. REISER SJ. *Medicine and the Reign of Technology.* Cambridge, England: Cambridge University Press; 1978.
11. Artaeus the Cappadocian [ca 100 AD]. In: MAJOR R.*Classic Descriptions of Disease.* Springfield, Illinois: Charles C Thomas; 1932:187.
12. BURTON R. *The Anatomy of Melancholy: What It Is, with All the Kinds, Causes, Symptomes, Prognostickes and Severall Cures of It* [1621]. Edited by JACKSON H. New York: Vintage Books; 1977.
13. KETY S. The biological roots of mental illness: their ramifications through cerebral metabolism, synaptic activity, genetics, and the environment. *Harvey Lect.* 1975;71:1–22.
14. HUSSERL E. *The Crisis of European Sciences* [1954]. Translated by Carr D. Evanston, Illinois: Northwestern University Press; 1970:5–6.
15. PELLEGRINO E. *Humanism and the Physician.* Knoxville, Tennessee: University of Tennessee Press; 1979:16.
16. GADOW S. Body and self: a dialectic. In: KESTENBAUM V, ed. *The Humanity of the Ill: Phenomenological Perspectives.* Knoxville, Tennessee: University of Tennessee Press; 1982:86–100.
17. BARON RJ. Clinical distance: an empathic rediscovery of the known. *J Med Philos.* 1981;6:3–21.
18. ·PHYSICIANS FOR THE TWENTY-FIRST CENTURY. Report of the Panel on the General Professional Education of the Physician and College Preparation for Medicine. Washington, D.C.: Association of American Medical Colleges; 1984. (Reprinted in *J Med Educ.* 1984:59 (11 pt 2):1–208.)
19. UPDIKE J. *Problems and Other Stories.* New York: Alfred Knopf; 1979:202.
20. SACKS O. *Awakenings.* New York: Vintage Books; 1976:102.
21. PINNER M, MILLER BF. *When Doctors Are Patients.* New York: WW Norton; 1952:18–31.
22. REUBEN DB. Learning diagnostic restraint. *N Engl J Med.* 1984;310:591–3.

4

GENESIS OF A COMMUNITY PSYCHIATRIST

Matthew Dumont

This selection is from Dumont's book *The Absurd Healer*. Dumont was one of the founders of the community mental health movement of the 1960s. He has served as director of a research institute at the National Institutes of Mental Health and as a psychiatrist in the slums of urban America, and he has written moving essays on the practice of psychiatry and medicine in the inner city. His career as a psychiatrist spans the development of psychotropic drugs, the subsequent release of patients from state mental hospitals (deinstitutionalization), and the ongoing struggle to develop community-based treatment for those patients.

Dumont believes deeply in the social and community side of medicine. His writing is about the realities of mentally ill people living in streets and shelters. His desire is for a community-based system in which people can be healed in supportive environments. Once healed (or better, never ill), they can live and work in communities with decent housing and schools.

Dumont claims that communities as well as individuals can need healing. He seeks to show that mental illness cannot be treated well outside a community. Rates of mental illness, or at least the concentrations of mentally ill people, are highest in poor communities where people experience extreme stress throughout their lives.

Recent studies of mental illness show that one in four Americans suffers from a mental illness (including alcohol and drug problems) once in a given year. Only about 28 percent of these individuals will seek treatment. Seven out of ten cases of mental illness go untreated. In this context, Dumont believes that psychiatrists need to work with other health and social workers to deal with a far broader range of personal and community issues than are addressed by conventional psychotherapies. If people are depressed because they do not have jobs or adequate housing, these are causes of mental problems on a par with other possible causes, such as brain chemistry. Adequate care and prevention, from Dumont's viewpoint, require treatment of both individual and community problems.

The community mental health movement, designed to develop mental health centers and treatment programs in communities, faces enormous problems of funding and acceptance. One consequence of the movement's relative lack of success is the number of mentally ill homeless people in U.S. cities. Another consequence is the high rate of untreated mental disorders in the communities most affected by the problems that help produce mental illness. Dumont's career is a testimony to the continuing effort to create a successful environment for community mental health.

One spring day I leaned over a dying man and watched as his last breath was drawn through rotted teeth. I listened to a silent heart with a stethoscope, and then with the prerogatives and licenses granted by a state, a city, a hospital, a university, and a three thousand year old tradition, I pronounced that a human life had ended.

In the middle of a spring night several years later, I strained to hear the drugged and sobbing voice of a woman who had just tried to end her life. Her chronic and hopeless illness had suddenly taken a turn for the worse, leaving her helplessly and incontinently awaiting an imminent death. She preferred to die by a last assertion of will. The prerogatives and licenses of the physician remained, but they did not seem very important as one human being tried to tell another about life and death.

On a spring morning two years later, I walked from the bright sunlight into a gray and shadowy tavern where the air was heavy with the smell of beer and stale breath. I shook hands with the bartender, nodded to a decrepit man next to me, and drank beer as I listened to the conversation and observed the interaction among a half-dozen homeless men.

In the barroom I had neither license nor sanction. I had even less a year later when I spoke with the administrative assistant of a United States Senator about police harassment of a gang of Negro youths who had turned their attention from extortion to voter registration.

These episodes highlight a strange career development for a physician. It is a career that departs in ever-widening cycles from traditional medical practice. It is a move from the medical model of individual patient care to a position of responsibility for large populations and involvement with social forces.

As a psychiatrist I was to minister to the needs of suffering individuals in a role protected and supported by centuries of respect and ascribed authority. My behavior was to be ordered by a body of ethics that was almost sacred and directed by an unassailable tradition of medical science. And now . . .

From Matthew P. Dumont, *The Absurd Healer: Perspectives of a Community Psychiatrist* (New York: Science House, 1968). Reprinted with the permission of Jason Aronson Inc.

Now I am a community psychiatrist and I function in an undefined role catering to undefined needs of an undefined clientele. This role has not been baptized by traditional medical prescriptions of confidentiality and responsibility. It is suspect among professional colleagues and responsive to no articulate demand from the community. I have moved from the respectable formality of psychodynamics to the ambiguity of politics and social change.

Where am I and how did I get here? Am I still a psychiatrist, still a physician? Or have I become an inadequately trained social scientist or some type of revolutionary?

I need to stand back for a moment, see what I am doing, and try to place what I find in a conceptual framework. I need to look at the forces that have propelled me in this direction. I need primarily to determine if the widening cycles of my departure from traditional medical practice are nonetheless securely rooted in that tradition. I need to do these things because it is inescapable that I will continue in the direction I am going.

The first challenge to my medical and psychoanalytically oriented focus on the individual patient was the residue of a social conscience. It was not a very large one, after all, but large enough to sensitize me to certain economic aspects of psychiatric care. It became very clear to me that psychiatry was a little inequitable. It is not just that 18,000 psychiatrists have preempted the job of looking after the millions of mentally ill, but that psychiatry's major treatment, psychotherapy, is predicated on social class. Psychotherapy, as generally practiced, requires a patient who is verbal, insightful and motivated, one who can delay gratification, and who, more or less, shares the values of the therapist, thereby virtually excluding the lower class person from treatment.

Psychiatrists are no more mercenary than other physicians, nor are they among the more affluent specialists. In other branches of medicine the *quality* of care will vary with the financial state of the patient, but only in psychiatry is the *method* of treatment determined by such factors.

A higher incidence of mental illness exists among the poor, and for this group there has been only the options of becoming psychotic and being hospitalized in a custodial institution or getting no care at all. Study after study has demonstrated the relationship between poverty and mental illness. We cannot say with any more certainty that poverty causes mental illness than that cigarette smoking causes cancer. The correlations are there, but the intermediate variables of a causative relationship are absent, giving the apologists of tobacco, for example, sufficient grounds to maintain a controversy. If, however, the medical profession devotes all of its effort in combatting lung cancer to thoracic surgery and none of it to programs aimed at reducing cigarette smoking, it will lose the battle. In the same way, if it is determined that mental illness is caused by poverty or by unemployment or by social discrimination, then it will be the responsibility of the mental health professions to devote at least some of their attention to these issues or the battle against mental illness will be lost.

The proponents of individual psychotherapy as the only model of psychiatric intervention are on shakier ground than the surgeons. A surgeon may insist that public education and legislative action are not his areas of competence, but he does at least devote his knowledge and skills to the individuals most in need of his care. The psychiatrists who insist on the practice of psychotherapy, and on that alone as their *raison d'être,* generally devote their attention to a middle-class population, and for the most part only to the mildly neurotic within that population. A tremendous effort of education, a huge outlay of public and private funds, and a scarce supply of human intelligence and sensitivity is expended on a small number of persons who probably have the individual and social resources to function adequately without treatment. Concern for this group is more a matter of level of performance, but this is in the face of a picture of overwhelming individual, family, and social disintegration among the poor. It is fascinating that every index of mental illness is highest among the poor except psychoneurosis—the one condition most amenable to individual psychotherapy. Psychiatry has generated a middle-class treatment for middle-class patients.

With the rationalization that his techniques of psychotherapy should be utilized on only those persons for whom they do the most good, the psychiatrist condones an outrageous misallocation of human resources. The rationalization is a poor one. A specialty of medicine has the responsibility to elaborate new techniques if old ones cannot help the most needful population.

In the final analysis, asking for definite proof that poverty "causes" mental illness is asking for the impossible. Scientists among us are devoting their careers to finding "the cause" of mental disorders. How can there be a single cause of anything so complex as an arbitrarily defined collection of behavior characteristics? We are not so naive as to believe any longer that any historical act, a war or a revolution, for example, has a single cause. We can be philosophical and ask if any iota of fact, like the falling of an acorn, has a single, ultimate or final cause. Causation is a fiction, an absurd abstraction, superimposed on a panoply of events to give it the semblance of meaning, order, and direction.

We say that the tubercle bacillus causes tuberculosis and take comfort in what seems like hard, indisputable, rational fact. What is factual is that tuberculosis cannot exist without the bacillus, but two individuals exposed to the same number of bacteria can respond in different ways depending upon a whole variety of host and environmental factors, some known, some unknown. The response may be a fulminating disease leading to death or an asymptomatic immunity. Poverty is a "cause" of tuberculosis as much as is the bacillus. Everything in medicine, everything in nature is the result of an infinite array of forces, actions, and reactions. Some of these are, however, more salient, immediate, potent, or remediable than others. Tuberculosis can be controlled by immunization or by early detection and treatment. It might also be controlled by the elimination of poverty.

To ask for definite proof that poverty causes mental illness is to deny that poverty acts as one of a number of salient influences on a set of behavior patterns which we call disordered. That poverty is highly correlated with these patterns has already been demonstrated. We know too little about the hereditary, biochemical, or developmental influences on these behavioral patterns to insist that the "truth" lies in these rather than in unemployment, segregation, anomie, inadequate housing or other aspects of social deprivation. Our responsibility as behavioral scientists is to determine which influences are more modifiable in their effects on specific patterns of behavior, not to determine which is the "true" cause.

The second train of thought that made it difficult to sustain the individual patient model came from the investigations of psychiatrists themselves. There are many differences between physical illnesses and psychiatric disorders. A major one is that while organic disease is limited to the physical organism, to the skin and its contents, mental illness is just as much a phenomenon of the environment around the patient. The violently deranged patients that Philippe Pinel encountered in the Bicêtre Hospital in 1794 were less violent and less deranged when their chains were struck off. More recently it was found that a patient in a mental hospital had a psychotic deterioration because of a covert disagreement between her therapist and ward administrator.

There is a village in Belgium called Geel where for a thousand years "possessed" patients have been cared for in the homes of peasants. My observations[1] of these patients demonstrated to me that the "social breakdown syndrome" of chronic schizophrenics is more an expression of custodial hospitalization and social isolation than something inherent in the illness. The greatest part of the social disability of this illness may derive from the way schizophrenics are treated. In Geel, on the other hand, where the patients are almost entirely unrestrained and where the tolerance to deviant behavior in the community is extraordinarily high, schizophrenia does not appear to be a very disabling illness. Apparently the degree of psychosis is related to the social and interpersonal setting of the patient.

The implications of these observations are more staggering than the statement of them. These observations mean, in short, that *mental illness does not entirely reside within the individual.* Community psychiatry, if nothing else, is an attempt to determine just how much of mental illness resides outside the individual, but this hurries my story too much. Conceptual leaps take place in small steps and it is only in retrospect that they are recognized at all.

Another major development from psychiatric research and practice added to the momentum of change: studies of family dynamics and attempts to treat the entire family as a unit. At first this was felt to be a new and effective way of approaching emotionally disturbed children. Soon, however, observers began to perceive a whole new dimension of psychopathology, i.e., disturbed relationships. The double-bind[2] was described as a situation in which contradictory messages are sent by a parent to a child in such a way that the contradiction cannot be recognized. It is as if a mother were to slap her child's hand as he reached for a piece of candy, and as the child withdraws his hand, his mother were to mutter, "You weakling."

In family dynamics it was too tempting to see explorations of such disturbances as attempts to find the "really sick one" in the family as other than the identified patient. A recently published and highly popularized book[3] which analyzes stereotyped relationships between people as "games" falls into this trap of looking for the real villain. Other therapists have gone further than this, and rather than see one or the other family member as the carrier of pathology or the focus of treatment, they have seen the patterns of communication, the interaction itself, as the disturbance. The "illness" was not within family members but between them.

One of the first families I had in treatment revealed this to me. A 17-year-old boy was sent to the clinic with a family friend who was to communicate to the psychiatrist the concerns of the boy's parents who themselves "could not make" the appointment. Their complaints, as communicated second-hand, were about the abrupt onset of the patient's argumentativeness, refusal to perform household obligations, and withdrawal from family life except for his incessant and belligerent demands to take over the family car and television set. The boy presented with a peculiar smile something between bravado and a smug, secret knowledge. He had strange repetitive gestures as if he were constantly picking minute, objectionable particles from his clothing. He said little other than giving evasive, disjointed answers to questions. Occasionally his sentences would become incomprehensible or suddenly stop midway. He acted indifferent to his parents and their complaints about him. A clinical impression of incipient schizophrenia was made but this diagnosis became less relevant when the family was prevailed upon to undertake treatment along with the patient.

This picture developed. For many years the mother had suffered from a chronic illness that required many operations, most of which left her more disabled and finally in endless pain. Despite her suffering, she never complained. She had a stiff-upper-lip attitude, never giving in to feelings of despair or hostility. She retained a childlike faith in her physicians despite their inability to relieve her. She was an "ideal" patient, even if she did not get better. Father was pillar of respectability, morality, and restraint. He stood by his wife with utter devotion and patience. He never permitted himself the slightest feeling of resentment towards his wife nor the barest wish to break away and find himself a mate who might be able to share the sexual, homemaking, and companionship aspects of marriage. They had two children, a year apart. The younger child, a girl, had nearly died in early childhood from rheumatic fever. Both parents spent sleepless nights for many months nursing her through her critical illness. They subsequently overprotected and catered to her and became terrified whenever she caught a cold. In the midst of this atmosphere of suffering, protectiveness, and selflessness, the son attempted to forge an identity for himself. Every normal impulse towards self-indulgence and every inclination to jealousy or hostility was laden with so much guilt by his parents' attitudes that he began to believe that he was evil. He found that he could not control his wishes and instincts so well as everyone else around him, and so he sought a sense of mastery by monopolizing the family car which he drove with endless fascination. He did well at school and spent many hours helping teachers or engaging in scout or religious activities. His symptoms began on the day that his sister got her driving license and demanded her share of the family car. As he fought for his need to preempt the only thing in the family he could master, he was made to feel more and more selfish. A vicious cycle developed as he acted increasingly like the image that was imposed upon him. The epitome of his role was described by Father as the day when Mother had to be hospitalized for an infection at the site of an operation.

Father approached the boy and, as if to get him to repent his sins and act like the concerned, helpful, generous child they had hoped to procreate, asked him if he wanted to see his mother's infection. The boy "arrogantly and callously" refused. According to Father, and with the tearful acquiescence of Mother and the self-righteous indignation of the daughter, the boy "didn't give a damn." It seemed as if the boy were the bearer of every vile, base, depraved, angry, and self-indulgent instinct in the family while the rest could carry on in their pure, guiltless suffering. Where was the focus of pathology? Who was the sick one? In whom was the illness when the illness lay in a family myth that anger and resentment are evil, when it lay in an unspoken, unrecognized conspiracy to expel hostility even if it meant expelling one of them with it? It was to this that the treatment was directed.

Measured dosages of confrontation with their own anger were administered to the parents. Anger was taught to be legitimate and benign, first when directed at the therapist and then at each other. They recognized with difficulty that one can be angry at someone for being sick, as unreasonable as this seemed, and it was seen not to be catastrophic. They had a reshuffling of "goodness and badness" and looked at themselves and each other in less stereotyped and rigid ways. When the parents could comfortably recognize hostility in themselves, they saw less in their son. Now they could understand that his disinclination to see his mother's infection was not because he did not care, but because he cared too much. The boy's symptoms abated and the diagnosis changed from "schizophrenic reaction" to "situational reaction of adolescence."

Still another professional encounter challenged the old psychiatric model. I spent one year as psychiatric consultant on a physical rehabilitation ward. Here were not psychiatric patients, not the mentally ill, just people. They were generally young men and women who would spend many months getting physical and occupational therapy: quadruplegics, hemiplegics, amputees, or multiple sclerotics. They were paralyzed, limbless, or in constant pain. They would never again be normal.

As I listened to them talk and watched them struggle, I found it increasingly difficult to formulate what I saw along psychopathological, or even psychodynamic lines. It was not that these were irrelevant, but they seemed so much less important than the existential reality of human beings trying to cope with an overwhelming stress.

Psychiatrists have a sense of understanding and mastery about the fantasy life of their patients. We can interpret dreams and explain the influences of unconscious wishes and fears on human behavior. But to the psychiatrist, the forces of reality are dark and inscrutable. What a paradox! To others it is the world of dreams and hidden thoughts and discordant behavior that are strange and frightening, but to psychiatrists, it is the reverse!

Psychiatrists tend to focus on the past. The more psychoanalytically oriented the doctor is, the more distant the past upon which he focuses. With these rehabilitation patients, the past continued to exert its influence, but that influence was unpredictable and much less salient than I had been led to believe. The here and now and the future seemed so much more important. They were faced with a greater stress on their coping resources than they had ever faced before, a crisis of incredible intensity. Psychoanalytic theory could not adequately explain why some patients were able adequately to grieve their losses and carry on despite them, to seek what fulfillment life had yet to offer them, while others became chronically depressed or denied unrealistically that a loss had ever taken place. To some patients this confrontation with a terribly harsh reality provided them with the means for a personality development that they had never had before. This served to confirm the ancient wisdom of the Chinese whose word for crisis is made up of two characters, one depicting danger and the other opportunity.

NOTES

1. DUMONT, M. P., and ALDRICH, C. K., "Family Care After a Thousand Years—a Crisis in the Tradition of St. Dymphna," *The American Journal of Psychiatry,* Vol. CXIX, No. 2, August, 1962.
2. BATESON, G., JACKSON, D. D., HALEY, J., and WEAKLAND, J., "Towards a Theory of Schizophrenia," *Behavioral Science,* Vol. I, No. 251, 1956.
3. BERNE, ERIC, *Games People Play,* New York, Grove Press, 1964.

5

THE ART OF SURGERY

Richard Selzer

Richard Selzer is one of the most insightful and lyrical contemporary writers on surgery and medical practice in the United States. As is evident from this selection, the experience of surgery has deep personal meaning for him, and he finds a quiet beauty inside the human body. Far from exulting in the surgeon's power and status, Selzer admits to wishing, at times, that he had the luxury to simply watch the intricate passage through human tissue and organs.

This selection from *Mortal Lessons,* Selzer's first collection of essays on the art and science of surgery, takes up in more specific terms the theme of medical humility developed in the essay by Lewis Thomas. The surgeon feels personally the loss of a patient's leg. A patient whose cancerous lesion is healed through what appears to be the power of faith arouses awe at the mysteries of healing.

The lessons Selzer draws from his experience are often mortal ones. Patients sometimes die on the operating table. Even the best doctors can be frustrated and feel helpless when confronted by the inevitability of death. Selzer's contribution is to make the lay public aware of the strong feelings of caring and love that often lie hidden behind a surgical mask.

I have come to believe that it is the flesh alone that counts. The rest is that with which we distract ourselves when we are not hungry or cold, in pain or ecstasy. In the recesses of the body I search for the philosophers' stone. I know it is there, hidden in the deepest, dampest cul-de-sac. It awaits discovery. To find it would be like the harnessing of fire. It would illuminate the world. Such a quest is not without pain. Who can gaze on so much misery and feel no hurt? Emerson has written that the poet is the only true doctor. I believe him, for the poet, lacking the impediment of speech with which the rest of us are afflicted, gazes, records, diagnoses, and prophesies.

I invited a young diabetic woman to the operating room to amputate her leg. She could not see the great shaggy black ulcer upon her foot and ankle that threatened to encroach upon the rest of her body, for she was blind as well. There upon her foot was a Mississippi Delta brimming with corruption, sending its raw tributaries down between her toes. Gone were all the little web spaces that when fresh and whole are such a delight to loving men. She could not see her wound, but she could feel it. There is no pain like that of the bloodless limb turned rotten, and festering. There is neither unguent nor anodyne to kill such a pain yet leave intact the body.

For over a year I trimmed away the putrid flesh, cleansed, anointed, and dressed the foot, staving off, delaying. Three times each week, in her darkness, she sat upon my table, rocking back and forth, holding her extended leg by the thigh, gripping it as though it were a rocket that must be steadied lest it explode and scatter her toes about the room. And I would cut away a bit here, a bit there, of the swollen blue leather that was her tissue.

At last we gave up, she and I. We could no longer run ahead of the gangrene. We had not the legs for it. There must be an amputation in order that she might live—and I as well. It was to heal us both that I must take up knife and saw, and cut the leg off. And when I could feel it drop from her body to the table, see the blessed *space* appear between her and that leg, I too would be well.

Now it is the day of the operation. I stand by while the anesthetist administers the drugs, watch as the tense familiar body relaxes into narcosis. I turn then to uncover the leg. There, upon her kneecap, she has drawn, blindly, upside down for me to see, a face; just a circle with two ears, two eyes, a nose, and a smiling upturned mouth. Under it she has printed SMILE, DOCTOR. Minutes later I listen to the sound of the saw, until a little crack at the end tells me it is done. . . .

One enters the body in surgery, as in love, as though one were an exile returning at last to his hearth, daring uncharted darkness in order to reach home. Turn sideways, if you will, and slip with me into the cleft I have made. Do not fear the yellow meadows of fat, the red that sweats and trickles where you step. Here, give me your hand. Lower between the beefy cliffs. Now rest a bit upon the peri-toneum. All at once, gleaming, the membrane parts . . . and you are *in.*

It is the stillest place that ever was. As though suddenly you are struck deaf. Why, when the blood sluices fierce as Niagara, when the brain teems with electric-ity, and the numberless cells exchange their goods in ceaseless commerce—why is it so quiet? Has some priest in charge of these rites uttered the command "Silence"? This is no silence of the vacant stratosphere, but the awful quiet of ruins, of rain-bows, full of expectation and holy dread. Soon you shall know surgery as a Mass served with Body and Blood, wherein disease is assailed as though it were sin.

Touch the great artery. Feel it bound like a deer in the might of its lightness, and know the thunderless boil of the blood. Lean for a bit against this bone. It is the only memento you will leave to the earth. Its tacitness is everlasting. In the hush of the tissue wait with me for the shaft of pronouncement. Press your ear against this body, the way you did as a child holding a seashell and heard faintly the half-remembered, longed-for sea. Now strain to listen *past* the silence. In the canals, cilia paddle quiet as an Iroquois canoe. Somewhere nearby a white whipslide of tendon bows across a joint. Fire burns here but does not crackle. Again, listen. Now there *is* sound—small splashings, tunneled currents of air, slow gaseous bubbles ascend through dark, unlit lakes. Across the diaphragm and into the chest . . . here at last it is all noise; the whisper of the lungs, the *lubdup, lubdup* of the garrulous heart.

But it is good you do not hear the machinery of your marrow lest it madden like the buzzing of a thousand coppery bees. It is frightening to lie with your ear in the pillow, and hear the beating of your heart. Not that it beats . . . but that it might stop, even as you listen. For anything that moves must come to rest; no rhythm is endless but must one day lurch . . . then halt. Not that it is a disservice to a man to be made mindful of his death, but—at three o'clock in the morning it is less than philosophy. It is Fantasy, replete with dreadful images forming in the smoke of alabaster crematoria. It is then that one thinks of the bristlecone pines, and envies them for having lasted. It is their slowness, I think. Slow down, heart, and drub on.

What is to one man a coincidence is to another a miracle. It was one or the other of these that I saw last spring. While the rest of nature was in flux, Joe Riker remained obstinate through the change of the seasons. "No operation," said Joe. "I don't want no operation."

Joe Riker is a short-order cook in a diner where I sometimes drink coffee. Each week for six months he had paid a visit to my office, carrying his affliction like a pet mouse under his hat. Every Thursday at four o'clock he would sit on my ex-amining table, lift the fedora from his head, and bend forward to show me the hole. Joe Riker's hole was as big as his mouth. You could have dropped a plum in it. Gouged from the tonsured top of his head was a mucky puddle whose meaty heaped edge rose above the normal scalp about it. There was no mistaking the an-nouncement from this rampart.

The cancer had chewed through Joe's scalp, munched his skull, then opened the membranes underneath—the dura mater, the pia mater, the arachnoid—until it had laid bare this short-order cook's brain, pink and gray, and pulsating so that with each beat a little pool of cerebral fluid quivered. Now and then a drop would manage the rim to run across his balding head, and Joe would reach one burry hand up to wipe it away, with the heel of his thumb, the way such a man would wipe away a tear.

I would gaze then upon Joe Riker and marvel. How dignified he was, as though that tumor, gnawing him, denuding his very brain, had given him a grace that a lifetime of good health had not bestowed.

"Joe," I say, "let's get rid of it. Cut out the bad part, put in a metal plate, and you're cured." And I wait.

"No operation," says Joe. I try again.

"What do you mean, 'no operation'? You're going to get meningitis. Any day now. And die. That thing is going to get to your brain."

I think of it devouring the man's dreams and memories. I wonder what they are. The surgeon knows all the parts of the brain, but he does not know his patient's dreams and memories. And for a moment I am tempted . . . to take the man's head in my hands, hold it to my ear, and listen. But his dreams are none of my business. It is his flesh that matters.

"No operation," says Joe.

"You give me a headache," I say. And we smile, not because the joke is funny anymore, but because we've got something between us, like a secret.

"Same time next week?" Joe asks. I wash out the wound with peroxide, and apply a dressing. He lowers the fedora over it.

"Yes," I say, "same time." And the next week he comes again.

There came the week when Joe Riker did not show up; nor did he the week after that, nor for a whole month. I drive over to his diner. He is behind the counter, shuffling back and forth between the grill and the sink. He is wearing the fedora. He sets a cup of coffee in front of me.

"I want to see your hole," I say.

"Which one?" he asks, and winks.

"Never mind that," I say. "I want to see it." I am all business.

"Not here," says Joe. He looks around, checking the counter, as though I have made an indecent suggestion.

"My office at four o'clock," I say.

"Yeah," says Joe, and turns away.

He is late. Everyone else has gone for the day. Joe is beginning to make me angry. At last he arrives.

"Take off your hat," I say, and he knows by my voice that I am not happy. He does, though, raise it straight up with both hands the way he always does, and I see . . . that the wound has healed. Where once there had been a bitten-out excavation, moist and shaggy, there is now a fragile bridge of shiny new skin.

"What happened?" I manage.

"You mean that?" He points to the top of his head. "Oh well," he says, "The wife's sister, she went to France, and brought me a bottle of water from Lourdes. I've been washing it out with that for a month."

"Holy water?" I say.

"Yeah," says Joe. "Holy water." . . .

With trust the surgeon approaches the operating table. To be sure, he is impeccably trained. He has stood here so many times before. The belly that presents itself to him this morning, draped in green linen and painted with red disinfectant, is little different from those countless others he has entered. It is familiar terrain, to be managed. He watches it rise and fall in the regular rhythm of anesthesia. Vulnerable, it returns his trust, asks but his excellence, his clever ways. With a blend of arrogance and innocence the surgeon makes his incision, expecting a particular organ to be exactly where he knows it to be. He has seen it there, in just that single place, over and again. He has aimed his blade for that very spot, found the one artery he seeks, the one vein, captured them in his hemostats, ligated them, and cut them safely; then on to the next, and the one after that, until the sick organ falls free into his waiting hand—mined.

But this morning, as the surgeon parts the edges of the wound with his retractor, he feels uncertain, for in that place where he *knows* the duct to be, there is none. Only masses of scar curtained with blood vessels of unimagined fragility. They seem to rupture even as he studies them, as though it is the abrasion of the air that breaks them. Blood is shed into the well of the wound. It puddles upon the banks of scar, concealing the way inward. The surgeon sees this, and knows that the fierce wind of inflammation has swept this place, burying the tubes and canals he seeks. It is an alien land. Now all is forestial, swampy. The surgeon suctions away the blood; even as he does so, new red trickles; his eyes are full of it; he cannot see. He advances his fingers into the belly, feeling the walls of scar, running the tips gently over each eminence, into each furrow, testing the roll of the land, probing for an opening, the smallest indentation that will accept his pressure, and invite him to follow with his instruments. There is none. It is terra incognita. Hawk-eyed, he peers, waiting for a sign, a slight change in color, that would declare the line of a tube mounding from its sunken position. There is no mark, no trail left by some earlier explorer.

At last he takes up his scissors and forceps and begins to dissect, millimetering down and in. The slightest step to either side may be the bit of excess that will set off avalanche or flood. And he is *alone*. No matter how many others crowd about the mouth of the wound, no matter their admiration and encouragement, it is *he* that rappels this crevasse, dangles in this dreadful place, and he is *afraid*—for he knows well the worth of this belly, that it is priceless and irreplaceable.

"Socked in," he says aloud. His language is astronaut terse. The others are silent. They know the danger, but they too have given him their reliance. He speaks again.

"The common bile duct is bricked up in scar . . . the pancreas swollen about it . . . soup." His voice is scarcely more than the movement of his lips. The students and interns must strain to hear, as though the sound comes from a great distance.

They envy him his daring, his dexterity. They do not know that he envies them their safe footing, their distance from the pit.

The surgeon cuts. And all at once there leaps a mighty blood. As when from the hidden mountain ledge a pebble is dislodged, a pebble behind whose small slippage the whole of the avalanche is pulled. Now the belly is a vast working lake in which it seems both patient and surgeon will drown. He speaks.

"Pump the blood in. Faster! Faster! Jesus! We are losing him."

And he stands there with his hand sunk in the body of his patient, leaning with his weight upon the packing he has placed there to occlude the torn vessel, and he watches the transfusion of new blood leaving the bottles one after the other and entering the tubing. He knows it is not enough, that the shedding outraces the donation.

At last the surgeon feels the force of the hemorrhage slacken beneath his hand, sees that the suction machine has cleared the field for him to see. He can begin once more to approach that place from which he was driven. Gently he teases the packing from the wound so as not to jar the bleeding alive. He squirts in saline to wash away the old stains. Gingerly he searches for the rent in the great vein. Then he hears.

"I do not have a heartbeat." It is the man at the head of the table who speaks. "The cardiogram is flat," he says. Then, a moment later . . . "This man is dead."

Now there is no more sorrowful man in the city, for this surgeon has discovered the surprise at the center of his work. It is death. . . .

I stand by the bed where a young woman lies, her face postoperative, her mouth twisted in palsy, clownish. A tiny twig of the facial nerve, the one to the muscles of her mouth, has been severed. She will be thus from now on. The surgeon had followed with religious fervor the curve of her flesh; I promise you that. Nevertheless, to remove the tumor in her cheek, I had cut the little nerve.

Her young husband is in the room. He stands on the opposite side of the bed, and together they seem to dwell in the evening lamplight, isolated from me, private. Who are they, I ask myself, he and this wry-mouth I have made, who gaze at and touch each other so generously, greedily? The young woman speaks.

"Will my mouth always be like this?" she asks.

"Yes," I say, "it will. It is because the nerve was cut."

She nods, and is silent. But the young man smiles.

"I like it," he says. "It is kind of cute."

All at once I *know* who he is. I understand, and I lower my gaze. One is not bold in an encounter with a god. Unmindful, he bends to kiss her crooked mouth, and I so close I can see how he twists his own lips to accommodate to hers, to show her that their kiss still works. I remember that the gods appeared in ancient Greece as mortals, and I hold my breath and let the wonder in.

6

THE ULTIMATE IN SURGERY

Marcia Millman

Medical sociologist Marcia Millman is a masterful observer of human behavior in the medical world. Few sociologists can portray the social interactions occurring in medical settings as vividly as she does in this excerpted description of the interactions among operating room personnel. In the details of how doctors and nurses go about their work, she shows that medicine is a complex world of human relationships that can be far different from the orderly, professional image presented to outsiders.

In her work Millman gives due credit to skilled and dedicated doctors, but she can also be a keen critic when the evidence demands it. From her observations of surgeons, she concludes that all too often, personality conflicts or the competition for prestige within the hospital leads to poor medical care. Self-importance, the desire to dominate others, or the pressures of the hospital bureaucracy can interfere with wise choices. These conditions can result in unnecessary and even deadly surgery, as in this account of an open-heart operation.

These excerpts from Millman's book *The Unkindest Cut* reveal the darker side of human behavior in medicine. Millman does not intend Dr. Dalton to represent all surgeons. Nor is the dissension among the members of this medical team typical. The social conditions and interactions that produced the tragedy described here, however, are typical of some of the situations she has observed.

The "ultimate" in surgery reveals how power relations in medical practice can interfere with the prospects of establishing healing relationships, especially in "heroic" areas of medicine like surgery. By describing them and showing the results of the social processes of group denial, poor communication with the patient and her family, and failure to challenge the surgeon's ultimate authority, the medical sociologist may contribute to positive change.

When Paul Lever arrived at Lakeside Hospital at 6:12 A.M. it was still dark outside. Being the surgical intern on the thoracic (chest) service, he had to make quick morning rounds of all the patients who were in the hospital for heart or lung surgery. Some were still having diagnostic tests and others were in various stages of recovery from their operations. They were spread out over several different floors in the hospital, so Paul had to run through the halls in order to get to the operating room by seven o'clock, when he would help the anesthesiologist prepare Mrs. Bergen for her surgery. He had looked into the patient's room before she was taken to the OR, but she was practically asleep from preoperative medication, so he hadn't disturbed her.

Earlier in the week Paul had told the resident he worked with that he felt uneasy about this operation because he knew that Mrs. Bergen was reluctant to have the surgery. The case had been discussed rather heatedly at the weekly cardiac conference, and Paul's surgical supervisor, Dr. Thomas Dalton, had made a strong case for the surgery. Dalton had asked one of the cardiologists (a medical, as distinguished from a surgical, heart specialist) at the meeting to perform a preoperative diagnostic procedure called a catheterization on Mrs. Bergen in preparation for the surgery. But the cardiologist had objected to the idea, arguing that he was not convinced that the possible benefits of the surgery outweighed the risks in the Bergen case. She was in a debilitated state, so chances were seven in ten that Mrs. Bergen would not survive an operation to replace two valves in her heart, and without the surgery she would probably live for six months to a year. Dalton, the surgeon, did not like being challenged, and he complained: "Oh, I know some criticize us because our statistics look bad, but after all, are we here to help the patients or have good statistics? No, I know that we can fix her up and give her ten good years and I think we should."

The cardiologist, however, had continued to object. There was no point in doing the diagnostic procedure, he argued, because the patient didn't want to have surgery. "She's not going to agree to this operation. Her family doctor told her that if she consents to surgery she's signing her own death certificate."

Dr. Dalton appeared to be irritated, but he persisted. "Oh, she'll have the surgery. I very rarely have a patient refuse me surgery." As Dalton drew the meeting to a close he concluded, "No, I want to help this lady. I *want* to do the operation if we can help her, and I believe we can."

Dalton was unaccustomed to resistance. He had made many important contributions to medicine over the years, and he was a prominent cardiac surgeon whose patients traveled long distances to see him. Those who worked closely with him, however, agreed that this aging medical celebrity was past his prime as a surgeon. He received very few referrals for surgery from the other doctors at Lakeside, and relied upon his reputation and the patients he had treated before for his current cases. Many of the younger doctors found it difficult to argue with Dalton. Because of his renowned achievements he commanded a great deal of respect, and even as he aged he had not lost his ability to dominate every situation with his sharp tongue and dramatic style. Most of the doctors at Lakeside admitted that they were afraid of Dalton and his caustic outbursts, and few refused him anything. It was only in the last few years, when his competence was reportedly slipping, that he had encountered any resistance at all.

As for the Bergen case, under Dalton's orders Paul Lever had booked the operating room for the case even before the advisory conference with the cardiologist had been held or before talking to the patient. Getting Mrs. Bergen to sign the consent form was not difficult. When Dalton heard that the patient didn't want to have the surgery but that her family was in favor of the operation, he declared that she was mentally "too obtunded" because of her medical condition to make a proper decision, and he called a family conference in the hospital. Paul had spoken briefly to Mrs. Bergen the night before the family meeting was to be held, and she had asked to know her chances of living through the operation. He had stated the matter as optimistically as he could: "Well, forty people out of a hundred having your operation would make it through." She had started to cry then, and told Paul that since her children were grown up they didn't need her to live beyond the year. But she wasn't ready to die the next day, so she preferred to settle for six more certain months.

As Paul later explained, he felt uncomfortable in these situations. He felt sorry for Mrs. Bergen, but her life could not have been very pleasant as it was. And, since she was Dalton's patient, he felt that he had no right to encourage the patient to resist her doctor's recommendations. Two hours after the family meeting, Paul heard that Dalton had gotten his way: Mrs. Bergen had yielded to family pressure and agreed to the operation. . . .

On the morning of Mrs. Bergen's operation, Paul changed into surgical clothes but did not scrub immediately. Instead he offered to help the anesthesiologist prepare the patient for surgery. He was doing this on the instructions of Dr. Dalton, who was annoyed that the anesthesiologists were so slow in setting up the patients. Dalton had requested that the anesthesiologists come into the hospital at six o'clock instead of their customary 7 A.M. when there was an open heart case on the schedule, but the Chief of Anesthesiology had refused to make special arrangements for Dalton's cases. . . .

Jerry Mandel was the anesthesiologist assigned to the case, and he was not very happy about it. He hated working with Dalton, as did all of the anesthesiologists, and so they took turns so that no one would have to do it more than once every two weeks. Jerry was about thirty-five years old, and since finishing his residency a few years before, he had spent most of his time working in the operating room of Lakeside Hospital. Although he sometimes had to work at night, his time off was generally uninterrupted. He worked fewer hours than many other physicians, and this was one of the reasons he had chosen the specialty. The work was fairly interesting, and in an ordinary day he was generally assigned to two or three cases, some of which he took care of himself and some of which were really managed by a nurse anesthetist who worked under his supervision. On the days of Dalton's open heart operations, however, the one case was the only job assigned to the anesthesiologist for the entire day. Dalton's operations were usually very long, and the double valve replacements (such as they were doing on Mrs. Bergen) could take him all day. . . .

Jerry Mandel, standing by the patient's head, looked up at the clock, since monitoring the passage of time was one of his responsibilities. It was ten o'clock, and Eric [the senior resident] and Juan Mendez, the thoracic surgery fellow from Argentina, were just beginning to "cannulate" the patient's heart: they were inserting large plastic tubes into the major blood vessels; these tubes would carry the patient's blood to and from the pump oxygenator at the foot of the table. This was a tricky part of the operation, as far as Jerry was concerned, because if the heart went into an irregular rhythm now, they were still not prepared to transfer the functions of the heart and lungs over to the pump. There was a sudden quiet in the room and Jerry looked up. Dr. Thomas Dalton had arrived. . . .

"Well, friends," he greeted everyone in the room, glancing around as if to take stock of who was there, and meeting everyone's eyes momentarily. "How are things looking?"

Juan and Eric nodded their heads and mumbled something incoherent as they continued to work on the cannulae. As Mary [the scrub nurse] helped Dalton into a sterile gown, vest and gloves, he looked over at the chest and remarked, "I see we're still not cannulated by ten-fifteen, as is our custom." Everyone recognized his sarcasm. He had told the residents over and over that he wanted the patients to be cannulated by the time he arrived to work on the valves. Now he would have to stand around and wait until they were ready. Dalton paced up and down the room, behind the residents. "Come on, boys. We should be moving like bats out of hell." He turned to the new assistant scrub nurse: "Well, young man, you're the fellow Mary told me about. Well, have a good look today and I hope you like what you see—it's the ultimate in surgery." . . .

Dalton peered over Juan's shoulder, just as the young man was completing the attachment of the cannulae. "Juan, how many times have I told you that you *must* wash your gloves every hour. Every single hour. I can't seem to get you to understand that concept. Now, tell me, are you really satisfied with those stitches you're making?"

Juan mumbled, "Yes, sir." The dark, quiet fellow struck a respectful look, but he seemed to pay no attention to Dalton's interruptions as he kept working. He had explained to Paul Lever some days before that he had come to the United States to learn cardiac surgery and he had made up his mind to simply ignore the way that Dalton treated him. "Are you *absolutely* sure that you have healthy tissue under those stitches, Juan?" Dalton persisted: "I know you say so, so I suppose I'll just have to take your word for it." . . .

Jerry Mandel was looking at the cardiac monitors when one of the pump nurses suddenly called out, "There's air in the arterial line." Such a situation is very dangerous, for air bubbles escaping into the circulatory system can cause fatal emboli. Dalton became excited. "Well, we have to remedy that fast, fast. Something's wrong and we can't go on like this." The pump nurse called out, "The air is coming up again in the arterial line." Dalton was turning red. "I know I can fix this. I know

I can. It must be fixed." Mandel was watching the blood pressure to see whether the air had created any damage yet. He murmured that everything on his end was okay.

Dalton snapped at him. "Will you talk out loud, for Christ's sake. If you have something to say, then say it so everyone can hear. If not, don't say it at all." Mandel's face flushed, and as soon as things quieted down, he stepped out of the room for a few minutes and asked Lisa [another anesthetist] to take his place. Dalton, noticing Mandel's departure, turned to his surgical team: "I *know* these anesthesiologists want to preside over their work, but in our kind of surgery it is *scandalous* that they don't know what they are doing. They *don't* tell us if they're not doing something we've asked them to do. They order drugs and don't use them. They *should* keep calling out the name and amount of drug they're giving until we acknowledge it, and we should keep calling the name and amount of the drug we want until they acknowledge it. . . .

Bill Cameron, the Chief of Anesthesiology, had heard by now that things were heating up in the thoracic room, so he dropped in to relieve the nurse anesthetist. Cameron had come to the hospital a year before, and had turned out to be an assertive and influential member of the staff. Recently, he had begun to make it known that he felt there were serious problems with the cardiac surgery program. Indeed, it was felt by many in the hospital that Lakeside was not doing enough cases to legitimately offer cardiac surgery, and some of the cardiac surgeons were not around the hospital enough to provide adequate leadership and instruction to the residents who were assisting on the cases. When the staff did only a couple of open heart cases a week instead of one a day, it was impossible for the residents and anesthesiologists to gain enough expertise to do a first-rate job. . . .

Dalton was cordial the moment that Cameron stepped into the operating room. "Hello, Bill. Boys, make some room for Dr. Cameron so he can take a look at what you're doing. Well, Bill, I know you fellows can't see much from there, but everything is going very well. We're a little slow today, but all the world would agree that it's going very well." . . .

The second artificial valve was practically inserted in Mrs. Bergen's heart. Installing these valves involved a long and tedious process of placing many stitches around the skirt of the prosthetic device and then pulling on the threads to draw the valve into place. Dalton called to the pump nurse and asked how long they had been on bypass. "Almost three hours, Dr. Dalton." It is not a good thing to keep a patient on the bypass pump for very long, because complications and mortality increase dramatically after the first two hours. Juan and Eric were about to draw the second valve into place and Dalton signaled to the Japanese visitor, who had been watching quietly. "Now I want Professor Shumate to see this valve and how well it is placed." He looked up at the huge, uncomprehending man, and Dalton grinned and added, "You see, nice little Japanese stitches." . . .

He turned to Mandel. "What's the mean blood pressure?" Mandel replied, "Seventy-nine, eighty." Dalton objected: "Oh no, that can't be. Something must be wrong with your measure." Mandel answered, "That's what it is, Dr. Dalton. I've checked it twice."

As Mandel had earlier explained to his assistant, Dalton never wanted to believe that the anesthesiologists were correct when they told him information he didn't like. Mandel had heard that in the hospital Dalton worked at before coming to Lakeside, the anesthesiologists had become so tired of arguing with him about the blood pressure that they installed a special monitor facing the surgeon which they would set permanently at his favorite reading. Meanwhile, they would use an accurate monitor that they kept hidden from his sight. The difficulty now was that Dalton was unaccustomed to hearing figures he didn't like, and when they told him the truth he insisted that they must be wrong. Mandel had come prepared for Dalton today. He had inserted a second, independent device to measure the blood pressure, and the next time Dalton told him that his reading must be wrong, he was going to have the satisfaction of demonstrating the corroborating second measure.

The stitching of the heart had finally been completed and they had begun to redirect the blood flow back into the patient's heart, gradually taking her off the bypass pump. Dalton asked how long they had been on bypass. The pump nurse answered: "It's been three and three-quarter hours, Dr. Dalton."

Dalton appeared nervous about the amount of time that had elapsed. "Well, it's been a long run, but it's been a good run. And she has solid valve placement." Since the valve placement was Dalton's special contribution to the operation, he often called attention to the masterful quality of this aspect of the operation.

Suddenly Mandel called out that the blood pressure had dropped from seventy-five to thirty, and he expressed his fear that this was the delayed consequence of the air bubbles that had escaped earlier into the arterial line and that might have finally formed an embolus.

Dalton disagreed. "That blood pressure drop is nothing. Are you sure you're reading it correctly? I don't trust those measures. I'm sure the drop is just coming from warming her up." But Juan and Eric simultaneously noticed that there was suddenly a lot of bleeding around the heart muscle. The heart was bleeding from somewhere. They quickly moved to fibrillate the heart out of its beat again and get the patient back on total bypass so they could find the tear in her heart and repair it. The fibrillator didn't work, and after investigation it turned out to have been unplugged. Dalton's rising voice started to plead: "Come on, folks. It's been *such* a good job. Let's not distintegrate now."

Back on bypass, they had trouble locating the leak because there was so much blood splashing around the heart. Dalton glared at Juan: "I bet someone poked one of his instruments right through her heart." Finally it appeared that a puncture had been made with a surgical instrument while they had been inserting the aortic valve. Dalton was beside himself with anger. "This happens to us too much, Juan. I don't know how to impress this upon you."

Juan had been ignoring Dalton's accusations and appeared to be concentrating on finding the tear so that he could repair it with surgical patches they called "pledgets." Every time Juan prepared a pledget Dalton would find something wrong with the way he was doing it. Finally, Dalton pushed Juan out of the way and started wildly to string up patches himself. While the blood oozed and obscured their view of what was happening, Dalton kept everyone informed. "Well, folks, I don't know if there's only one hole here or more, or where it is. The truth be told, I don't really know what I'm doing. I only hope to God there's a hole where this patch is going."

The repairs would not hold. Once again they had to cut open the heart to locate the puncture site in order to stop the bleeding. Mrs. Bergen had been on bypass for six hours when Dalton felt satisfied that they had stopped the bleeding. He was worried: "Well, folks, I don't know if were gonna get away with this one, but I hope we do. I *do* want so much to help this woman." . . .

Mandel indicated to his assistant that he had mentally given up on the case a long time before. He was no longer actively watching, but was sitting quietly on his stool behind the patient's head. He was going through the motions of his activities, but he no longer carried any hope for the patient's survival. He knew of no recorded case in surgical history of a patient successfully brought off the pump after as long as six hours, and he saw no chance that it could happen in this case.

They were gradually coming off bypass when they noticed blood slowly and stubbornly oozing across the heart once again. Dalton saw that his meticulous patching had failed. He stepped back from the surgical field, leaned against the wall and crouched down on his legs, holding his head in his hands. He looked up, his face red and sweaty. "Well, friends, I'm almost to the point of despair. We don't have any choice anymore. I think we're just going to have to redo the entire suture line." He stood up and changed into a new sterile overgown and gloves for a final attempt to hold the heart together.

Once the heart begins to shred apart, it is very difficult to keep it repaired. The muscle becomes more and more damaged and increasingly vulnerable to further rips. For the third time, they put Mrs. Bergen back on total bypass, so that they could cut the heart open again and once more repair it from the back. . . .

The oozing would not stop. Angrily, Dalton pushed Eric and Juan out of the way and stood over the patient by himself. "Okay, now *I'm* gonna do it. I'm certainly tired of everyone else getting in the way. I'm going to sew the rest of this."

Eric and Juan shrank back and silently exchanged blank expressions. Like the anesthesiologist, they expressed through their gestures that there was nothing left to do, but Dalton kept patching. Every few minutes he would look up from his stitching with a hopeful expression and say: "I think we have it now, don't you?" The others, seeming reluctant to argue, would weakly agree.

Finally, Dalton seemed satisfied with the repair and ready to start the heart beating again. He reminded everyone that the heart had responded nicely after the first pump run, before the tear had appeared, and there was no reason why it shouldn't do so again. He called out to anyone in the room, "How long have we been on bypass? Five hours?"

Mandel wearily raised himself from his stool. "No, Dr. Dalton, it's been seven and a half hours."

Dalton made a face of disbelief. The pump nurse repeated the time. "Seven and a half, Dr. Dalton."

He still looked determined. "Seven and a half hours. That means if we get her off the pump alive we will succeed in having the longest pump run yet resuscitated in history. Isn't that right?"

Mandel answered patiently, "Yes, Dr. Dalton. I've never seen it go beyond six hours."

Dalton nodded his head excitedly, up and down. "Well, I think we're gonna make it. She's had good perfusion, hasn't she?" He looked around at everyone in the room. "There's no reason why she shouldn't make it I think we'll do it. I've closed those holes with good, solid sutures."

At 6:37 P.M. it was at last time to try to shock the heart back into beating, to push it into taking up its work again after all those hours of tearing and cutting and sewing and after being allowed a long period of rest while the mechanical pump had done its job. Eric and Juan grasped the paddles. Everyone stepped back from the table. Dalton orchestrated the application of the current: "One, two, three, *shock!*"

The heart was too tired. There was no response. They increased the voltage of the current and tried again. There was still no response. They turned up the current again, and still there was no response. They tried for a fourth time. No beat was recorded. Finally, Dalton injected a chemical stimulant and massaged the heart with his hands. But the heart would not beat.

Now, there was no longer any delay. Dalton looked carefully around the room at the dozen or so people who had been collected together for the past twelve hours. Without much expression he announced: "Well, I'm ready to quit if you all are." There was no objection. Everyone nodded their heads. Most had believed the patient was lost hours before, and now they seemed anxious to go home.

Dalton went on: "I just want to say that it's been a tremendous effort you've all shown here today, and you shouldn't feel discouraged."

Mandel humored the surgeon, while everyone else was silent. "Yes, Dr. Dalton, it really looked like we would make it for a while."

Dalton crouched down on his legs again, leaning against the wall, with his face in his hands. He looked up at Eric. "I'm truly sorry that this had to happen to you, Eric. You've been *such* a good resident. You've worked so hard here these four months and I wanted so badly for you to have a good case on your last day."

He stood up, pulled off his gown and gloves, and left the room. Without a word, Juan and Eric started to sew up the chest cavity and Paul and Mary quickly disconnected the lines, tubes and equipment. As they finished their work, Dalton hurried off to his dinner party at home. Those left in the operating room heard him toss his final remark over his shoulder. "It's just not fair. To have gotten so far and done so well, and lose so badly."

7

THE JOY OF MY LIFE

James Jones

This selection by medical historian James Jones portrays a dedicated nurse who spent most of her career caring for participants in a medical experiment. Nurse Rivers used her considerable interpersonal skills to help the patients feel at ease in a highly ambiguous situation. Unfortunately, the experiment to which she devoted so much attention is among the best-known examples of racism and callousness in medical research. In a sense, Nurse Rivers's care and dedication went for naught.

The infamous Tuskegee syphilis experiment traced the course of this deadly sexually transmitted disease in a group of impoverished black men living in rural Alabama. Of the subjects, 399 had been diagnosed as being infected with the syphilis spirochete, the microorganism that causes syphilis, when they were in their young-adult years; they were assigned to the experimental group. Informed that they had "bad blood," they and a control group of 201 men from similar backgrounds who had been found not to have contracted the disease were followed by Nurse Rivers and her supervisors for the next fifty years.

Syphilis causes lasting damage to the bones and nerves and often leads to death, but its early signs are rather mild. It can persist for decades before causing serious damage. When the experiment was designed, during the 1930s, there was no known cure for syphilis, although there were treatments that themselves caused damage. When antibiotics were discovered in the 1940s, it became possible to use penicillin in the treatment of syphilis. The men in the Tuskegee experiment, however, were never offered penicillin. The doctors running the experiment refused to prescribe it for them and continued their research in order to observe the course of the disease.

Designed well before the civil rights movement or the imposition of strict regulations on experimentation with humans, the Tuskegee experiment is a shocking reminder of why such controls are needed. The doctors who designed the experiment were violating their own norms of professional practice in the interests of research. They rationalized their actions on the grounds that the men would not have had access to health care in their backward rural county anyway. Clearly, the fact that the subjects were black and poor made the doctors feel, at least intuitively, that they could be experimented on in ways that the doctors would not have recommended for white middle-class people like themselves.

Nurse Rivers was an unwitting and unquestioning accomplice to this travesty of medical ethics. Her story is a poignant reminder that improvements in healing are often blocked by social ills like racism and class bias.

The first few autopsies upset Nurse Rivers. Drs. Peters and Dibble actually performed them, but she was required to assist. "I hadn't had that experience," she stated. "It wasn't an easy thing to see them do those autopsies." In fact, she reacted to them much like a layman. Cutting dead men open, removing their vital organs, brains, and spinal cords, seemed "crude" to Nurse Rivers, and because she felt squeamish she found it hard to fulfill all that was expected of her, especially securing permission for the autopsies from the men's families. "I wasn't sold on autopsy," she admitted, "so I had a problem selling it to other people."[1]

Nurse Rivers worked hard to overcome her personal feelings. She considered herself a professional woman, a nurse who could do what the doctors ordered. Assisting with the autopsies and obtaining permission from the families were among the most important of her duties, and she was determined to do her job well. She wanted to cast a happy reflection on the nurses' training program at the Tuskegee Institute and on Dr. Dibble for recommending her to Dr. Vonderlehr. Gradually, her distaste for the autopsies decreased and then vanished entirely, making it easier to deal with the relatives of the men. "I would come to find out that I was worse off than the family," she recalled. "The family would immediately say, 'All right, Nurse Rivers.'" Indeed, she went on to compile an incredibly high consent rate. During the first twenty years of the experiment, she approached 145 families and all but one granted permission.[2]

Nurse Rivers's success was no accident. With only slight variations she followed the same procedures with each family. Immediately after a subject had died, she would break the news personally to the next of kin, who, in most instances, was the man's wife. Her sense of timing was acute. "I wouldn't go right on in to the autopsy," she explained, "and I'd stay with the family because they would expect me to come and console them." Hours would pass with nothing more than sobs of grief breaking the silence.[3]

Often the family would create the opening. Faced with the loss of a loved one, they turned to her for some explanation. Many feared that they might be suffering from the same sickness and sought reassurance that they, too, would not die. But if such convenient lead-ins were not forthcoming, Nurse Rivers was prepared to initiate the subject of autopsies herself.[4]

The request was always conveyed in highly personal terms and with great sensitivity to the family's wishes, for Nurse Rivers had a gift for using the right language: "Now I want to ask you a favor," she would entreat the wife soon after they both had stopped crying. "You don't have to do it; we don't have to do it." She would then explain that the doctors wanted to learn what had caused the man's death, but instead of mentioning the word "autopsy" she employed a term that was sure to be understood. "You know what an operation is," Nurse Rivers would say reassuringly. "This is just like an operation, except the person is dead."[5] . . .

Beginning in 1935 her work became easier because the PHS began offering burial stipends in exchange for permission to perform the autopsies. The idea seems to have originated in a request for a cash payment from the widow of the first subject on whom an autopsy was performed. According to Nurse Rivers, the woman asked "for a hundred and fifty dollars for her husband's body as we performed an autopsy." Though the request was politely refused, Dr. Vonderlehr was quick to perceive in burial stipends an excellent means of enticing the families.[6] . . .

The burial stipends were a strong incentive for cooperating with the experiment. "For the majority of these poor farmers such financial aid was a real boon," declared a PHS report published in 1953, "and often it was the only 'insurance' they could hope for." According to the report's principal author, Nurse Rivers, Macon County's black people "didn't have anything for burials."[7]

Nurse Rivers saw the burial stipends as a godsend for people who could not afford decent funerals. The cash payments also provided protection against losing the autopsies of men who did not die in the hospital. "They would let me know when somebody died," she observed, "because in those early days fifty dollars was a whole heap of money for a funeral." Occasionally, one of the men might balk, complaining that he needed help while he was still living, not after he was dead, but whenever this occurred, explained a PHS report: "She appealed to him from an unselfish standpoint: What the burial assistance would mean to his family, to pay funeral expenses or to purchase clothes for his orphaned children." Most of the families accepted the offer without hesitation, considering themselves fortunate to receive burial aid. Nurse Rivers, too, felt personally grateful because the money kept her from having to face them empty-handed. "I could go to them and ask for an autopsy because I knew the fifty dollars was coming."[8]

Nurse Rivers's interest in the families did not end once they had granted permission for the autopsies. She attended every funeral service and often sat with the relatives of the deceased. "I was expected to be there," she said. "They were part of my family."[9]

Her success rested in large measure on the rapport she had with the families, relationships that were close and ongoing. Keeping in touch with the men was essential, for if contact were broken, autopsies might be lost. In the early years of the experiment, there was a tendency to underestimate the difficulties that would confront Nurse Rivers as a follow-up worker. "The Negro in Macon County appears to be an individual who remains in the same place over a period for many years," wrote Dr. Cumming. "Old Negro men are frequently met who report that they were born within a mile or two of the meeting place and have never moved out of the County." He saw Macon County as a hermetically sealed laboratory, an ideal setting for studying syphilis "not presented in many places in the civilized world today."[10] . . .

Home visits became an important part of her follow-up activities. Through them, she came to know the men and their families well. "Miss Rivers would come by and check on us between times we see the doctors," recalled one of the men. "Yes, sir, she sure would. Come in and visit with us and talk to us and ask us how we doing," the man continued. "Sometime she'd feel our pulse, see how our pressure was doing. . . . It was very nice," he added gratefully. Similar testimonials make it clear that the PHS did not exaggerate when it reported: "A single home visit is worth more than a dozen letters on impressive stationery."[11]

Nurse Rivers visited the ill more frequently. A subject who was sick in bed for two weeks on one occasion remembered her making "three or four different trips" to his home. To keep herself abreast of illnesses, she relied upon direct notifications by physicians, the men's families, and the men themselves. The men were especially helpful. In addition to contacting her about themselves, they reported on each other, giving Nurse Rivers eyes and ears everywhere. She did her best to be omnipresent because sick men could take a turn for the worse at any moment, and it was her job to be there just in case a trip to Andrew Hospital seemed advisable. Men who were amazed to see her appear unannounced at their sickbeds often inquired how she had learned of their illness. "Oh, a little bird told me," Nurse Rivers would reply with a smile.[12] . . .

For their part, the physicians came to respect her knowledge of human relations and to value her advice. One health officer probably spoke for his colleagues when he described Nurse Rivers as "a good right hand, an excellent person." What commended her most, he confessed, was that she "would indicate to me the things that she thought I could or couldn't do with them. . . . She would not let me fall into any pitfalls. She was very careful about keeping me out of trouble."[13]

If Nurse Rivers served as "cushion," she also served as a "bridge" between the doctors and the men. The health officers occasionally complained that the men were uncooperative or responded to instructions too slowly. She handled these situations by paraphrasing what the doctors had said so the men would understand exactly what the doctors wanted. Nothing angered the health officers more than subjects who refused to be examined because they did not feel sick. The doctors interpreted this attitude "as rank ingratitude for a thorough medical workup which would cost anyone else a large amount of money if sought at personal expense." On those days, the PHS report explained, "the nurse reminded the doctor of the gap between his education and health attitudes and those of the patients."[14]

Rushing through examinations without giving the men time to talk about their aches and pains was a serious offense for young clinicians to commit. The men felt neglected, uncared for. But instead of confronting the doctors whenever this occurred, they turned to Nurse Rivers, who listened to their complaints and offered soothing explanations. "She tried always to assure them that the doctor was a busy person interested in many things, but that they really were first on his program," declared the public health report.[15]

Though the men probably believed these reassurances, many wondered why the same doctors seldom returned. "They sent a different crew every year when they sent a doctor," a subject observed. "You never did see them others no more." Another man, whose eight years of schooling made him one of the best-educated subjects in the experiment, expressed his suspicions more strongly: "I tell you the only thing on down through the years that made me think on my way was that we never had the same doctor. . . . That's why I maybe begun to wonder." Struck by the absence of older faces among the doctors, he added: "They were young men and that's what made me curious. I said [to myself]: 'I wonder if they were doing their intern or practicing on us or what?' But nobody ever said nothing."[16]

Few questions of this sort ever reached the doctors. The men preferred to devote their discussions to matters of health rather than personnel changes. Besides, the familiar figure of Nurse Rivers remained a constant, appearing like an old friend at each roundup. Her presence no doubt made the rotation among the doctors seem less important.

Most of the men never raised questions about the experiment, at least not outside their own circle. To them Nurse Rivers offered no explanations; one of her characteristics was knowing when to remain silent. "She never did tell us nothing about what they [the doctors] was doing," complained one subject bitterly. But when the men did raise questions, they asked them of Nurse Rivers. She parried each with consummate skill, varying her responses to match her listeners and imparting only as much information as the moment demanded.[17]

Often her replies merely echoed what the men had been told at the beginning. "The answer she would give me was: 'You just got bad blood and we is trying to help you,'" a subject recalled. While generally vague and elusive, Nurse Rivers also knew how to trade upon the men's ignorance and need for medical care to fashion explanations for the experiment that they would find compelling. One subject who complained of being in chronic poor health and asked why he should remain in the study remembered her replying: "You may be suffering with something you don't know it, and if you go through this study then you'll know what's wrong with you and you'll know how to remedy [it]."[18]

The relationship that evolved between Nurse Rivers and the men played an important role in keeping them in the experiment. More than any other person, she made them believe that they were receiving medical care that was helping them. "She knew them [and] they knew her and trusted her," stated Dr. Heller. "She would keep them satisfied that our intentions were honorable and that we were out for the good of the patient."[19]

How well she did her job is evident from the comments of the subjects. "We trusted them because of what we thought that they could do for us, for our physical condition," said one of the subjects. "We were unable to do anything for ourselves physically." When asked about his participation in the experiment, another man replied: "We [were] just going along with the nurse." He, too, definitely believed that he was benefiting from the study for he added: "I thought they [the doctors] was doing me good."[20]

If the men trusted and respected Nurse Rivers it was no less true that she became genuinely devoted to them. Among all the researchers, she alone came to know the men as individuals. She visited in their homes, ate at their tables, sat at their sickbeds, and mourned at their funerals. Her life became intertwined with theirs, and a bond that transcended friendship developed between them. A young woman when the experiment began, she grew old with the men who survived. In a real sense, she shared their lives and they became her life. After watching her interact with the men and their families, one of the "government doctors" observed that for her "the Study has become a way of life."[21] . . .

For most of her life the men in the experiment were the closest thing Nurse Rivers had to a family in Tuskegee. Her blood relatives lived elsewhere. She did not marry until she was well into her fifties, and when she finally did wed, she remained within the experiment, marrying Julius Laurie, an orderly at Andrew Hospital and the son of one of the controls. After her marriage the "government doctors" addressed her as "Mrs. Laurie," but to most of the men in the study she remained "Nurse Rivers."

Nurse Rivers's ability to recognize the men on sight helped the PHS prevent them from obtaining treatment. During the first few years of the experiment there was no real danger that the men would receive medical care. But in 1937 the Rosenwald Fund decided to renew its support of syphilis control programs and sent a black physician, Dr. William B. Perry of the Harvard School of Public Health, to Macon County. Fearing that the resumption of treatment activities might endanger the experiment and aware that Dr. Perry needed help badly, Dr. Vonderlehr shrewdly arranged to have Nurse Rivers assigned as his assistant. Dr. Perry agreed to cooperate fully with the experiment, and he and Nurse Rivers worked together for several months. Her presence at the treatment clinics no doubt guaranteed that the men in the experiment were not treated. . . .

Nurse Rivers was not troubled by the duties she performed. Indeed, she never thought much one way or the other about the ethics of the experiment. She saw herself as a good nurse, one who always did what the doctors ordered. Not once did she advocate treating the men. In fact, she never raised the matter for discussion. She did not do so, she explained, because "as a nurse, I didn't feel that that was my responsibility. That was the doctors'." Any other response would have been unthinkable for a nurse of her generation, argued Nurse Rivers, because "as a nurse being trained when I was being trained we were taught that we never diagnosed; we never prescribed; we *followed* the doctor's instructions!"[22] . . .

Nurse Rivers did not give penicillin a second thought, at least not in connection with the men in the experiment. By the time it became widely available more than a decade had passed since the men had been given any form of treatment for syphilis. A momentum had developed; not treating them had become routine.

Ironically, Nurse Rivers's real concern was that the men had become a privileged group. Compared with their neighbors, she saw them as "the cream of the crop" in terms of the health care they received. She formed that attitude in the early years of the experiment and maintained it for the remainder of her professional career. When the study began, the black population in many parts of Macon County lived outside the world of modern medicine. Though hookworm, pellagra, tuberculosis, and syphilis (to mention only a few diseases) were endemic in the area, many people went from cradle to grave without ever seeing a physician.

In Nurse Rivers's view the experiment lavished medical attention on those fortunate enough to be selected. Instead of being neglected, the men were examined by a team of physicians every year, received free aspirin for their aches and pains and "spring tonic" for their blood, and had their own nurse to look after them. "They didn't get treatment for syphilis, but they got so much else," she stated. Arguing that medicine is as much art as it is science, she also explained the therapeutic value of what the subjects thought was being done for them. "They enjoyed having somebody come all the way from Washington or Atlanta down here [to Tuskegee] and spend two weeks riding up and down the streets looking at them, listening to their hearts and [having] somebody to take their blood pressure and this sort of thing," she declared. "That was as much help to them as a dose of medicine."[23] . . .

Nurse Rivers devoted her life to the experiment with a clear conscience. For her the men were the experiment, and she saw herself as serving them well. She had been trained to follow the doctors' orders and to take good care of her patients. Nothing in her nurse's training had prepared her to recognize that there could ever be a tension between doing what the doctors instructed and looking after the best interests of her patients. Her former teachers at Tuskegee, the private doctors in the area, and the PHS officers who served as her supervisors were all involved in the experiment. It never occurred to her to question their judgment. . . .

Class consciousness offers the best explanation of her denial that the experiment was racist. The dilemma confronting her was the same for all the black professionals who were involved in the experiment: on the one hand scientific energy and money were to be devoted to the study of diseased blacks, long ignored by science and medicine; but, on the other hand, the whole notion of framing the experiment as a study of "the diseased" instead of "disease" smacked of racism. The social gap that existed between her and the men made Nurse Rivers less sensitive to the full implications of attempting to prove that blacks really were different from whites. Class consciousness, stoutly reinforced by professional loyalties, served as the functional counterpart of race in placing her and the other black clinicians on the side of the white researchers. As upwardly mobile blacks they did not seem to feel personally threatened by working to prove still another way in which blacks could be labeled "different."

If Nurse Rivers avoided the difficult confrontation with racism posed by the experiment, she did not shirk her duty to the subjects as she saw it. To the physicians the men remained subjects, but to her they were patients. Her supervisors had decreed that the men would remain untreated for syphilis. That decision set the limits of what she could do. But within the confines of doing as she was told, Nurse Rivers struggled to preserve her professional integrity and personal humanity vis-à-vis the men. . . .

Though the experiment was not mentioned by name at the ceremony, Eunice Rivers Laurie was given the Oveta Culp Hobby Award for her role in the Tuskegee Study. She received a framed certificate praising her for "notable service covering 25 years during which through selfless devotion and skillful human relations she has sustained the interest and cooperation of the subjects of a venereal disease control program in Macon County, Alabama." It was signed by Marion Fulsom, the secretary of HEW. She hung it on the living room wall of her home in Tuskegee, proudly displayed between a photograph of Martin Luther King and a plaque on which the Florence Nightingale Pledge was inscribed.

Nurse Rivers continued to work for several years after receiving the award. In her final years, she stated, people often stopped her on the streets and said: "Nurse Rivers, how in the world you still following them old people?" Her reply was always the same: "Yes, I'm following them. They're friends of mine and I'm trying to keep up with them so that the department can keep up with them. . . . I love those people. I enjoy going out there and sitting down and talking to them." Old age forced Nurse Rivers to retire in 1965, but she continued to come out of retirement for a few weeks to help with the annual roundup every year until the experiment ended.[24]

NOTES

1. Author's Interview, Eunice Rivers Laurie, May 3, 1977.
2. Laurie Interview; Eunice Rivers, Stanley H. Schuman, Lloyd Simpson, and Sidney Olansky, "The Twenty Years of Follow-up Experience in a Long-Range Medical Study," *Public Health Reports* 68 (1953): 394.
3. Laurie Interview.
4. Rivers et al., "Twenty Years," p. 394.
5. Laurie Interview.
6. Rivers to Vonderlehr, January 3, 1934, Records of the USPHS, Venereal Disease Division, Record Group 90, National Archives, Washington National Record Center, Suitland, Maryland [hereafter NA-WNRC].
7. Rivers et al., "Twenty Years," pp. 391–93; Laurie Interview.
8. Laurie Interview; Rivers et al., "Twenty Years," p. 393; Laurie Interview.
9. Laurie Interview.
10. Cumming to Gentlemen [Milbank Memorial Fund], November 29, 1935, TF-CDC.
11. Author's Interview, Carter Howard, May 2, 1977; Rivers et al., "Twenty Years," p. 394.
12. Author's Interview, Charles Pollard, May 2, 1977; Laurie Interview.
13. Author's Interview, John R. Heller, November 22, 1976.
14. Rivers et al., "Twenty Years," p. 393.
15. Ibid., p. 392.
16. Howard Interview; Author's Interview, Frank Douglas Dixon, May 2, 1977.
17. Pollard Interview.
18. Howard Interview; Dixon Interview.
19. Heller Interview.
20. Author's Interview, Herman Shaw, May 2, 1977; Pollard Interview, both quotes.
21. Joseph G. Caldwell to William J. Brown, June 29, 1970, TF-CDC.
22. Laurie Interview.
23. Ibid.
24. *Washington Post,* April 19, 1958; Laurie Interview.

8

EMERGENCY ROOM NURSE

Echo Heron

In this account of her apprenticeship on the Emergency Room staff, Echo Heron portrays some of the typical human scenes that make ER work so stressful and compelling. The cases coming her way on this particular shift demand a great deal of emotional self-awareness and self-control on the part of the nurse. Treatment of a vermin-infested street person, a severely burned but drunken and disorderly woman, and an abandoned baby requires a sense of professional detachment that writer Heron understands but nurse Heron has yet to fully develop. Nurse Heron implicitly learns that she needs to vent her anger with a balky and unruly patient, but not to such an extent that her behavior prevents her from carrying out her work. She also learns that the ER is a medical setting in which acts of great human kindness can coexist with acts of almost unimaginable callousness or despair.

An important feature of the ER world revealed in this selection is the extent to which indigent and poor patients use the ER as their primary source of medical care. The abusive street woman is part of a much larger world of people who have no personal physician and know of no other source of medical care than a trip to the ER when their condition becomes intolerable. Eventually our society may develop approaches to community medicine that will make other avenues of routine health care available to needy persons—through improved access to neighborhood clinics, for example. In the meantime, ER nurses like Echo Heron will continue to juggle the conflicting demands of true emergencies and illnesses resulting from chronic neglect and poverty.

The wheelchair and its owner came to an abrupt halt in front of bed one.

To set the brake, I leaned over the old bag lady, known throughout the county as Wheelin' Wilma, and two things happened: I saw her hair, looking very much like an abandoned winter nest, *move* by itself. Then I smelled her.

Without giving thought to how it looked to the other patients, I put my hand to my mouth and backed away, gagging. The rancid smell of her filth stung my nose, making my eyes water. I turned my face to the wall and breathed in a gulp of untainted air, hoping the childhood ability to hold my breath for long periods of time had not left me.

I scrunched up my eyes, to clear away any momentary hallucinations caused by some foreign crustation on my contact lenses, and moved closer to stare once more at the back of Wilma's head.

No! Yes, there it went again; I wasn't losing my mind. The top layer of the matted clump of hair which rested heavily on the old woman's neck actually (my stomach did not want to hear the word) *swarmed.*

"What's yer problem, girlie?" Wilma shouted testily. "Whaddaya doin' behind there anyway? I want some service!"

I finished locking the brakes, and into Wilma's good ear, the one without the hearing aid, I excused myself in the strained voice of one who is holding her breath and backed away from the wheelchair. A few feet away I let out my breath, wiped my eyes, and went in search of someone to confirm what I'd seen.

Despite the sting of Wilma's lingering odor in my nose, I was in excitement heaven. The longest, dreariest winter of my life had followed the inevitable path of nature and ended in spring semester. As far back as January I had begun counting the hours to graduation night; from 2,880 I was down to 201, and 15 hours into the instructors' new brainchild known as the "student forty-hour week."

Since the beginning of March the instructors had hinted there would be a wonderful, mysterious "surprise" for us at the end of the year. In the middle of April each of us was asked to list three areas of medicine in which we would most like to work and indicate the hospitals of our choice.

I figured I'd beat the system and signed up for emergency at Redwoods Memorial as my first, second, and third choices. . . .

Wilma, Irene told me, was a "repeater," one of ER's regular weekly customers. Sometimes her complaints were legitimate; mostly she was just looking for a warm meal and a little human companionship. Furtively looking around, Irene "confidentially" informed me that after Wilma's husband had died and left her penniless ("Well, actually I'd heard he left her twelve dollars"), her children ("My husband's sister read there was a boy and a girl") deserted her. Unemployable, Wilma took to the streets of San Francisco, taking an advanced course on how to be a proper bag lady. For a few years Wilma did pretty well for herself, living in the lap of bag lady luxury ("Those women make a lot of money off the junk they collect, you know!"), until she'd been hit by a speeding taxicab, which had left her paralyzed from the waist down. ("The papers said she was drunk, you know, stepped right out in front of the car . . . tried to sue the company . . . didn't get a dime.") Tsk-tsk.

Now, as a recipient of the state's generosity ("That means out of our pay-checks!"), Wilma lived with her four cats and faithful spotted mongrel in a deserted school bus on the outskirts of Sausalito and in her spare time, which was most of it, took in more stray cats and dogs.

She loved her animals as a mother loves her children ("God knows her own were failures!"), and with the money from her meager welfare checks, she fed them, groomed them, and turned over whatever was left to a local veterinarian who checked them over and cared for their wounds.

When the animals were restored, Wilma personally found homes for each one of them. It was, in certain sophisticated circles about the county, *très chic* to own one of Wilma's former strays.

While Wilma took excellent care of her animals, she paid very little, if any, attention to her own personal hygiene. On this visit Wilma's complaint was a sore, itching scalp. From what I'd seen and smelled, I believed she had a legitimate gripe.

Dr. Mahoney and Katy were busy pulling a piece of steak out of an inebriated man's windpipe, so I accosted Gus, who was just taking her first bite of lunch.

"Sorry to do this while you're eating, Gus, but would you help me out with Wheelin' Wilma? There's something making her hair move," I said, "and it ain't the wind."

Gus looked past me and waved to Wilma. "Sure. Wilma and I have a great respect for each other, especially after she bit me the last time she was here."

Gus moved into the suture room, where she donned a long-sleeved isolation gown, a pair of rubber gloves, and a paper surgical cap over her hair. She waited for me to do the same.

"You never know with Wilma," she explained, "living in that truck out there in the swamps with those animals and no water or facilities; I wouldn't touch her without protection if I were you."

I put on the gloves but couldn't go to the extent of the isolation gown and cap. "That's going to make her feel terrible, Gus. She's going to feel like some kind of freak leper if we both go over there looking like that."

"That's up to you, Ec," Gus said, shrugging her large, rounded shoulders. "As for me, I've got two more hours of contact with other patients, and then I go home to my husband, two kids, and one dog, and I'll guarantee you none of the afore-mentioned need whatever Wilma's got. By the time you finish dealing with her, you'll wish they made condoms big enough to fit your whole body into."

I considered what Gus said, and a few minutes late we both approached Wilma looking like something from outer space. She glanced first at me and then at Gus. I expected a caustic remark. Instead, she just shook her head and clicked her tongue. "That bad, eh?"

Gus nodded, and holding our respective breaths, we picked Wilma up out of the chair and put her on the gurney. Our neck veins bulged with the effort; for someone who reportedly didn't have enough to eat, Wilma was keeping up on her weight.

Not seeming to mind the rank odor as much as I, Gus drew the curtains around the gurney and was soon breathing normally.

"For God's sake, Wilma, why don't you take a bath? You smell awful."

Gus had a rare quality to her tone of voice, which, when combined with her southern accent, came out sounding kindly and maternal no matter how harsh the words or how stern the reprimand.

"Aw, come on, Gussie, you know I don't got no water or washtub at my place, and them public showers aren't made for wheelchairs." Wilma sniffed. "Besides, the animals don't care, and I quit goin' to all them fancy dignitary dinners a long time ago, ya know." Wilma's cackle sounded like the scream of a wounded peacock.

Gus and I removed the top layer of Wilma's various coats and sweaters.

"That's no excuse, Wilma," continued Gus. "If you can take care of those stray animals, you can clean yourself."

Without warning Wilma jabbed a dirty, discolored finger into Gus's shoulder. "Just do your job, sister, and take care of my head!"

Gus ignored Wilma's jabs and continued what she was doing without comment, but I took exception to the incident. There was a certain hostility in the old woman's demand that disturbed my initial impression of Wilma as a "character," eccentric but likable.

After removing a third coat, we got down to Wilma's shirt. Stiff with soil and any number of caked-on substances, the material tore easily under our hands.

Naked to the waist, Wilma's skin looked like a work of modern art, covered with splotches of different-colored dirt and grime. The areas under armpits and around her neck were red and irritated. I handed Wilma a patient gown and told her to put it on. She shoved it back at me.

"You do it," she said indignantly. "I'm tired!"

Rather than hassle with her, I slipped the thin piece of cotton over her arms, feeling a small dose of resentment creep into my throat.

Gus pulled the exam light over to Wilma's head. From a fair distance she studied the old woman's hair and then the skin of her neck. Involuntarily she shuddered and stepped back. Pointing at the back of Wilma's head, she mouthed the word *lice.*

I leaned closer to look. The small gray-white parasites crawled at a steady pace through her hair and in the folds of her neck. An innocent, subconscious curiosity caused me to pick up the matted bun so I could see Wilma's scalp.

A shiny brown cockroach dropped to the floor and scurried under the bedside cabinet with the greatest of insect speed. Gus, half laughing, half screaming, jumped up against the wall. I clung to the far end of the curtain, whimpering. Cockroaches were to me what the rats in room 101 were to Winston in George Orwell's *Nineteen Eighty-Four.*

Immediately my head began to itch, and I was sure I felt something crawling on my scalp over my left ear. I moved to scratch my head and realized I was about to touch myself with the same hand that had just touched Wilma's hair. I froze, and my arms started to feel crawly. I glanced over at Gus; she was scratching the side of her face with her shoulder.

"Wilma, you got a bunch of creatures taking up residence on you," said Gus, briefly blotting her perspiring upper lip with her shoulder.

"Well, hell, get 'em off me. That's what I came here for!" Wilma said, scowling.

Gus moved around to face Wilma. "I think you've got to let us cut that wad of hair off so we can see why you're sore underneath. I'm sure Dr. Mahoney will send you home with some special shampoo and soap, and you'll have to wash all your clothes and linen. Can you do all that?"

We watched Wilma while she chewed on the idea. After a minute she stared at us, wearing a belligerent expression. "Naw. Sounds like too much work for this old crip."

Gus gave one of her more expressive sighs. "Okay, Wilma, in that case, I think we've got to get county services involved. Maybe they can find you a temporary place to stay and somebody who can help you, but we really can't let you wander around in public like this, spreading these critters all over the place."

Wilma was stunned by the unexpected turn of events, and her eyes filled with tears. "What about my animals? I got a new kitten that needs to be eyedropper-fed every few hours; who's gonna take care of him, huh?"

Gus knelt and looked kindly into Wilma's face. "I'll make arrangements with the SPCA to take care of all your animals until this is over, but from now on, Wilma, I want to see you take better care of yourself. You've got to promise you'll do something about the way you're living. People won't be as nice to you if you don't try to help yourself; you know that, don't you?"

Still tearful, Wilma nodded her head reluctantly in agreement.

Gus left me to shear off the infested chignon alone. Taping one side of a plastic trash bag to Wilma's neck, I opened the top, and readied my bandage scissors.

I wanted to get the bugs contained as quickly as possible, but after making one cut into the thick gray hair, I stopped abruptly. The sound of the hair being cut brought me to the edge of a dark memory. Skirting around the unpleasant thought, I made another cut, and the sound again roused a hazy memory picture.

Disregarding my conscious wish, my mind rebelliously stepped into the cold fruit cellar of the house where I grew up. Sitting on a high wooden stool, I sat quietly weeping while my mother placed a bowl over my head and sheared off the ends of my already short hair. Vanity in a girl of thirteen, she told me sternly, was a sign of shamelessness and a most grievous sin.

I released Wilma's hair from the grip of the scissors.

"Whaddya stoppin' for?"

Snapping to, I finished cutting off the clump and let it fall into the bag. The newly exposed section of Wilma's scalp was raw and infected from her scratching.

"God, Wilma, you've scratched yourself raw." I showed her the mess of infested hair before I tied off the bag with a piece of string.

Wilma looked at the matted stuff dubiously and shrugged it off. "Lookit, sister, don't bother me with the gory details. It's your job to take care of it."

Fury hit me like a twenty-foot wave. I felt used. The woman was a taker, and nothing anyone could do for her would ever be enough; she would always expect, *demand* more.

I swallowed, gritted my teeth, and let go. "You got that wrong, lady!" The statement came out of me with such sudden force and volume that Wilma jumped, and her watery eyes widened with surprise. "It's not *my* job. It's yours, damn it! You come off with this I'm-a-cripple attitude and that we're some subservient group of butt wipers, obligated to take care of your whims. If you really want to know, Wilma, you are so far off base, it makes me sick! There's a lot of people worse off than you who have really done something for themselves. Stop expecting other people to pull you up. Work a little, Wilma. Struggle a little; go for something better than just surviving."

Self-control grabbed me by the throat and choked me. All of a sudden I was in the throes of remorse. Surreptitiously, I looked around the curtain to see if anybody besides Wilma had heard me.

Dr. Mahoney, standing by the next gurney, looked up from the wrist she was examining. "Subservient butt wipers?" she mouthed, raising her eyebrows. I shrugged, my face burning with embarrassment, and closed the curtain.

Wilma had started to cry and hyperventilate at the same time. She tried poking her finger at me, but I moved out of the way. "You git somebody else to take care of me, somebody who's nice, you dirty-mouthed snot! I got my rights! Git that other nurse back here, or I'll sue you for malpractice!" Wilma blew her nose and wiped her eyes on the hem of her gown.

She looked away from me and muttered, "Little snipe! Treating a poor cripple like that. . . . "

The conflicting emotions of wanting to scream at her and pity triggered an instant fantasy in which the basic Wilma, meticulously manicured and dressed, sat in a clean and cozy living room, reading a book on flower arrangements. At her feet lay a snoozing spotted mongrel and four cats; there was not one flea among them.

"Okay, Wilma, just relax," I said. "I'll have Gus come back." Plaintively I sealed my gown and other protective paraphernalia in a plastic bag and left the woman alone.

I was in the middle of explaining to Gus why Wilma had "fired" me when the triage buzzer sounded once. I signed Wilma's chart over to Gus and walked to the lobby. . . .

Irene came in, moving languidly, but not without some purpose, toward the coffee. Greeting us, she poured a cup and leaned against the sink. Her eyebrows knitted tightly together, she sipped her coffee with a certain amount of delicacy.

"You know," she said uneasily, "I think I should tell you two there was something very suspicious going on in the parking lot when I came in just now." She stopped for an uncharacteristic pause, then went on. "I overheard, only briefly, mind you, an argument in the big light-colored car that's parked right out in front of the lobby doors. It wasn't any of my business, of course, but when I passed by, I heard a woman say something like 'I'm hurt; you've got to help me.' Now I could be wrong, but—"

Gus and I left Irene talking to herself and went to the parking lot. Just as Irene had said, there was a big light-colored car parked by the doors. Cautiously moving closer to the auto, we heard a man yelling and stopped to listen.

"Hey, asshole, didn't you hear me? I said I'm *not* taking you in there! You did it to yourself! Get out and walk yourself!"

Reactivated by the abusive language, Gus hurried around the car and knocked, none too gently, on the driver's window. A moment passed. Gus raised her hand again when the window rolled down with a high-pitched mechanical whir. A large, red-faced man in his sixties focused with difficulty on Gus's white uniform and name tag. Weaving, he looked back at the passenger.

"Here! Here's a nurse. Get her to help you." He turned to Gus. "My wife has had an accident with a cigarette"—he slurred the words—"and she wants to talk to you." Gripping the steering wheel, he stiffly pushed himself back into the plush seat so Gus could see the passenger.

Peering around the man's head, Gus froze, then jerked her head up. "Get a gurney!" she screamed. "Stat!"

I raced into the trauma room and grabbed the gurney. Irene looked at me questioningly.

"Find Dr. Mahoney. Tell her we're going to need her for"—I realized I didn't know what was in the front seat of the car—"for something stat!"

When I got the parking lot, Gus was standing just inside the opened passenger door. Hearing the squeak of the gurney wheels, she turned around, looking wild.

"Quick, Ec! Help me get her up."

I situated the gurney as close to the passenger door as I could and got a whiff of what smelled like a smoldering campfire.

"Thank God she's as drunk as he is," whispered Gus. I glanced down at the passenger.

The only things I recognized were a huddled human form, a pair of half-melted slippers, and the sleeve of a quilted plaid houserobe. From those starting points I was able to put together the charred figure.

My eyes traveled from the slippers to the head, which was like that of a hairless mannequin painted glossy black. Sticking out over her ears were straggling wisps of burned hair. I leaned closer, trying to discern the nose and mouth, when two blue eyes opened and stared into my face.

"Hi, honey, I'm Estelle," she said in a voice that could have belonged to Froggy in *Our Gang*. Her teeth were badly stained with nicotine, and her breath was loaded with booze. "Could you get me a hanky so I can cough up some of this crap from my throat?"

"Sure, sure," I answered, feeling nervous as a cat; my experience in dealing with burns of this magnitude was nil. "Let's get you onto this gurney first, and I'll get you all the Kleenex you can use in just a sec, okay, Estelle?"

Her head wobbled drunkenly, and she laughed a little. "Okey-dokey, pokey."

The woman couldn't have stood more than five feet and weighed less than a hundred pounds. Easily we lifted her onto the gurney. As soon as we were clear of the car, the man slammed the door shut from the inside, gunned the motor, and squealed out of the parking lot. The woman didn't look in the direction of the car but raised her voice. "You miserable bastard! I hope you run into a pole and break your goddamn head!"

As we sped through the empty corridor into the trauma room, Gus told me the only information she'd got from the man was that his wife had fallen asleep smoking and woke up in flames. He couldn't, however, remember how long ago that had been.

As we flew past Irene's desk, she caught a glimpse of the burned form and pivoted away from the sight.

I grabbed a box of Kleenex and, in my nervousness, took out too many, spilling half of them on the floor. The spindly right arm and hand, the only unburned part of her, came up to grab the tissue. With a wet, rumbling cough, she brought up a glob of gray mucus streaked with black.

Gus grabbed my arm. "Oh, shit!" she said under her breath. "Her airway is involved. We're got to move fast." She placed a two-pronged oxygen cannula in the woman's nose, being careful not to irritate any of the burned skin, and turned the flow to high.

Irene hurried to the door. "Dr. Mahoney is in ICU reintubating a patient. She said to hold down the fort as best you can and she'd be here as soon as she could."

I shot a look at Gus. "Help!" I said, panicking. "I don't know what to do. I've never seen anything like this before. You're going to have to walk me through there."

"Sure," she said. I could see her mind was racing. "Sure. It's okay, don't worry, we can do it. The airway is the main thing, but that's okay for right now, so you get her vitals and I'll start the IV."

I cut away the scorched sleeve of Estelle's right arm and took her BP and pulse, while Gus assembled the IV equipment.

We were so intent on what we were doing that when the woman suddenly spoke, we both started. "Yeah," she said loudly, "I tried to get that son of a bitch to bring me in before, but he was too drunk." The woman giggled. "Of course, he wasn't as drunk as me. . . . "

Gus applied the tourniquet to Estelle's arm and sponged off the skin with an alcohol wipe. She picked up the large-bore angiocath. "What do you mean, 'before'? When did this happen?"

Estelle ignored the question and pulled her arm out of Gus's grip. Tentatively she touched the top of her head and pulled off a clump of the burned hair. Her hand wove as she tried to study it. "Yeeech! What a mess! I must look like hell," she murmured.

I wondered if she knew the irony of her statement.

Gus gently pulled her arm back down and probed for the large antecubital vein. Finding it quickly, she slipped in the angiocath and released the clamp, letting the IV solution run in wide open.

Together we cut away what was left of the robe. Pieces of black cotton, mixed with strips of what must have been a flannel nightgown, lay in a small heap on the floor.

In the fastest mathematical calculations I'd ever done, I added up the percentage of Estelle's body which had been burned, using the rule of nines. Her chest, a mixture of third- and second-degree burns, accounted for eighteen percent; her left arm added another nine percent; the head nine percent, and so on, until I came up with a total of seventy-two percent. From the burned pattern of her clothes and limbs, I guessed the fire had started at her feet and spread upward. Besides her right arm, which must have been under something or outstretched, her buttocks and upper back, which had pressed against the chair, had also escaped harm.

Gus tried to ease off Estelle's right slipper and had to cut around the plastic that had melted into the skin. When I removed the left slipper, four of her toes were missing. Checking inside the slipper, I found the remains of the woman's foot mixed with a gob of plastic and nylon. . . .

At two, the pneumatic doors opened at the same time the buzzer went off. The hard, squealing howl of a baby reached our ears.

"At least we know this child is not in respiratory distress, a good sign," said Dr. Mahoney as we rushed, single file, toward the noise.

All of us came to a halt in front of a giant of a man in overalls, holding the squalling child as if it were some faintly disagreeable foreign object.

Shyly he handed the baby to Dr. Mahoney and we all moved, as if chained together, to the nearest gurney. She removed a large blue bandanna from around the baby. The little girl was covered with scrapes embedded with road dirt.

The man took the soiled piece of cloth from her apologetically. "Sorry, ma'am, but I didn't have anything else to wrap it in."

Dr. Mahoney felt the baby's skull, looked into her eyes and ears, and ran her expert hands over the miniature body while the man spoke.

"My name's Paul Jepson, and I'm a driver for a trucking company out of L.A."

Mr. Jepson followed Dr. Mahoney over to the sink. She lined the bottom with soft towels and ran in warm water. The baby's crying died down to a soft whimper as she played with Dr. Mahoney's glasses.

"I was driving my rig along the highway . . . just coming into San Rafael, when I noticed this passenger car about a quarter mile in front of me start slowing down and weaving off to the side, like it's got trouble.

"The next thing I know, this lady sticks the top part of her body out the back window, screaming like she's getting killed or something, and throws this thing out onto the road. At first I thought it was a bundle of rags, but then I see this kid fall out of the middle of the bundle. I pulled off and ran to pick it up as quick as I could; I was afraid somebody might think it was just a doll or somethin' and hit it.

"Anyway, I left the rig there since it's one of those big piggyback jobs and flagged down the next car. It seemed to be the fastest way to get the baby to the hospital."

Silently we all watched the baby splash at the bubbles as Dr. Mahoney gently soaked off the road dirt.

Two minutes later she picked up the child and wrapped her in a warm flannel blanket. "Well, all I've got to say is it's a good thing these little people bounce. There's no damage that I can see other than the road burns."

Irene was leaving to pick up a bottle of formula and some flannel sleepers from the nursery when two California Highway Patrol officers came in to ask about the baby and the truck driver who had picked her up.

Relieved his truck had not been cited, Mr. Jepson gave his statement and was allowed to go.

The officers helped themselves to the cake and hot coffee while they filled in the blanks of the story.

"The baby's name is Phoebe. She's six months old. Our unit in San Rafael picked up the mother about fifteen minutes ago hitchhiking along the freeway, spaced out of her mind on something, looking for the child.

"According to her, she and the baby's father were out for a ride when they got into an argument over drugs. The father said she threatened to kill herself and the baby but decided to throw just the kid out and let it go at that."

Dr. Mahoney stopped playing pattycake with the baby and looked over at me. "Remember the other day when I was telling you that I didn't let things get to me anymore?"

I nodded my head.

"I lied. This makes me sick."

9

RAPE KIT

Perri Klass

In this selection Perri Klass describes her experiences as a medical resident in pediatrics. This is a fine example of the way doctors write about their own professional socialization. At first, the long hours and the many different people one encounters are among the more challenging aspects of learning to be a pediatrician. Later, everything seems routine and the resident may develop a blasé attitude. But then there are new shocks arising from the social dimensions of medicine, especially the pain of dealing with reprehensible aspects of human behavior such as child molestation.

Child molestation is on the rise in the United States. One explanation for this trend is the improved training and increasing sophistication of medical professionals, who are better able to recognize and report cases of abuse and molestation. A more fundamental cause, however, is the decline in the material well-being of many families with young children. A higher rate of adolescent fertility among poor populations also increases the probability of child abuse.

One of the humorcus and poignant episodes that Klass describes is a reflection of the difficulty Americans have discussing sexuality and the biology of sex among themselves and with their children. The more tragic episodes deal with the effects of the use of sex as a weapon to do harm. Klass learns that the things she says to a young rape victim are helpful and appropriate when an older, more experienced doctor says virtually the same thing. But her experiences dealing with rape and child sexual abuse lead her to realize that doctors are extremely limited in their ability to address the larger social and psychological issues that produce rape victims and their tormentors.

The agonies of residency are the stuff of medical folklore. In recent years, they have also at times been front-page news, as the question is raised: does sleep deprivation mean poor medical care? New York has made laws limiting the hours residents can work, and many people believe that such laws will soon be passed everywhere. But a week ago, in 1992, I heard a senior obstetrician assuring two exhausted residents that there is no scientific evidence anywhere that any amount of stress and sleep deprivation affects resident performance. And then he went on to give his version of the speech that so many senior doctors give: when I was a resident, we lived in the hospital, we fought for the complicated cases, we loved our work, we begged for more. And that's the only way to learn medicine. As I said, medical folklore, medical legend. The proverbial days of the giants (a phrase which never fails to make the residents snicker).

So anyway, when I started my residency I was more or less prepared for some of its harsher aspects. I was nervous about being away from my family so much, about how I would function under hospital pressures, how I would cope with the schedule. And, speaking of stress, I guess I had some vague rather mushy idea that there would also be something sad about seeing all those sick children. Since I had every intention of being a deeply sensitive doctor, I probably saw myself helping some generic grieving family, acting as a tower of strength to children in pain, parents in distress.

But there are no generic families. Children are specific, their stories are specific, and their pain is specific. I would not have been able to predict the most strikingly difficult encounters, the lessons hardest to learn. The horror of a day when the world seems to be full of raped children. The repeated awful sense that I am myself in the business of hurting babies, sticking them with needles, making them cry. The tension of judging a parent competent or incompetent. Or the feeling of a baby actually dying under my hands.

Death is a hospital familiar. By the end of internship, we all knew the rituals of death, the bureaucracy of death. Forms to fill in, and if you use the wrong color ink, the morgue won't release the body to the family. Phone calls from the medical examiner. But before I got used to it (and I did get used to it, more or less), there had to be a first death, a night when the ending of a life had its full and proper impact.

After my first stint on the wards, I rotated through some of the other parts of the hospital. Some time in the emergency room, learning to handle the widely varied complaints: the child with a stuffy nose at three in the morning, the child with high fever and rash, the baby who might have stopped breathing for a few seconds earlier in the evening, and the adolescent with chest pain. I went back to the wards, back to the NICU, back to the emergency room. I was taking things in stride which would have terrified me only a month or two before: another sick preemie, another kid in respiratory distress in the emergency room, another chronic patient with multisystem disease. This next section is about those things which jolted that new-found complacency, that ridiculous attempt to prove to myself that I could take any-thing the hospital cared to hand me.

Sometimes medical training feels almost parasitic. To put it baldly, you are picking up your learning and your experience and your professional qualification out of the suffering of sick people. Yes, you are taking care of them, yes, you are try-ing to help, but it's also true that for you, this is a learning experience, while for them it's life and death. And so when I look back on my own growing pains, on the unexpected griefs and guilts of my internship year, I am looking back on patients and their parents who were living with pains of a very different order. . . .

The rape kit is a small plastic box, and it actually says RAPE KIT on it in red let-ters. We keep a supply of them in the emergency room, and no one looks forward to using them.

In a pediatric emergency room, you see a lot of sniffles. You look in a good many ears. You hear yourself asking, again and again, "Now, when you say diarrhea, how many bowel movements a day do you mean he's having?" A great many parents use the emergency room for every small ailment of childhood, and it can be a long time between true emergencies. And that is probably all for the best, since no one can really live in an atmosphere of one crisis after another, one near death after an-other, one death after another.

Life in the emergency room has its comic moments, too. At 2 A.M. on one hideously cold rainy night, I walked into a room to be confronted by a perfectly well-appearing boy, about thirteen years old, and his father.

"What seems to be the problem?" I asked in my most professional and-what-brings-you-out-on-a-night-like-this tone.

"There's no problem," said the father, flatly.

"Oh," I said. "Well, good."

"I want *you* to tell *him* there's no problem." He indicated his son. "Go ahead, tell the lady what happened."

The boy wouldn't look at me. He wouldn't talk to me either, at first, but his fa-ther insisted, and finally he whispered to the wall, "Something came out of my penis when I was sleeping."

"There!" said the father triumphantly. "Go ahead, tell him it's normal."

Now, sensitive doctor that I am, I did not say to this man, you mean you dragged your son out in the rain and brought him to the emergency room because you couldn't bring yourself to explain to him about wet dreams? Instead, I excused myself, quietly, and went to find one of the senior doctors working in the emer-gency room, an older man with children of his own. It seemed to me that after what this boy had already been through, he was entitled to get his little your-body-is-changing lecture from a father figure, not a young woman.

Days I worked in the emergency room sometimes seemed to have patterns to them: one asthmatic after another, one small baby with fever after another, one nonsense case after another (a nonsense case is a fifteen-year-old who has had a wart on this thumb for six months or so and has suddenly decided to come to the emergency room at noon on a Wednesday and would like a note for school saying he couldn't come because he was being treated in the emergency room). And then this one horrible day which was one rape after another.

She was thirteen and a young thirteen, and I really did believe her when she told me she wasn't sexually active. I had asked her father to leave the room while I examined her, and I had put the question cheerfully, in the midst of a string of other questions. (Emergency room lore: the adolescent girl who was asked whether she was sexually active and replied, no, she just lies there, her boyfriend is the active one.) I believed her, but she was a thirteen-year-old female with abdominal pain, and it is a truism of emergency room medicine that all females past puberty are pregnant until proven otherwise (this is just a harsh way of saying that people don't always tell the truth or even know the truth about their level of sexual activity, and before you do X rays or give any medications or take someone off to surgery, you have to verify that she isn't pregnant). So when I sent her urine off to be analyzed, I also sent a pregnancy test.

Abdominal pain and vomiting are extremely common complaints. People come into the emergency room all the time with stories of abdominal pain and vomiting. Sometimes they have stomach bugs, and sometimes they have acute appendicitis. Sometimes they're having miscarriages or ectopic pregnancies (pregnancies outside the uterus, usually in the fallopian tubes). Sometimes they hate school so much it makes their stomachs hurt, and sometimes they've taken overdoses. Abdominal pain is always a hard complaint to evaluate, since the treatment for a stomach bug is to rest in bed and drink lots of fluids, and the treatment for an ectopic pregnancy is to go immediately to the operating room and have your belly cut open. And with all the most careful diagnosis in the world, you can't always say what someone has; the surgeons preach that unless 20 percent of the appendectomies you do are unnecessary, you aren't doing enough operations. In other words, if you aren't operating on a certain number of the people without appendicitis, your index of suspicion is too high, and you're bound to miss some of the acute appendix cases—and if you miss those, they can get very sick indeed.

With this particular patient, I wasn't really thinking surgical emergency. She said she had been having a little belly pain, not too severe, for almost a week, and she'd been doing a lot of vomiting. Her father thought she had lost a little weight, and she wasn't interested in food. I thought maybe a stomach bug, but I wasn't sure.

When the urine pregnancy test came back positive, I needed to get her father out of the room again. One of the other doctors in the emergency room took him aside for me and began asking him some questions about his daughter's medical history. I went back into the little examining room and closed the door, faced the thirteen-year-old. Idiotic sentences occurred to me. ("The good news is, you don't have appendicitis.") Finally I said, "You probably aren't going to be happy to hear this, but your test shows that you're pregnant."

She stared at me for a minute, then shook her head. Then she began asking me how she could have gotten pregnant. As I said, she was a young thirteen. I told her what I thought had to have happened, and she considered for a minute, then asked, "I could get pregnant even if I didn't want him to do it?"

"Did someone do it when you didn't want him to?" I asked, and she began to cry, and then she told me a long and miserable story about a much older boy who she didn't know who had given her a ride home from school one day, saying her mother had sent him. This had happened three weeks earlier.

"Did you tell anyone about this?" I asked.

"He said he would come back and get me if I told," she said.

I told her that it was now up to her whether or not her father was told, that I could tell him or she could tell him, or else she could keep it secret for now. She wanted me to tell him, so I brought him into the room and told him, and then she blurted out her story one more time. I was grateful to him for being tough, for not doubting her story, for putting an arm around her and comforting her. He'd been worried about her, he told me, for a couple of weeks; she'd been acting very quiet, very unlike herself. I made a little speech to the two of them about what her options were, about the clinic I was going to refer her to, about gynecologic exams and pre-natal care, about adoption, about abortion. Then the girl's father went out to call her mother, and I was left alone with my patient again. Without planning any such speech, I heard myself saying, "One thing, you know, you mustn't think of this as being about sex." She looked at me in confusion, and I knew I was making a mess of it. "This isn't what sex will be for you," I said. "This was an act of violence; someone did this to you out of anger and hatred. This has nothing to do with making love, and you'll find out about that someday when you feel ready for it, when you agree to it. It's something different." She said nothing, and I wondered whether I should have kept my mouth shut.

Later that afternoon when the police brought in the nine-year-old boy, I actually volunteered to be the one to see him. They had called to tell us they were bringing in a kid who had allegedly just been raped, and I wanted a chance to collect evidence, to do something that might help chase down and convict the offender.

He was a nice bright boy, and I sat in our conference room with him, his parents, the social worker, and the police detective, and he told us what had happened; he had been playing with friends in a field and a couple of older guys had come and watched them, and his friends and he got nervous and decided to go home, but one of the guys followed him and made him go behind an empty building and raped him. The detective asked him a long list of questions about what the man looked like and exactly what he did, and the boy answered patiently, looking from his mother to his father, and his parents smiled at him and encouraged him, and then exchanged very different looks when they thought he wouldn't see.

After all this, I took him into the examining room. His mother came too (his father said he didn't think he could) and a nurse, who would help me and also act as a witness. I did a quick general physical, looked his whole body over for bruises and other marks. Then I opened the rape kit. We examined his anal and genital areas with ultraviolet light because dried semen fluoresces, and we carefully noted all the areas of white glow. Then I rubbed up some of those areas on a gauze and we did an acid phosphatase test, testing the samples with a chemical that turns purple if the substance is indeed semen. It turned purple, and we put the gauze and the acid phosphatase strip into the special plastic evidence bag and sealed it. We looked carefully for pubic hairs or other clues. We documented every small scrape and laceration.

I took swabs from his mouth and his anus to culture for gonorrhea; if a child has a sexually transmitted disease, this is considered good evidence in court that the child has been molested. The boy was very quiet while I did this, holding his mother's hand. I kept up a rather meaningless flow of talk, trying to encourage him and reassure him and continually promising him that I was almost done. When I finally *was* done, we sealed all the little evidence bags into the rape kit and closed it with stickers and I signed the stickers. And then finally we told him he could go home and take a bath, and I went out and wrote a careful description of the physical examination. A few minutes later the boy's father came up and asked whether I had tested his son for AIDS. No, I said, we don't do that routinely. In fact, I knew, there had been no time for this boy to develop antibodies to the virus, even if it had been transmitted, and the test checks for antibodies. On the other hand, AIDS is a sexually transmitted disease, and it made sense to me that it would be useful to document that this boy was originally negative—just in case he was unlucky enough to turn positive later. Besides, the father said his son had already asked him about it, so I figured that I might as well do the test and let it come back negative. I explained all this to the father, then drew the boy's blood. The boy asked if I was testing him because the rapist was homosexual, and I tried to explain that men who rape small boys are not necessarily homosexual, and anyway, that men who are homosexual do not necessarily have AIDS. But what if he used drugs, the boy said, he might have AIDS from that.

I took the tourniquet off his arm, and just then the psychiatrist knocked on the door. While I was putting the blood into tubes and labeling the tubes, I listened to hear how the psychiatrist would approach this situation.

The psychiatrist looked the boy in the eye, and said, "You know, this man was using his penis as a weapon. This had nothing to do with sex or love."

I have no particular wisdom to offer on the subject of men who rape children or even adults. In medicine, especially perhaps in pediatrics, the villain is supposed to be disease, malformation, bad fortune. If I wanted to deal regularly with situations where there really is a villain, I would have gone into some other field. It makes me angry, it makes me upset, and there's nothing I can do about it.

The next case I took that day was a young couple with their first baby, eight days old. They had come to the emergency room because they were very upset; the baby was spitting up a little bit of milk every time she ate. The nurse described the case, and I immediately volunteered to see them.

"No more rape kits today," I said. "I'm in the mood to give burping lessons."

10

DARING TO HEAL

Kathleen Hunt

This account by medical writer Kathleen Hunt portrays the work of Médecins Sans Frontières (Doctors Without Borders). It is an outstanding example of how dedicated health care providers respond to crises in the contemporary world despite all the obstacles in their path. Daring to heal in famine-stricken and anarchic Somalia, in war-torn Kurdistan and Afghanistan, and amid the natural and social disasters of Bangladesh, nurses, doctors, and other medical personnel volunteer their time and risk their lives to offer their medical skills in emergencies.

Hunt's account touches on a great many problems of emergency medical care in the world's most troubled regions. Note that none of the situations described originated as a medical problem. Famine, dehydration caused by diarrhea, cholera, and untreated wounds all cause severe medical emergencies. But the origins of these problems are more fundamental than lack of immediate medical attention. Diarrhea (and the high rates of infant mortality it causes) is a consequence of contaminated water supplies. The remedy is redesign of the water system, which requires cooperation and investments that go beyond immediate medical attention. In the case of Somalia, the anarchy and violence that produced famine cannot be healed by providing medical care to famine victims. The solution lies in creating political order—an extremely difficult challenge, as international relief organizations have learned. Heroic as the work of these medical professionals is, therefore, their work will be fruitless without other forms of healing at a broader social level.

In the United States there are neighborhoods and communities that resemble war-torn areas of the third world. One does not need to go as far as Kurdistan to find people in dire need of better medical attention and emergency care. A volunteer organization like Médecins Sans Frontières, which draws attention to these areas of high violence, disease, and addiction and provides needed, immediate care, could help spur longer-term and more fundamental remedies.

Few countries exemplify the world's forgotten catastrophes more graphically than Somalia, which had the ill fortune in January to see the violent overthrow of its aging dictator eclipsed by the countdown to war in the Persian Gulf.

Since the outbreak of civil war in 1988, Somalia had unraveled into lawlessness, falling to the mercy of rampaging soldiers and armed highwaymen. By January, when the climactic battle began for control of the capital, Mogadishu, most of the international aid community had pulled out of the ancient Arab seaport. Only a handful of Europeans remained, most affiliated with a small Austrian charity, SOS Children's Village. As the havoc spread north toward the city of Berbera, even the International Committee of the Red Cross withdrew. Telephones and telexes were cut, and commercial transportation was paralyzed.

But one relief group defied conventional wisdom and headed in rather than out. On Jan. 7, a small team of surgical volunteers from Médecins Sans Frontières (M.S.F.) flew into Somalia from neighboring Kenya to operate on the war-injured. Twice in the next few weeks, M.S.F. volunteers were forced to flee the country, first when waves of marauding Government troops invaded the hospital they were working in and later when rebels from the United Somali Congress overran Government headquarters and threw open prison dungeons and arms depots. Each time, the group slipped back a few days later. As Government forces and rebel factions filled the skies with artillery fire, Somalia's only contact with the outside world was the radio line between the M.S.F. volunteers and their regional office in Kenya.

Two decades after its birth in Paris, Médecins Sans Frontières (Doctors Without Borders) has grown from a band of swashbuckling young crusaders to the largest—and some would argue most efficient—medical relief organization in the world. With an annual budget of $30 million to $40 million, the group sends 2,000 volunteers a year into the field. And with 70 full-time staff members in Paris and more than 500 professionals on reserve, they are able to instantly dispatch an exploratory team of medical and logistic experts to the scene of a breaking emergency. Within hours of the team's report, they may begin to charter cargo planes and mobilize the M.S.F. logistics center in the town of Lézignan, in the south of France.

Spawned by a group of radicals from the Paris revolt of 1968, M.S.F. and its two offshoots, Médecins du Monde and Aide Médicale Internationale, have forged a movement of medical volunteers impelled by the duty to speak out against the suffering they witness and to go where other groups will not. For much of the last decade, the French doctors acted almost as a medical cavalry as the mujahedeen fought the Soviet Army in Afghanistan. Not only were they one of the very few relief organizations in the country, but they also brought eyewitness reports of the atrocities to the attention of the West.

Over the last 12 months, a year of disasters that left even the International Red Cross and the United Nations reeling, Médecins Sans Frontières and Médecins du Monde were consistently on the front line. Last July, they were with the rebels as Liberia was falling apart, and a month later, they were in Syria and the Jordanian desert building camps for some of the 700,000 refugees fleeing Iraq. In January, there was Somalia. Since February, they have battled the cholera epidemic that began in Peru and is threatening all of South America. Barely had their weary volunteers brought shelter and medicine to thousands of Kurds last April when a cyclone swept over a third of Bangladesh, prompting Paris to dispatch an exploratory team to assess the destruction.

It's early May when a photographer and I arrive in Somalia. In Mogadishu, M.S.F. volunteers are still performing surgery day and night, hunkered down in the rambling, single-story pavilions of Medina Hospital. Filled to its 130-bed capacity, the hospital has expanded outdoors, engulfed by patients with festering wounds, lying on foam mattresses under the flat-topped thorn trees. Except for the Red Cross, which has ventured back with a staff of three, the international relief community is still waiting it out in Nairobi.

The crackle of gunfire is commonplace in the Somali capital, and explosions shake the single-story hospital. In the stifling emergency room, there is no respite. A harried, sweat-soaked French nurse named Sabine Brunello plunges to the floor to examine a patient who has just arrived on a stretcher. Looking back over her shoulder at the crowd of spectators, she shouts in English: "Please! I want some help!"

A few feet away, the body of a little girl, cut down by a stray bullet, lies abandoned by her despondent parents. The floor is littered with saturated gauze and discarded rubber gloves, and flies have begun to swarm around a souring puddle of blood. Glancing across the room. Brunello murmurs, "The kids are really the toughest."

Across the compound, the team's medical coordinator, 32-year-old Jean-Hervé Bradol, is taking a short break in the kitchen of the former nurses' quarters. "I wanted to work here precisely because it's not in the spotlight, because no one cares about it," he says, slouching in the heat and humidity. "In fact, that's always been the great merit of M.S.F., they go to places others don't go." Bradol is married to a physician, who is back in Paris with their small child. "We take risks," he says of his colleagues, "financially, personally, with no feedback." The Somalia group was well aware of the disparity between the publicity surrounding the Kurdish disaster and that in Somalia.

Spirits are low on the M.S.F. team, which works from 8 A.M. until well after midnight. Relations have not been smooth with the local medical staff, who were alienated by the rigid work style of one of the first M.S.F. doctors to arrive. After weeks of diplomacy, M.S.F. has mended the rift, but recently some Somali doctors threatened to quit unless they were paid cash salaries in addition to the food rations they receive. "What are we doing here?" wonders Dr. Lionel Raffin, an anesthesiologist from Paris. "Now we are exhausted and our morale is destroyed. Are we doing anything worthwhile?" Since Raffin arrived two weeks ago, the team has performed 82 major operations and stitched up or set bones on scores of other patients. To Raffin, this seems like a drop in the ocean.

But his colleague Bradol sees the group's role more broadly, as independent witness to Somalia's agonizing upheaval. "We're not here to show people how to run a hospital," he argues. "We want to pressure the Government to act well." Their presence also provides a gauge of the level of stability of the new Government. "It would be very negative if we pulled out," Bradol says. Indeed, Charles F. Laskey, the director of CARE's Somalia program, says other agencies take their cue from M.S.F., although they also criticize them. "Some say they're too brash, won't cooperate too much with other nongovernmental organizations," he says. But "they dropped in and came out two or three times and that told us a lot. If those guys can't work there, then we can't."

Monitoring the ephemeral state of order is central—indeed vital—to M.S.F.'s daily work, and the delicate task of keeping in touch with all the contentious factions in Somalia falls to Wim Van Hauwaert, a nurse from Belgium and the team's overall coordinator. At 28 and built like a bear, Van Hauwaert moves easily among his roles as manager, morale-booster and diplomat. Every day, he makes at least one tour through the rubble-strewn capital with his well-informed young Somali driver to assess the balance of power among the rebel factions and to evaluate the general level of anarchy.

One morning, I go with Van Hauwaert to inspect two huge water purification tanks that the team has provided for several thousand people in a shantytown on the outskirts of the city. Like everyone else, we take along an armed guard. The whole city has been on alert today after fighting broke out between rebel factions last night.

As the driver turns down a main boulevard, 50 men and boys spring out of nowhere and surround us, swinging rifles and rocket launchers and pistols and shouting guttural orders all at once. "Stop!" they holler. "No photos! No PHOTOS!" The tension mounts as we continue past a charred Government tank, near the Hotel Towfiq. Van Hauwaert signals with a low hand gesture for our driver to stop; both of them now seem alarmed by the number of machine-gun-mounted cars in front of the hotel and by the bands of heavily armed men who are shrieking, "Get into the hotel!"

Inside, the hotel receptionists stiffen as two gunmen, slung with bandoliers, storm past and up the stairs to the roof. Another four men are standing on the rooftop across the street, all aiming their machine guns at our hotel. Half an hour later, we slip out and continue on our tour.

Most of the M.S.F. volunteers to Mogadishu are veterans of other difficult missions, but no one expected the workload, tension and deadly anarchy they found here. For the first three months, Medina Hospital was overrun with weapons; volunteers had guns pulled on them by families demanding that their relatives be treated ahead of others. "This is my toughest mission ever, and I've worked in Kurdistan, Mali and Niger," says Jeanne-Marie Gomis, a nurse who specializes in war surgery. "One patient threatened, 'If you don't help me, I'll beat you!'"

Despite the exhaustion, isolation and unnerving volleys of gunfire and grenades as they work, a strong feeling of camaraderie exists among the M.S.F. staff. Each evening, they break for dinner about 9, heading for the refuge of the old nurses' quarters. One by one, they flop down around the long table, to discover that once again, in the throes of Mogadishu's madness, their Somali cook, Didi, has managed to whip together a tasty meal of fish, meat stew and rice. Didi wears a snow-white chef's hat, which Bradol jokingly insists was not provided by M.S.F.

Determined to relax during mealtime, no one even blinks at the persistent machine-gun fire that seems 10 feet outside the window. Rather, they lose themselves in anecdotes that capture the utter chaos of the place. The table erupts in laughter over the story of the visit a month before by Dr. Bernard Kouchner, who was appointed French Minister of State for Humanitarian Action in 1988 and who was a founder of M.S.F. When he asked Somalia's interim President what kind of humanitarian aid the French Government could provide, even Kouchner, who has undoubtedly heard his share of unorthodox requests, was taken shack by the President's instant response. "Arms," he told Kouchner. "We need weapons for our policemen, so they can try to bring some order to this place."

At 51, Bernard Kouchner still resembles a slight, sandy-haired youth, though his face has become leaner with age, etched with intensity and anger. His lips, usually pursed in impatience, occasionally relax into a charismatic movie-star smile.

As a young physician and member of the Union of Communist Students, Kouchner was active in the Paris protests of May 1968. Later that year, he and other young doctors went to Biafra with the Red Cross, to work with the Ibo secessionists who were being bombed and starved out by the Nigerian Government forces. For many, it was their first exposure to genocide, and it was a cruel test of their Hippocratic oath.

"Some of the team decided to leave," Kouchner recalls, "and the rest of us organized a meeting to plan how we could protect our patients." The group brought together pragmatic political activists like Kouchner with traditional Christian humanitarians. One of these was Dr. Max Récamier, who impressed his colleagues with his spiritual commitment to serving humanity and influenced the group's mandate to help without regard to national or political identity.

"We are facing a mass murder," Kouchner told the group, "so if we are good doctors, we have to stop the bombing." Haunted by the echoes of World War II, when the International Committee of the Red Cross chose not to denounce the Nazi extermination camps, the group decided to break the oath of confidentiality they had signed with the Red Cross and to report what they saw. As healers, they argued, they had the duty to alert the world to the agony they witnessed, and to condemn the oppression causing it.

They also took exception to the Red Cross policy of respecting sovereign authorities and going only where they were authorized to go. Doctors, they argued, had a "duty to interfere," clandestinely if necessary. "You do not ignore a bleeding man simply because he happens to be bleeding across a border," Kouchner still insists. Emboldened by their new philosophical commitment, they named themselves Médecins Sans Frontières and rounded up a corps of doctors who would be on call for emergency deployment. Surviving on small donations, hitching rides on Air France or paying their own way, they navigated perilous situations with little more than their medical bags and political wits.

"At first, people saw us as crazy leftist Boy Scouts," remembers Dr. Patrick Aeberhard, a cardiologist in his mid-40's and a former president of Médecins du Monde. "Then we were seen as agents of the K.G.B. and C.I.A. alternatively, which was a good thing for us—at least we weren't politically aligned. But gradually they saw that we criticized things from the place where the *people* were"—that is, from the point of view of the population under attack.

The brashness and defiance of M.S.F.'s founders propelled the movement and gave it its élan. "The thing that is so incredible about Kouchner is that he will tell anyone what he thinks," Aeberhard says, recalling a 1976 incident in which Kouchner stormed out of a hospital in West Beirut that was being shelled by a Christian militia unit. "He crossed through an incredibly dangerous zone, marched up to the Christian militia and starting yelling at them for attacking the hospital. Kouchner told them, shaking his finger, 'Listen, some day *you're* going to be on the side that's getting bombed, and I'm going to come and help you, so you'll see I'm not taking sides.' But the militiamen sneered and said, 'Yeah, but we're going to kill you before that.'"

If their courage and conviction launched the young doctors into the field, their first stabs at humanitarian relief were pure improvisation. On a recent trip to the United States to promote Doctors Without Borders, M.S.F.'s new American affiliate, Dr. Francis Charhon shared memories with Dr. Rony Brauman, M.S.F.'s current president, of the days when they knew so little about relief supplies that they had to search the Yellow Pages to order blankets and other materials in bulk. At 45, prematurely white-haired, Charhon still has a schoolboy swagger. "Perhaps we had the imagination," he says, his eyes alight with amusement. "Having no background gave us the freedom of mind, and we did it."

Like many who joined M.S.F. in the 1970's, Brauman was inspired by Marxist ideals, believing that peasant revolutions would change the world. Nothing crushed the vestiges of that theory more than the savagery of the Khmer Rouge, Cambodia's revolutionaries, who left more than a million dead in their wake. Brauman was in Thailand in 1979, when thousands of ghostly Cambodians stumbled out of the jungle along the Thai border.

"We were lost at first," he says, wincing. "Nobody can be rational in a situation like that. You could only hear the groaning, and the wind in the trees. I had nightmares for weeks after that."

At the end of the 1970's, Médecins Sans Frontières split into two camps, driven apart by a controversial scheme of Kouchner's to publicize the plight of the Vietnamese boat people by launching a ship—the Île de Lumière, Island of Light—

to rescue refugees at sea. The plan triggered a bitter political debate, which brought to a climax a personality conflict and power struggle among the movement's founders. Critics denounced Kouchner's mission as self-promoting. He defended it as an act of bearing witness.

Eventually, Kouchner and his followers broke away, founding the rival Médecins du Monde (M.D.M.), which has remained smaller and more loosely structured than the parent group. (Aide Médicale Internationale, also formed at about this time, specializes in sending tiny teams behind the lines of conflict.) Brauman regards the split as the final collision of two generations of volunteers: Kouchner and the older generation wanted to remain small and informal, leaving large-scale relief efforts to the major international organizations.

Housed in a cobbled courtyard a few blocks from the Place de la République in Paris, M.D.M. deploys about 500 volunteers a year to some 40 countries. Operating with an annual budget of about $20 million, over 60 percent of which comes from private donations, M.D.M. has put special effort into domestic programs for AIDS victims and the poor. It has also opened chapters in several Eastern European countries, where local physicians seek to promote health and human rights.

Since assuming his role as politician in 1988, Kouchner's relations with both M.S.F. and M.D.M. have been stormy. His reputation as a "media animal," as he has been called, was fueled by his highly publicized liaison with the leading television anchorwoman on France's Antenne 2. While the rival relief agencies squared off in the battle for funds and news teams jockeyed for access to disaster zones, Kouchner's critics accused Médecins du Monde of giving an unfair advantage to Antenne 2.

Kouchner is unrepentant. "This is the success of the French doctors," he says, defending his pursuit of media coverage. "Without photography, massacres would not exist. Nothing can be done without pressure on politicians."

As further justification for courting the media, Kouchner points to three United Nations resolutions France has successfully proposed since 1988 that have brought the guiding principle of both organizations—the duty to interfere—closer to becoming an inalienable right. On April 5, amid the urgency of the Kurdish crisis, the longstanding sanctity of national boundaries took an unprecedented blow when the United Nations granted states, as long as they are operating under the flag of the United Nations, the right to cross into Iraq to reach civilians in distress, a right that formerly applied only to private relief agencies.

Meanwhile at M.S.F., the "new generation" as Brauman calls it, has systematically forged the group into a large, formal organization, focusing on large-scale disaster relief and public health issues.

With spirited self-confidence, they slash through the political thicket in which they invariably land. When necessary, they are willing to irritate a host government in order to protect the lives of civilians, as M.S.F. did in exposing the forced resettlement of Ethiopian villagers in 1985. Some 100,000 people perished in the moves, the group estimates. The reminder of that terrible year brings Rony Brauman's fist down on a table. "This was not the peak of the famine," he insists. "But we could see that the forced relocation was killing an incredibly high number of people." Finally, in December 1985, the Mengistu Government tossed the French team out of Ethiopia.

From every crisis they have distilled essential lessons. Perhaps their most renowned innovation has been the development of prepackaged "kits" for every conceivable disaster situation, ready to be airborne in hours. A "kit sanitaire" weighs 1,790 pounds and contains all the materials needed to provide potable water and sanitation for 10,000 people for three months. Kits for setting up field offices include typewriters, stamps and hole punches. A meal kit, a French version of K-rations for the volunteers, consists of dried soup, cheese, conserve, chocolate and wine.

Over the last few years, M.S.F.'s achievements have been gathering recognition. Its "Clinical and Therapeutic Guide" has been adopted by the World Health Organization, and in 1987 the French Government named M.S.F. a Grande Cause Nationale. Last year, when thousands of refugees from Iraq were stranded in the Jordanian desert, M.S.F. was designated by the European Economic Community to coordinate its border relief effort.

From the day in early April when Médecins Sans Frontières received word of the Kurdish exodus from a volunteer in eastern Turkey who had made the terrible journey with the refugees, it cranked into high gear, and within a week had cargo planes in the air and dozens of volunteers in Turkey and Iran.

Casual and hip, with spiky haircuts and the latest in cowboy jackets and jeans, the young staff at M.S.F.'s high-tech headquarters in Paris convey the inimitable French air of effortlessness, but it is working at furious speed, devouring information on recruits, supplies and charter flights and shuttling it to the Kurdistan control room on the second floor. There, surrounded by maps, flow charts, computers, phones and faxes, a half-dozen staff members run the nerve center for the M.S.F. affiliates across Europe and the permanent logistics center in southern France.

In the reception area, over the steady din of telex printers and the beeping of fax machines, volunteers stream in, with backpacks and bedrolls. Within 36 hours of M.S.F.'s first public appeal for volunteers, 1,500 calls jammed the phone lines.

Two days later, the new recruits arrive in the harsh, craggy mountains of Kurdistan. Here, for the past two weeks, in the remote Turkish border post of Cukurca, Médecins Sans Frontières has been the sole international relief agency working with the 70,000 Kurdish refugees, battling the diarrhea and dehydration caused by the camp's contaminated water.

The air is motionless in the 15-by-18-foot hospital tents, and by midmorning the sour smell of fever and diarrhea is intense. Reinardt Byl, 29-year-old nurse from Holland, has been here since the beginning. He has tired gray eyes and several days of sandy stubble. "The first day, we had five dead babies in five minutes," he says. "There were so many people." At least 700 Kurds have died over the course of 12 days. Two-thirds of them have been children.

The efforts of M.S.F. and other organizations have helped reduce the daily death rate by one-third, but 70 percent of the 2,300 patients a day still suffer from diarrhea. The doctors and nurses are anxiously waiting for results from the foot of the steep rocky slope, where Guy Jacquier, a young engineer, toils in the mud with a team of American soldiers. The Americans arrived a few days ago to hook up the final pipelines for the clean water system he has designed. Cooperative and unassuming, and speaking English with a balmy French lilt, the 27-year-old Jacquier is a hit with the G.I.'s.

"It was great to find they already had the system in place and we could just build on it," says Sgt. Ken Smith. "They're better than we are at brainstorming and planning; they've got more experience in this than we do. But we're better at getting the people to get it done." Now, with the help of a newly arrived sanitarian from the International Rescue Committee and the 30-man military detachment of engineers and medics, they have just begun to pipe water from nearby springs into several gargantuan inflatable tanks with spigots.

Relief is written on Jacquier's sun-bronzed face. "Two days ago, we had nothing," he says, playing down his own efforts as he lights a cigarette with his mud-encrusted fingers. "I feel really better. By the end of this week, we should have the water system in place for all the people."

Further up the road, a medical epidemiologist from the United States Centers for Disease Control in Atlanta emerges from a tour of the camp, impressed to discover that a French epidemiologist has already done the standard survey of mortality and health status, which he had intended to do.

"I remember these guys 12 years ago," says Dr. Ronald J. Waldman, marveling at how much M.S.F.'s approach has evolved. "They'd arrive like medical cowboys, set themselves up and let people come to them. They did pretty wild things, like intricate surgical procedures by their headlights."

But over the last decade, an increasing number of French volunteers have sought solid public health training in the United States, which has a stronger tradition of public health than France. The emphasis has shifted to the less glamorous but lifesaving activities of sanitation, nutrition and oral rehydration. At M.S.F.'s Epicentre in Paris, modeled after the Centers for Disease Control, it compiles and analyzes health data that are vital to fighting outbreaks in settings such as this.

Ask any of the French doctors "Why the French?" and you get a shrug, a pout and a gaze of bewilderment. There is no doubt that one source of inspiration for the founders of the movement, a generation raised on Jules Verne and Cyrano de Bergerac, was the spirit of adventure and panache these figures symbolize. Add to that the anticolonial backlash dating from the French wars in Algeria and Indochina and the American sequel in Vietnam. While political activists in the United States tended to turn their attention to poverty at home, their French counterparts found a focus for their commitment in the nascent field of international human rights.

Over the last 20 years, the French groups have dispatched 20,000 volunteers to 85 countries across the globe. There is no mistaking them for the traditional, bland charity workers or idealist missionaries who sometimes stalk the same territory. I first came across them in 1980, in the sprawling bamboo-and-thatch refugee camps on the Thai-Cambodian border. Shaggy-haired and trailed by a curl of acrid

Gitane smoke, they cut distinctive figures among the legions of sweltering relief workers who flocked to the malaria-infested area.

M.S.F. and Médecins du Monde have brought to France a glory and respect that rivals that of the French Foreign Legion. The risks have usually been high, and several volunteers have lost their lives. Scores of others have been detained, kidnapped and taken hostage. Every year, at least a million Frenchmen send contributions to one of the groups—ordinary people like the car mechanic in Lille who vowed to donate a day's wages to M.S.F. when a customer, Dr. Marie-Bertille De-Houk, told him she was about to spend a month in Kurdistan. Schoolchildren have flash cards and coloring books featuring the French doctors, and French television has broadcast a popular six-part series inspired by the movement.

Dr. Jonathan Mann of the Harvard School of Public Health, the former director of the World Health Organization's AIDS program, recently joined Médecins du Monde as president of its new American affiliate. "The concept of bearing witness is not a very developed one in American health training," he says. But Mann is convinced that the movement will take hold in America: the French groups address a need "specific to our time . . . not met by some of the traditional humanitarian organizations."

In the wake of this year's unending calamities, there has been renewed discussion of the need for an international rapid deployment force that can kick down doors to help victims of disasters. And if the breathless momentum of the French doctors is any sign, the call to action will resonate with young volunteers as it has for Médecins du Monde's Patrick Aeberhard. "There's something unforgettable about the look in the eyes of people who feel you have not abandoned them."

11

STARTING OUT

Robert Coles

In the 1940s and earlier, polio was a scourge of childhood. An epidemic as sensational as AIDS is today, polio withered the limbs of young people, leaving paralysis and broken lives in its wake. The epidemic waned with the development of an antiviral vaccine by Jonas Salk. However, many medical professionals who are in their middle years today can remember their helplessness and sense of futility in the face of this disease. From this experience they gained a healthy respect for what patients feel when their doctors cannot perform miracles and they must rely on their own inner resources to heal their physical and psychic wounds.

Robert Coles, arguably the most prolific and influential psychiatrist in the United States, was beginning his psychiatric residency during the polio epidemic. He was also struggling, as many sensitive health professionals do, with conflicts that naturally arise between the science and the humane art of medicine. His more rigidly scientific mentors in the hospital urged him to resist the temptation to trade anecdotes with patients, in the interests of objectivity and professional detachment. Other medical mentors and his wife urged him to share his feelings and thoughts with patients.

In this moving account from Coles's book *The Call of Stories,* we watch the patient "teach" the doctor. The lessons concern the therapeutic importance of stories about fictional heroes and their trials. In talking about these stories, Coles and his patient discover a route to healing. The well-known stories of Huck Finn and Holden Caulfield become powerful metaphors for dealing with and eventually mastering the strong feelings that trouble the polio victim's mind and sap his will to adapt to a new life.

The youth of fifteen had polio; he would lose the use of both legs. His father had been killed in the Second World War; his mother had died in an automobile accident when he was ten. A grandmother, a sensitive and thoughtful widow in her sixties, had become his main family. The young man had no brothers and sisters. He had two uncles, whom he yearned to see more often, but they were living in Texas and California. (Like him, they were born near Boston.) I came to know this fellow fairly well. I first met him in the emergency ward of a Boston hospital when he came in with a sore throat, feverish, and, alas, weak in the legs. My work with him as a pediatrician gave way eventually to my conversations with him as a child psychiatrist. He was "moody," by his own description, and he was not averse to long talks.

We always started with sports, especially baseball and hockey, his two loves. In time we'd drift toward the hospital scene as he saw it: the nurses, the virtues and faults of various ones, and the doctors, mostly their faults. He regarded us residents with a skeptical eye. We strutted, were all too cocky. "The doctors give so many orders, it goes to their heads." He said those words so many times that I found myself, in retaliation, observing his "hostility." It was hard for him to accept the bad deal life had given him. He was angry, I knew, and needed a target, someone or something to attack, lest he turn all the fury on himself and become depressed. As he described us doctors, scurrying around, always on the move, collaring people with our orders, he seemed wistful. He would look past me, toward a window, and I always hesitated to press our conversation. He seemed gone—his mind was out there, free of his body.

Once, as we talked about the body's prospects, he became philosophical. He wondered whether the soul is always confined to a given body. Might it become migratory? What did I think? I was stupid enough to shun the question and to throw it back at him. He was smart enough to spot my pose—a shrink in action—and irritated enough to give me a dose of his bile. He spoke at considerable length; one remark has stuck with me for the many years since he made it: "If you would tell me what you think, then I could answer better." At the time I wasn't getting any wiser, however. I interpreted that comment as an effort on his part to hide behind me, as it were—to let me know that he would pretend to oblige me by taking cues from me, but not deliver to me what I wanted, his own unvarnished self. He spotted a coy reserve in me at that moment, which must have told him what was crossing my mind. He changed the subject abruptly, instructively. Had I read *The Adventures of Huckleberry Finn*? Yes, I answered, wondering what the question meant. He said no more. It was left to me, during the silence that followed, to figure out what to say, if anything. I waited just long enough to realize that the youth, whose name was Phil, had no intention of proceeding further in any direction. My wife's and supervisors' faces, their voices, rushed to my head. A week or so earlier my wife had urged me to "exchange stories" with the children I was interviewing in the hospital; Dr. Ludwig had agreed: "Why don't you chuck the word 'interview,' call yourself a friend, call your exchanges 'conversations'!"

Suddenly I heard myself talking about Huck and Jim, about the mighty river, about my own experiences as a child when my mother took my brother and me to visit her family in Sioux City, Iowa, located on the Missouri River. I told Phil that my grandfather used to take me to that river, point south, indicate the destination of the water: the Mississippi, then New Orleans and the ocean. "Those rivers are arteries of the American heartland," he'd tell me—the farmland expanding and contracting, opening up and offering crops, then retreating into the winter lair, and all the while the water flowing, keeping an entire region alive and fertile.

Not brilliant imagery, but enough to shed me of my scrutinizing, wary reticence; enough to involve Phil in a bit of a personal story, which in turn was connected to a reading experience he had recently had, and one I had also had, though about seven or eight years earlier. I was almost ready to tell him how young he was to have read the Mark Twain book—to patronize him foolishly and smugly—when Phil began talking about the book. He had read it as a school assignment before he fell sick. When he'd been in the hospital a week or so and began to realize that he was "really paralyzed" and that his disease might be "for a lifetime," he became morose, more so than others on the same ward with the same disease, for whom the bad news had yet to sink in. All he could think of was "the black space" of his future life. But a teacher came to visit him on a Saturday afternoon, and the result was a reacquaintance with the Twain classic. Not that young Phil relished the idea at first. Here is how he described what happened (his remarks have been edited and on occasion reconstructed because my tape recorder intermittently broke down):

"I was surprised to see him [the teacher]. I'd liked him, but he was gone from my life, the way a teacher is when you go on to the next year of school. I guess he heard I was sick. We all knew he was a softie! Some of those teachers don't give a damn for you as a person. They talk to the back wall, and if you hear, fine, and if you don't, you flunk! This guy we all knew—he was different. I guess I didn't learn how different until he showed up here.

"He came in and smiled and said hello. I was surprised. I said hello back. I didn't have anything more to say, though. He was quiet, too. I was glad! I was tired of people coming and expecting me to talk with them. I wanted to lie there and think. I felt like crying, but I didn't; I couldn't; I think I was afraid that if I started—once I started, I'd never stop. He just sat there and smiled; then he asked if he could go get me something—food, or a glass of juice. I was thirsty, and I said, 'Yes, orange juice'; and he left, and came back with orange juice and with some peanuts. I liked that, the peanuts. I used to nibble on them a lot before I got sick. I remember my mother saying they were better for me than chocolate. I got a little choked up then, thinking of her and the peanuts and looking at my legs. No more baseball. No more hockey. No more walking, either.

"I saw him looking at the magazines I had on the table near my bed. He leafed through them; then he asked me if he could bring me some books, maybe. I shook my head. I didn't want any books. I was beginning to think I didn't want any teachers here either—*him.* Then he said he was gong to go! I guess he'd read me! I felt like I was going to cry, but I didn't know why. I was afraid of breaking down in front of him. I tried to tough it out. I became flip. I joked about having a ball when I came back to school—speeding down the corridors at sixty in a wheelchair. He smiled, but he didn't laugh as much as I did. I knew when I was laughing that it was fake. In a minute he was gone—and then I did cry. I didn't even want to see another day. It was raining outside, and I was crying, and my legs were useless, and I haven't even graduated from high school, that's how young I am, and all I can see ahead is those rehabilitation people, and nurses, and my grandmother looking so worried, and she looked so sick, once I got sick. For a while I thought she was going to die, and then there'd be no one.

"He came back a few days later; he had this book under his arm. He didn't push it on me. He stood there and talked, small talk, and I talked. After a few minutes there was nothing more to say. Suddenly, without saying anything, he up and left. I thought it was strange, the way he left. But he hadn't left; I mean, he came back. He had orange juice in one hand, a glass, and peanuts in the other. I couldn't help smiling. That was the first smile on my face, I think, since he'd been to see me. We talked a few minutes more, about the lousy weather, and then he said he was going. He shook my hand, and just as he was saying good-bye, he took the book from under his left arm with his right hand and put it on my table. He didn't say anything, and he was out of the room before I could say anything.

"I was really curious to see which book he'd brought. I looked, and saw it was the Mark Twain one, *Adventures of Huckleberry Finn.* I started flipping through the pages. I wondered why he brought it. I'd already read it—in his class, last year. What was the point? I guess I was a little annoyed with him. I wondered what was wrong with him, at first. Why that book? What's he got in mind? I asked myself those kinds of questions. I didn't go near the book for a few days. It was just there, with the magazines my grandma brought. I didn't read them much either. I'd look at the pictures, and I'd read a paragraph—and you know what? I'd get sick to my stomach. I'd feel like puking. I thought it was part of the sickness. I told the nurse, and she told the doctor, and he asked me, and I explained to him what was going on. He examined me, and told me it was all in my head. I joked with him: I said, 'All'?

"When the doctor left the room, I decided to pick up that book; so I did. I flipped through the pages, and then I started reading it, and then I didn't want to stop. I read and I read, and I finished the whole book that night; it was midnight, maybe. The nurse kept coming in to tell me I should put my light off and go to sleep because I needed my rest. What a joke! Are you kidding! I said to her. I'm going nowhere. I'll be in bed for the rest of my life. What difference does it make to me, night and day? She backed off. I read, and when I was done with the story, I felt different. It's hard to say what I mean. [*What do you think happened?*] I can't tell you, I can't explain what happened; I know that my mind changed after I read *Huckleberry Finn.* I couldn't get my mind off the book. I forgot about myself—no, I didn't, actually. I joined up with Huck and Jim; we became a trio. They were very nice to me. I explored the Mississippi with them on the boats and on the land. I had some good talks with them. I dreamed about them. I'd wake up, and I'd know I'd just been out west, on the Mississippi. I talked with those guys, and they straightened me out!"

At that point he paused for a long time. He shook his head. He stared out the window. Then he abruptly put a question to me: "Have you ever read a book that really made a difference to you—a book you couldn't get out of your mind, and you didn't want to [get out of your mind]?"

Yes, I said, and knowing he wanted an example, I told him: *Paterson,* William Carlos Williams' long poem. We got into a long talk about Dr. Williams' medical work with mostly poor and working-class people, about his effort through stories and poems to understand America's social history and moral values. He asked for examples, which of course I didn't have on hand. But he was obviously setting the stage for another conversation. I got my Williams books out of a box, brought a couple of them to his room the next day, and read from the first two books of *Paterson* and from various poems Williams had published in the course of his long writing life. I will never forget the direction of our discussion afterward. Phil wondered whether Williams would ever have been able to accomplish what he did, were he not inspired by what he saw all the time as a practicing physician. Then he wondered whether Mark Twain, whose life he had briefly studied, would have been able to do the kind of writing *he* did, had he not been such an inveterate wanderer before he found himself having much to say. The reason for Phil's interest in pointing out the connection between art and life was not too hard for me to comprehend—or for him, either.

He began musing out loud about his future prospects, with discouragement and dismay. In reply, I pointed out that writers are constantly creating their own worlds, not necessarily needing to travel far and wide in order to gather the particulars for so doing. He once more wanted examples, and our next minutes were taken up with Jane Austen and *Pride and Prejudice,* which I'd read in high school and which his closest friend, a year older, was about to read at the behest of an English teacher. Well, Jane Austen was a novelist, a writer—lucky to be able to achieve what she did, living the life she did. Things would be different for him. He was no writer, would be no writer, had never even thought of becoming one. Now, significantly paralyzed, he could not even be the day-to-day athlete he'd been; nor did books seem the most inviting of alternatives. He politely but firmly reminded me that he was not "the greatest of students," that he was a "slow reader," that he was struggling with his own worries and terrors, not those described by a novelist in a story: "I wish one of those writers had written about the mess I'm in!"

I did not, then, try to come up with a novel that might pass his muster. Even if I had known of a novel with a polio victim of his age, sex, and background as the hero, I would not have mentioned it at the time. His complaint went deeper; like Job, he was puzzled in the most profound way possible and wanted to find his own voice, use it to make his own plea, his own cry, though he had already begun to regard the world as largely indifferent to him and his situation. I decided to await his decision: whether to do some reading as a means of reflecting indirectly, but with emotional resonance, on his personal situation; or to reject such a way of trying to come to terms with his ongoing situation. A week later, as I was talking with him in his room, I noticed a new box of candy on his bedside table, and underneath the candy box a book. The title was not immediately obvious; I had to move toward the window on a pretext—a bit of sun in my eyes, so best to pull the shades. As I did so, I saw that the book was *The Catcher in the Rye.* I didn't say anything; neither did Phil.

A few days later, as we talked about the rehabilitation efforts taking place, Phil suddenly changed the subject: "I've discovered a book that has a kid in it like Huckleberry Finn." I said nothing but looked interested. He asked me, "Have you ever read *The Catcher in the Rye?*" Yes, I answered. "Do you see what I mean about Huck Finn and Holden Caulfield?" Yes, I answered. Silence. I got alarmed. Why wasn't I feeding our conversation? Why my terse yes, two times spoken? But he began a lively monologue on that novel, on Holden, on Pencey Prep, on "phonies," on what it means to be honest and decent in a world full of "phoniness." Holden's voice (Salinger's) had become Phil's; and uncannily, Holden's dreams of escape, of rescue (to save not only himself but others), became Phil's. The novel had, as he put it, "got" to him: lent itself to his purposes as one who was "flat out"; and as one who was wondering what in life he might "try to catch." He lived on a city street rather than near a field of rye. He was not as utopian, anyway, as Holden. But this youth had been removed by dint of circumstances from the "regular road" (his expression) and he was trying hard to imagine where to go, how to get there. *The Catcher in the Rye* enabled him to return at least to the idea of school—to consider what kind of education he wanted, given his special difficulties.

He had been getting some tutoring in the rehabilitation unit of the hospital. Now he began teaching himself—leaving the building for Huck and Jim on the Mississippi, for repeated excursions to meet Holden. A friend of his invited him to expand his travels, to visit Ralph and Piggy and Jack and Simon on the tropical island in William Golding's *Lord of the Flies.* But Phil resisted that invitation; the book, brought to him by the friend, remained unread. He had glanced at it, seen its charged symbolism, its mix of hard realism and surrealism. Huck and Holden stirred him, brought him to reflection; Ralph and the band of boys on the island were "not for me." When Phil said that, he looked at me and saw my curiosity rising; he decided to give me a terse explication, one I would never forget: "I'd like to leave this hospital, and find a friend or two, and a place where we could be happy, but I don't want to leave the whole world I know."

My wife was quite taken by Phil's way of putting those books into a perspective that suited him. He was calling on certain novels in his own manner and turning away from others for his own reasons. (Phil also rejected the detective stories his friends brought to him, and the Westerns.) A week or so later I heard him again talk about Huck and Jim and Holden. They had become, for him, a threesome. Rather, he had joined them; they were a foursome. His misfortune had evoked in him a wry, sardonic side. He was quick to notice hypocrisy or deceit in the world as it came to him—on television, in the newspapers, in reports from friends and family members, and through hospital personnel. One particular doctor especially offended him, reminding him of a certain teacher and also of an uncle, his mother's older brother. They all "pretended to be nice," but were (in his judgment) "phonies." How he loved that word; what palpable pleasure it gave him! Once, using it, he must have noticed something cross my face—an expression in my eyes, a tightening of my face—and he must have guessed that I thought his use of the word was significant and perhaps inappropriate. He called me on my heightened response to the word "phony"; he told me that both Twain and Salinger were warning the reader to take a hard, close look at the world. If I did so; if I read those two books as he had recently done; if I would "stop and think," then a recognition would descend upon me, too—or so he hoped. He loved the blunt, earthy talk of Twain, and Salinger's shrewd way of puncturing various balloons. He didn't like being paralyzed; but he did like an emerging angle of vision in himself, and he was eager to tell me about it, to explain its paradoxical relationship to his misfortune: "I've seen a lot, lying here. I think I know more about people, including me, myself—all because I got sick and can't walk. It's hard to figure out, how polio can be a good thing. It's not, but I like those books, and I keep reading them, parts of them, over and over."

12

PAUL O'BRIAN

Renée C. Fox

Renée Fox is the most accomplished medical ethnographer in the United States, with many years of close observation of medical practices to her credit. Her record of research and writing on social aspects of medicine is long and varied. Her recent work has explored the social issues involved in organ transplants and artificial heart surgery. Her earlier work, especially *Experiment Perilous*, from which this excerpt is taken, caused her to become especially well known for her vivid accounts of interactions among patients and medical professionals under conditions of great uncertainty and stress.

This selection deals with the untimely death of a young, once vigorous man. Although he has lost his long battle against cancer, the patient never fully gives up or accepts death. This spirit has kept him going through years of uncertainty and long bouts of enervating medical care (the mustard treatments used in the early days of chemotherapy). A lively concern for the course of his disease, and a persistent habit of demanding to know what the doctors are learning about it, are important aspects of the way he fights against it.

Just beneath the surface of Paul's running commentary about his failing health is the feeling that many doctors are not sensitive enough to the needs of the individual patient; they treat the disease but not the person. Paul's resistance to passivity, his anger, and his humorous but pointed efforts to rally other patients are all part of his personal strategy to stay alive as long as possible.

In this selection Fox does not choose to include a great deal of commentary and analysis. A few epigrams, a descriptive passage, a transition paragraph here and there are sufficient to convey her purpose. In presenting this articulate patient's battle against a terminal illness she allows him to convey the meaning of the situation.

Through the use of details such as the repeated mention of Ward X, the sociologist enables us to share the experience of a patient whom we come to know briefly as a singular human being.

Hodgkin's Disease: a painless, progressive and fatal enlargement of the lymph nodes, spleen, and general lymphoid tissues, which often begins in the neck, and spreads over the body . . .
—*The American Illustrated Medical Dictionary*

I only know that one must do what one can to cease being plague-stricken, and that's the only way we can hope for some peace or, failing that, a decent death . . .
—Albert Camus, *The Plague*

Disease so adjusts its man that it and he can come to terms; there are sensory appeasements, short circuits, a merciful narcosis . . . But one must fight against them, after all, for they are two-faced. If you are not meant to get home, they are a benefaction, they are merciful; but if you mean to get home, they become sinister.
—Thomas Mann, *The Magic Mountain*

Our family doctor's a good doctor, but he's not very good at handling patients in a social way, if you know what I mean. When I got sick, he told my father that I had only five years to live. If he had told *me,* I wouldn't have cared at all. But Dopey there had to go and tell my father and worry him half to death! That's why he won't believe my sister when she tells him how well I'm getting along in the hospital this time . . . Because this is the fifth year, you see . . .

With full knowledge of the nature of his disease, and the imminence of his death, Paul O'Brian, twenty-seven, lived out his days. From his doctors, he had demanded and received this merciless knowledge. ("I asked him whether he could tell me anything about the progress of Hodgkin's disease; how far it had gone . . . I asked him how long he thought I had to live . . . ") His ferocious drive to "find out" had made it imperative for him to ask these questions; and with a kind of savageness, he had come to terms with the unequivocal answers.

The coming-to-terms struggle had been a desperate one: a literal life-and-death battle. At first, a terrible void seemed to stretch before him:

I wasn't working. And I was looking for a job, but not really very hard. I slept late every morning; went to bed late every night. And I had nothing to do . . . absolutely nothing to do. Nothing to look forward to . . . no one to see. I even went out one day and got drunk, thinking maybe that would help. But it didn't . . . You see, before I was sick, I was so active. I went to school, and to work. I had dates, and went dancing and to parties. I just never had a moment to spare, my life was so full . . . So to have my life so empty and so unbusy was a hard thing to get used to . . .

Paul's days were taken up by strenuous treatments, but they still seemed "empty" to him—without meaning, beginning or end:

> I don't know which of the two treatments they're going to give me this time: mustard or X-ray. I'd rather have X-ray, I think. No, I'd rather have mustard. I don't know . . . (*pointing to his upper chest*)—I guess I'd rather have X-ray if it's going to be from here up, and mustard if it's going to be from here down. Because X-ray goes on forever. Day after day they drag you down for your treatment, and you're as limp as a rag. Nitrogen mustard gas only lasts two days, and most of the time you don't know what's going on . . .

All of this involved "coming to the hospital, and going out—coming in and going out": a senseless repetition of arrivals and departures. There were days when Paul O'Brian longed for the ultimate certainty of his death:

> Listen, Dr. W., this is all stupid. What's the use of going on with these treatments? Just let me go home and forget about it. It's going to get me sometime or other, anyway.
>
> You know, if I thought I was going to have to go on like this for years—for more than five years, even . . . coming in and going out, coming in and going out—with only short intervals in between—I'd rather not live. Really, I'd rather die and get it over with.

And yet, Paul O'Brian refused to surrender himself. Move in the pattern of wellness, he affirmed. And "keep endless watch . . . lest you join forces with pestilence."[1]

> This time when I go home, I'm not going to wear a suit like I did last time. Last time, I sent for my favorite blue suit, and a special tie and shirt. And then, when I put them on, I discovered I'd lost so much weight that nothing fit and I looked just terrible. Like death warmed over . . . This time, I'm going to wear slacks, and a sport shirt, and a sweater . . . What I'd really like to do is drive my car home from the hospital. And when I finally do get to my house, I'd like to open the front door, run upstairs carrying my suitcase, and then rush downstairs again to the kitchen, and take a nice, cold beer out of the refrigerator. . . . If I did all those things, then my family would really believe that I was well . . . and home to stay . . .
>
> I hope I get out of this hospital mood before I get out of here, though. Like I'm sitting her now and saying to myself as I watch the people in the corridor and on the ward, "That's a nurse; and that's a dietician; and that's a famous doctor." I wish I didn't know anything about anything here—about who people are, and what's going on. I'd like it if I could feel and act as if I'd never been here . . . When I get out of here, I'll probably have to come back for a check-up once a week, for about a month or so. But do you know something? No matter how many times I have to come in for a check-up, I'll never come up to this ward. Never! Once I get out, I want to leave it all behind me . . .

Even when the ward claimed him, Paul O'Brian kept faith with nonappeasement. Every drop swallowed, every pound gained, he regarded as a triumph. For with each progression, no matter how small, he advanced his return to the outside world:

> I remember when I was so sick for a while when I first came in . . . I'd lie there in bed and say to myself, "All I want for tomorrow is to be able to swallow a little tea." And when I finally succeeded in keeping that down, I'd say, "All I want now is to be able to drink a little tea, and eat a piece of toast, too." . . .

Paul had no tolerance for the supine. There was "something *wrong*" with a patient who "rested all day long," he declared. And when the whole of F-Second turned into a "stay-abed ward . . . with everyone in his cubicle by 9:30 at night"—that was the time Paul "*really* wished [he] could get out of the dump!" For him, a "quiet" ward was a "half-dead" place. And Paul O'Brian craved the "bustle," the clamor of life. As he envisioned it, the "perfect ward" would be a living defiance. "Graveyard roses" and "sickroom bonbons" would be outlawed. Beds and wheelchairs would stand empty. And "from every cubicle . . . you would hear all this laughter."

Death and disease would have no sovereignty in a world of Paul's making. They were his mortal enemies. Against all the ways in which they could seduce or overtake a man, Paul fought his neverending battle:

> So far as I'm concerned, Mac is a bore and a regular hypochondriac. Do you know, he keeps a record of everything that has happened to him since his operation? He writes it all down in that big fat notebook of his. His temperature, his weight, his headaches—even a pain in his toe. That annoys me to death!
>
> When I look at Sam, I do more than wonder about that adrenalectomy operation. It certainly doesn't seem to have done him much good! All that trouble with his eyes. There's something terribly wrong with them. This morning he could hardly find his orange juice or his toast on his tray. His hands kept reaching in the wrong direction. His eyes must be all out of focus . . . So far as I'm concerned, it's just not worth having that operation. One thing for sure—they're not going to get *my* adrenals! . . . I don't see why anyone would want to be experimented on, anyhow!
>
> This place keeps drawing you in toward itself, and the world outside starts to get smaller and smaller—farther and farther away . . . I wouldn't want to adjust perfectly to any place. And particularly not to *this* place.

10/22/51: Discharge Note
27-year-old white male with Hodgkin's disease known for four years. Entered hospital 21 days ago for sixth admission. Ran a progressive downhill course with increasing pulmonary difficulty and pain. For the past four days patient has been in severe respiratory distress, and during past 36 hours has required constant oxygen, and large amounts of sedation. For the past 10 hours has been cyanotic, chest filled with large rhonci, gurgles, etc. Conscious until last hour when respirations became irregular, gasping and quite noisy. Patient finally stopped breathing, and some 30–50 seconds later heart sounds ceased. He was discharged to Ward X at 9:55 p.m.

Paul O'Brian's last days were a testament to his credo. He cried bitterly because he was "coming back to the hospital." ("The tears kept rolling down my face.") In spite of "a temperature of about a hundred-and-three," the morning of the day (October 1) he left home, he shaved himself. And he arrived on the ward resolutely determined to "do nothing but get well and go home again." ("This is the Jewish New Year, isn't it? Well, maybe things will start afresh for me.") Feverishly, he battled narcosis. ("I don't even know if I slept last night. That's how befuddled I am. It's all that dope I'm getting. It's changing my personality so that I hardly know myself. And I don't like it one bit. I'm just not going to take any more medication.") With unblurred contempt, he looked out on the ward. ("This place is dead! No one on the ward is funny any more. And everyone's in bed all the time. It's awful! A bunch of mourners, that's what they are. Take Mr. Kaye, for instance. He looks as if you could hire him to cry.") Shattering the funereal silence, Paul's voice rang out: "Come on, somebody! Make a little noise, won't you? Talk! Laugh! Do anything! But don't just lie there like a bunch of mummies!"

On October 13 Paul was still not "bedridden." On October 15, he launched himself on a "rehabilitation program":

> They're going to try to rehabilitate me—Miss P., and the others. She's going to get someone up here to show me how to make a wallet. And she's going to bring me a book of funny stories. And I've asked her to get Father Mac to come up and see me. . . All that's to get me out of the apathy I'm in . . . Because it's not natural to feel as hopeless as I do now . . .

On October 19, Paul was put on the Danger List. ("My sister told me that I was on it, and I couldn't take it. I shouldn't care about dying. But I do . . . ") On October 22, Paul O'Brian was "discharged to Ward X."

The day he died, Paul held fast to consciousness. (Dr. L.: "I've never seen anything like it! Most people aren't aware of everything happening to them like Paul is.") Through his oxygen mask, in a loud unmodulated voice, he talked on and on. ("How's everyone on the ward? Go see if my bed in the cubicle is made up, will you? Because I intend to get back there.") His family arrived. ("Hi. I had a pretty good night, last night . . . Why did you all come? It wasn't necessary. That means you had to leave work and everything. How did you get here? Did you take the car . . . ?") Paul lapsed into unconsciousness, and then aroused himself with a bitter reproach. ("You can go on talking to me, you know, even when I can't talk to you! I can hear every word you say! What's new in the outside world?") The O'Brian family departed. ("They're too sentimental. I don't want consolation.")

Paul had a choking spell. ("Open the windows! All the way from the top!") He said he felt "very hungry" and wanted "something to eat." ("Chow! I want some chow!") In spite of his difficulty in breathing and swallowing, Paul downed a glass of orange juice, a poached egg, and a cup of coffee, in huge, frenetic gulps. ("Hurry, hurry! The next bite!") The nurse arrived with the medicine tray, and Paul swallowed three pills at once.

Before he became unconscious for the last time, he asked for his "square crucifix with the special blessing"; and he made a deadly joke with the newspaper boy who appeared in the doorway. ("No, I don't want a paper! I'm dying!") Reverence-and-blasphemy.

At 9:45 and-a-half, Paul "finally stopped breathing." At 9:55 p.m. when his "heart sounds ceased" and he was "discharged to Ward X," the battle Paul O'Brian had waged ended.

NOTE

1. ALBERT CAMUS, *The Plague* (New York: Alfred A. Knopf, 1950), p. 229.

13

THE USE OF FORCE

William Carlos Williams

The poet's business, William Carlos Williams wrote in the preface to his poetic masterpiece *Paterson,* is "not to talk in vague categories but to write particularly, as a physician works, upon a patient, upon the thing before him, in the particular to discover the universal." In this short story from his book *The Doctor Stories,* Williams must use force to pry open a sick girl's mouth, making some discoveries about the human will in the process.

Widely recognized as one of the foremost poets of the twentieth century, Williams worked for his entire adult life as a family doctor in the manufacturing town of Paterson, New Jersey. His practice spanned the development of antibiotics and other miracle drugs, which vastly improved the ability of doctors to heal diseases like diphtheria (the hidden illness in this story). However, the majority of his patients were from working-class families, and many of their health problems stemmed from the pinched and unhealthy social environment in which they lived.

During his later years Williams was frequently asked how it was possible to maintain two successful but demanding careers. He disliked this question. To him it was evident that his life as a doctor and his life as a poet were intimately intertwined. His poetry was enriched by all the rickety stairs he climbed to treat the ill, for along the way he learned many lessons about the human spirit. The images of life in the neighborhoods of Paterson gained through his medical practice became the stuff of which his poetry was made.

Williams's doctor stories have influenced hundreds of medical professionals to commit to writing their thoughts and feelings about the healing experience. One of these, Robert Coles (also represented in this volume), publicly acknowledged the influence of Williams's work on his own development as a doctor and a writer. Unfortunately, Williams's stories about the medical profession are few in number and not widely known. As this sample shows, however, they offer powerful insights into the life of that vanishing species, the family doctor on a home visit.

They were new patients to me, all I had was the name, Olson. Please come down as soon as you can, my daughter is very sick.

When I arrived I was met by the mother, a big startled looking woman, very clean and apologetic who merely said, Is this the doctor? and let me in. In the back, she added. You must excuse us, doctor, we have her in the kitchen where it is warm. It is very damp here sometimes.

The child was fully dressed and sitting on her father's lap near the kitchen table. He tried to get up, but I motioned for him not to bother, took off my overcoat and started to look things over. I could see that they were all very nervous, eyeing me up and down distrustfully. As often, in such cases, they weren't telling me more than they had to, it was up to me to tell them; that's why they were spending three dollars on me.

The child was fairly eating me up with her cold, steady eyes, and no expression to her face whatever. She did not move and seemed, inwardly, quiet; an unusually attractive little thing, and as strong as a heifer in appearance. But her face was flushed, she was breathing rapidly, and I realized that she had a high fever. She had magnificent blonde hair, in profusion. One of those picture children often reproduced in advertising leaflets and the photogravure sections of the Sunday papers.

She's had a fever for three days, began the father and we don't know what it comes from. My wife has given her things, you know, like people do, but it don't do no good. And there's been a lot of sickness around. So we tho't you'd better look her over and tell us what is the matter.

As doctors often do I took a trial shot at it as a point of departure. Has she had a sore throat?

Both parents answered me together, No . . . No, she says her throat don't hurt her.

Does your throat hurt you? added the mother to the child. But the little girl's expression didn't change nor did she move her eyes from my face.

Have you looked?

I tried to, said the mother, but I couldn't see.

As it happens we had been having a number of cases of diphtheria in the school to which this child went during that month and we were all, quite apparently, thinking of that, though no one had as yet spoken of the thing.

Well, I said, suppose we take a look at the throat first. I smiled in my best professional manner and asking for the child's first name I said, come on, Mathilda, open your mouth and let's take a look at your throat.

Nothing doing.

Aw, come on, I coaxed, just open your mouth wide and let me take a look. Look, I said opening both hands wide, I haven't anything in my hands. Just open up and let me see.

Such a nice man, put in the mother. Look how kind he is to you. Come on, do what he tells you to. He won't hurt you.

At that I ground my teeth in disgust. If only they wouldn't use the word "hurt" I might be able to get somewhere. But I did not allow myself to be hurried or disturbed but speaking quietly and slowly I approached the child again.

As I moved my chair a little nearer suddenly with one catlike movement both her hands clawed instinctively for my eyes and she almost reached them too. In fact she knocked my glasses flying and they fell, though unbroken, several feet away from me on the kitchen floor.

Both the mother and father almost turned themselves inside out in embarrassment and apology. You bad girl, said the mother, taking her and shaking her by one arm. Look what you've done. The nice man . . .

For heaven's sake, I broke in. Don't call me a nice man to her. I'm here to look at her throat on the chance that she might have diphtheria and possibly die of it. But that's nothing to her. Look here, I said to the child, we're going to look at your throat. You're old enough to understand what I'm saying. Will you open it now by yourself or shall we have to open it for you?

Not a move. Even her expression hadn't changed. Her breaths however were coming faster and faster. Then the battle began. I had to do it. I had to have a throat culture for her own protection. But first I told the parents that it was entirely up to them. I explained the danger but said that I would not insist on a throat examination so long as they would take the responsibility.

If you don't do what the doctor says you'll have to go to the hospital, the mother admonished her severely.

Oh yeah? I had to smile to myself. After all, I had already fallen in love with the savage brat, the parents were contemptible to me. In the ensuing struggle they grew more and more abject, crushed, exhausted while she surely rose to magnificent heights of insane fury of effort bred of her terror of me.

The father tried his best, and he was a big man but the fact that she was his daughter, his shame at her behavior and his dread of hurting her made him release her just at the critical moment several times when I had almost achieved success, till I wanted to kill him. But his dread also that she might have diphtheria made him tell me to go on, go on though he himself was almost fainting, while the mother moved back and forth behind us raising and lowering her hands in an agony of apprehension.

Put her in front of you on your lap, I ordered, and hold both her wrists.

But as soon as he did the child let out a scream. Don't, you're hurting me. Let go of my hands. Let them go I tell you. Then she shrieked terrifyingly, hysterically. Stop it! Stop it! You're killing me!

Do you think she can stand it, doctor! said the mother.

You get out, said the husband to his wife. Do you want her to die of diphtheria?

Come on now, hold her, I said.

Then I grasped the child's head with my left hand and tried to get the wooden tongue depressor between her teeth. She fought, with clenched teeth, desperately! But now I also had grown furious—at a child. I tried to hold myself down but I couldn't. I know how to expose a throat for inspection. And I did my best. When finally I got the wooden spatula behind the last teeth and just the point of it into the mouth cavity, she opened up for an instant but before I could see anything she came down again and gripping the wooden blade between her molars she reduced it to splinters before I could get it out again.

Aren't you ashamed, the mother yelled at her. Aren't you ashamed to act like that in front of the doctor?

Get me a smooth-handled spoon of some sort, I told the mother. We're going through with this. The child's mouth was already bleeding. Her tongue was cut and she was screaming in wild hysterical shrieks. Perhaps I should have desisted and come back in an hour or more. No doubt it would have been better. But I have seen at least two children lying dead in bed of neglect in such cases, and feeling that I must get a diagnosis now or never I went at it again. But the worst of it was that I too had got beyond reason. I could have torn the child apart in my own fury and enjoyed it. It was a pleasure to attack her. My face was burning with it.

The damned little brat must be protected against her own idiocy, one says to one's self at such times. Others must be protected against her. It is social necessity. And all these things are true. But a blind fury, a feeling of adult shame, bred of a longing for muscular release are the operatives. One goes on to the end.

In a final unreasoning assault I overpowered the child's neck and jaws. I forced the heavy silver spoon back of her teeth and down her throat till she gagged. And there it was—both tonsils covered with membrane. She had fought valiantly to keep me from knowing her secret. She had been hiding that sore throat for three days at least and lying to her parents in order to escape just such an outcome as this.

Now truly she *was* furious. She had been on the defensive before but now she attacked. Tried to get off her father's lap and fly at me while tears of defeat blinded her eyes.

14

THE ROAD BACK

Joseph Heller and Speed Vogel

This selection is a patient's account of the healing influence of friends. The patient, a famous novelist, was struggling against a potentially fatal illness, one that had paralyzed him and threatened to cause lasting damage to his nervous system. Guillain-Barré disease is a devastating viral illness. It attacks the nervous system and paralyzes its victims for many months, but with intense care it can eventually be defeated.

The patient is Joseph Heller, author of *Catch 22* and other well-known novels. He is one of the most revered humorists in the United States, although his writing touches on serious themes as well. The friends who appear in his hospital room are famous as well. But his closest friend, Speed Vogel, is not featured in this selection. Vogel visited Heller constantly, and the writer credits him with being the friend who did the most to pull him through his nearly fatal illness.

The two friends who figure most centrally in this account are Mel Brooks and Dustin Hoffman. To both it is clear that the patient feels a need to take care of the caring visitor, and this unstated demand affirms the patient's desire to live and to fight the disease. The friends' concern and their demonstration of love for the patient are themselves healing influences.

Hoffman brings the gift of music. He also aids and abets Heller in his desire to find out as much as possible about the illness. By the end of the excerpt, it is not clear what the actual outcome of the illness will be, but there is no doubt that the visiting friends have played a significant part in taking the patient some distance along the road back to health.

$\mathbf{M}$el Brooks materialized out of nowhere to pay me the first of his visits. Nothing could have been more unexpected to me than the sight of him in my intensive-care unit at about 9 P.M. on a frigid, black winter evening in late December. I had not even known he was in New York. For reasons no more arcane than a very solid and self-centered intelligence, Mel does not take any more warmly to the idea of dying than I do. His face was pinched and gloomy, he regarded me sorrowfully. I could see he had not come to make me laugh. He had bigger fish to fry.

"Tell me honestly," he said right off, "did it begin with a numbness or tingling in your feet and work its way up along the peripheral nerves of the spine and into your cranial nerves to affect your pharynx and face?"

I shook my head and studied him with amazement and respect. "You know about Guillain-Barré?" I exclaimed.

"Of course, I do," he answered matter-of-factly. "Who doesn't? Landry's ascending paralysis. Eighteen-fifty-nine, right? I know all about the polyneuritises."

"How come?" I questioned him. "I never even heard the word *polyneuritis* before, and I've been a hypochondriac longer than you. I'm older."

"How come?" He seemed surprised by my question. "I've got my medical dictionaries, of course. Why are you looking at me like that? Lots of people have medical dictionaries."

"But not everybody memorizes them," I said as a joke.

He took me seriously. "I do. Was there any paresthesia anywhere beforehand? Did you have a respiratory infection of any kind? Any other viral infections? No bronchitis? No rabies shot? Get any other vaccinations? How about childhood viral diseases? Smallpox, measles, hepatitis. . . ."

"Mel, Mel," I broke in benevolently when it began to dawn upon me what lay most heavily on his mind. "I know why you're here. I think I can give you what you've come for, the protection you want. I know how to immunize you." I paused to clear my mouth with the suction tube. "I'll have them shave my head and let you rub my baldy for good luck."

The laugh he gave was perfunctory. "It isn't funny, you know," he admonished me somberly. "Guillain-Barré is no joke. As many as 1.6 to 1.9 per hundred thousand get it every year. That's between 16 and 19 people per million."

Who could help being impressed? "Let me try to build up the odds for you," I said, going all out to comfort him. "Not many people have *two* close friends who get it, right? Can we begin with that?"

"Practically no one," he gave in, after considering.

"Well, you and I have some of the same friends, Julie and Speed and George, and they've already got me. Now all three are not going to have *two* friends with Guillain-Barré, are they? Statistically, you're practically guaranteed."

Reassured a little by that line of reasoning, he talked of other things for a while. He whirled and tongue-lashed the resident on duty severely when he learned

I was unable to sleep. Valium relaxes the muscles and sleeping potions depress the respiratory system, and Mel was not disposed to prescribe either.

"Give him tryptophan," he then commanded in that same brusque tone which I imagine resonates for years in the recollection of film editors with whom he has worked. "It's mother's milk to him. You can get it in any health food store. I'll send up a bottle of tablets tomorrow," Reminded that I couldn't swallow tablets, he exploded: "Pulverize them in the blender and pour them down his Levin tube. Do I have to tell you people everything? And give him a clean Yankauer tube. That one's filthy. I don't like the color of those secretions."

Among the tests to determine the cause of my condition was an electromyographic examination which they gave me on my second full day in the hospital. The test establishes neurological damage by studying the conduction velocity of stimuli along nerve fibers. Put plainly, I think, this EMG test measures the speed with which sensations of pain induced by needles and electric shock travel along specific nerves far enough to be recognized as pain. The EMG test I was given that day, though sufficient to the purpose, was superficial compared with one I was to undergo at a later time.

Wheeled out on my stretcher after it was performed, I was surprised to see my old friend George Mandel, the novelist, in the waiting room, leaning on the counter in his unbuttoned brown sheepskin coat and conversing gravely with the clerk there. I was stunned by his wan and dejected expression. My humanitarian impulse was to spring up off my stretcher and bid him please, please lie down, at once, and let me get or do something for him.

George and I have been friends since I was about 14, for close to 50 years. We met while I still lived in Coney Island. I have known George through thick and thicker, in sickness and in health—I had seen him after World War II, from which he had returned with a head wound from a German sniper's bullet; I had seen him during an episode of heart trouble, and I had seen him with a stone in his salivary gland—and I had never seen him looking worse, more glum, than he did just then. He looked just awful, and what was making him look so bad was the way I looked to him, lying on a stretcher, limp and exhausted, with a tube in my nose. He had just been told by the clerk that the test to which I had been subjected was experienced by many as excruciating, intolerable. This would have been news to me had he come right out and said so.

But instead he asked solemnly, "How're you feeling?"

"O.K., I guess," I answered promptly. I knew I felt tired.

"Did it hurt a lot?"

"What? No, not really. What's the matter?"

His look was a startled one. "No? Are you really O.K.? Are you sure it didn't hurt?"

"Of course, I'm sure. What are you talking about?"

George stared at me piercingly. "Do you know who I am?" he demanded: "Do you know where you are? Do you know why you're down here?"

"Sure, I do. Why are you asking me that?"

"I was checking your memory. Are you sure it didn't hurt? Maybe you forgot already."

George, who by instinct is both heroically diplomatic and infinitely tolerant, assumed control of the area of human relations in the division of labor that began to evolve about me among a rather sizable and growing number of people who would visit frequently and upon whom I knew I could depend.

It was he who received phone calls and letters from old friends and others who did not know how to reach me and did know how to reach him. There was the shocked phone call from Marian Berkman, who'd been friends with me since the seventh grade in elementary school in Coney Island, and who'd been widowed earlier that year when her husband, Lou, who'd been a friend of mine since the fifth grade, had died of cancer. He tactfully put off other would-be visitors to allow me to adjust more stably to my plight and my surroundings. To George came a phone call from Mario Puzo, who was the first to use the paralyzing word "paralyzed" to describe me and then was curious to learn if I was going to "croak." I had met Mario through George, back about 1950 or so, before any of the three of us had published a novel. George was in communication with my friend Marvin Winkler in California, with whom I had shared a playpen as an infant, if both our mothers were to be believed, and who maintains to this day, calumniously, that I used to empty both our milk bottles. With finesse, George undertook the ticklish assignment of telling the woman who had been my literary agent for 30 years, Candida Donadio, that, because of the expenses I envisioned, I wished to spare myself her commission in connection with my newest novel.

"Candida, I've got some bad news for you about Joe," was the inspired way George Mandel began.

And after that, of course, whatever he had to say could only come as a relief.

George showed the most devotion and nobleness of all, though, in submitting at my bedside with unflagging grace, politeness, and self-control to the company of several people I knew he could not stand—including, at times, me.

Early in the morning of the day an item about my illness appeared in The New York Times, which was the Monday of my second week in the intensive-care unit, a nurse surprised me with the message that Dustin Hoffman was on the telephone. He had seen the newspaper and had already been told by the information desk that I was discouraging visitors. Now he had called the nurses' desk in the unit to find out from me if it was all right for him to come. Of course, I said yes.

I made certain to be out of bed by the time Dustin arrived; and all of the flushed and fluttery nurses made certain that I'd been shaved, bathed and otherwise groomed. At that time, it still required but two people to move me from the bed to a wheelchair. By the end of that week; when I could no longer assist with my shoulders, trunk or legs, it took at least four; six generally cooperated in sliding me horizontally from my bed, on my bedsheet, at the count of three, to a stretcher-mechanism placed alongside whose different sections were dropped and raised to transform it into a chair.

Dustin and I had met about 10 years earlier and would get together for dinner or lunch from time to time. A reason we have remained such good friends is that we have never been close ones. We have never worked together, and that, too, has undoubtedly helped, leaving each of us with an unmarred respect for the judgment and consideration of the other that is probably unwarranted by both. Between us, as the foundation for our friendship, are the ground rules I promulgated once, only partly in jest: He doesn't have to read my novels, and I don't have to see his movies. I think a year or two must have passed since we'd last spoken. But I was not surprised he was so solicitous or that he would hurry to bring me what consolation he could supply.

We greeted each other with the somber good humor of a friendly and resigned philosophical ritual.

"You look terrible," was the way I welcomed him. "What in the hell has been happening to you?"

"I've been having a rough time," was his straight-faced reply.

Dustin was another one of those people of mine who, on first visit, looked alarmingly ashen and grave, fearful, and I could see it was going to take a very heavy effort on my part to boost his spirits. He had already, it turned out, telephoned his own physician, who was not yet at his office, and had left some questions and the message that he would soon call again for the answers. Within minutes of arriving, he requested the loan of a pencil and pad from one of the nurses and went outside to use the pay telephone. He returned in about 15 minutes with jottings on his pad indicating to me that he had called a medical man for the inside dope on Guillain-Barré, of which he himself, like Mel Brooks before him, was now visibly in terror: I saw the words "peripheral," "paretic," "paresthesia," "self-limiting" and "autoimmunological," all of which were now familiar to me, along with a few that in this context were entirely new, such as "stress" and "triggering factor."

"Most people," Dustin notified me encouragingly, improvising from his notes, "make a good recovery."

"Is that so?" I said with a hint of sarcasm that I'm afraid went right by him.

"Yeah," he grunted seriously. "The outlook is favorable, very favorable. In anywhere from. . . . "

And here there followed the phenomenon which is often portrayed in imaginative literature as "a voice trailing away."

"Did he also tell you," I kidded him, "that it's catching?"

He ignored this. "There also may sometimes be a triggering factor," he went on like a pedagogue. "Yeah, a triggering factor, something that triggers it. Have you been under any stress lately?"

"Naaah," I replied.

"Really?"

"Haven't you?"

"Who hasn't?"

Then he offered to give me anything I might need.

I shook my head. "Like what?"

"A private nurse, an attendant, a guy just to hang around to wait on you and give you exercise."

"Take a look," I answered, and indicated with a turn of my head the large number of staff members in the unit, most of whom would peek in our direction every chance they got as they continued about their business. "Maybe later on. Right now, I've got plenty."

And at just about that second, a "Team 7000" alarm sounded (the code words will vary in different places, but in the medical intensive-care unit at Mount Sinai, it was "Team 7000"). The call was for immediate life-sustaining aid for the comatose woman in the bed opposite mine. Her name was Rose and we were near the entrance of the unit. Suddenly, nurses, residents, respiratory therapists and all else came gathering in full haste, and there were quick comments about such things as blood pressure and pulse rate and commands for atropine and oxygen and God knows what other things. And Peggy Dunne, an able, pleasant woman who was one of the day supervisors, ever so softly asked if I'd mind requesting my visitor to wait just outside until the crisis was past. Dustin overheard and nodded politely and left on tiptoe, looking apologetic and saying he would wait and be back. And as I watched him moving away, I felt for the first time a pang of humiliation and shame at being seen in such surroundings by people I knew.

The emergency was attended to successfully that time, and Rose was kept alive. (But I will give large odds that she was not for much longer among the quick.)

"Why did they want me to go out?" Dustin inquired with more interest than petulance after he was allowed back in. Like many of the famous practitioners of what he sometimes calls his art and at other times speaks of as his profession, he has an attention span that can at times grow short; but I know from experience that his curiosity is genuine and intent once it is aroused. "Is there some kind of rule, or did they think I wouldn't be able to take it?"

"It could be," I answered with a playful irony that I knew would not be wasted upon him, "that they had no part for you."

He smiled wryly at this and inquired again if there was not something he could get me, give me, or do for me. I could think of nothing. He was better here than I was. Dustin is smarter and more inventive than many of the people he deals with, which may explain the occasional conflicts with motion picture producers and directors we hear about, and he came up with a suggestion now that hit the bull's-eye: a Sony Walkman. To me, this was that kind of pure inspiration one thinks of as genius. I had never listened to a cassette player of that kind, but I knew what a Walkman was and what it could do for me in my present straits. Here was a gift that would bring me the music I missed and also shield me somewhat from the distressing commotion intrinsic to the functions of the place, which included not merely the noise of machines and the comings and goings and natural conversation at the nurses' station in the late evening, but also the insufferable din from the radio there.

What recordings would I want? Dustin's pencil moved rapidly as I rattled off the compositions that came to mind: concertos by Brahms, Beethoven quartets, anything and everything by Bach. Dustin had an assistant named Julius working for him then who knew what to do. The package arrived no more than three hours after. Much of the music I'd asked for was not available on cassettes, but Julius had filled in admirably. Here, along with much else, was the "Archduke" Trio. And here also was more, much more, than I or anyone could have hoped for, the "St. Matthew Passion," more than three hours of choral music as soothing and sublime as anything ever conceived by the mind of man.

I had never listened to a Walkman before and was enchanted by the engulfing clarity of the sound. None of the nurses on duty then had ever listened to one either; nursing is not a high-paying occupation and buying one would have meant more than a day's take-home pay. One by one they came to sample the experience, their faces brightening as they donned the headset. On the evening shift, in one of those eerie lulls that settled in regularly, the headset was tried on by a nurse who was thrilled as much by the music as by the quality of the transcription, and she let out a cry of delight to one of the other young nurses working with her. I suggested she put it on the cassette player on the radio, at the nurses' station. There followed an extraordinary 10 minutes, both charmed and unreal, in which everyone present was brought to a standstill by the bars of music flowing out suddenly that seemed so melodic and ethereal, of a different world—everyone sentient, that is. The other three patients in the unit with me that evening were on their backs, unconscious (they indeed seemed part of a different world), and one or two of them, perhaps all three, were attached to the mechanical respirators or to other pieces of pumping and suctioning equipment that huffed and puffed in the background night and day. The music on the cassette chanced to be the andante from the second Brahms piano concerto, and Misha Dichter has never sounded more beautiful to me or to the others in that small body of rapt listeners who heard him that night in those macabre surroundings.

True to his promise, Dustin returned in the morning two or three days later, bringing a present that again was an inspired choice. This time he arrived with a newly purchased electric toothbrush, an appliance with which he was not acquainted, but he did not hesitate to plug it into the outlet he spied in the panel of equipment on the wall in back of me. Curious as to its application and potential usefulness to me, which turned out to be enormous for almost a year, he could not wait to learn how it worked. I had owned one before and instructed him, and he began brushing my teeth.

Now here is something that was like a scene from a movie, to me and to those there with me: Dustin Hoffman brushing my teeth—and in that place!

When Dustin is working at anything, he knows all that he is doing at every moment, and he was no less conscientious brushing the teeth of a friend in an intensive-care unit than he would have been in a different role on stage or before a camera. He took seriously what he was doing. People stopped what they were doing to watch. I was as fascinated as the rest as I listened to him relate without affectation that one of the first jobs he found upon coming to New York to seek his fortune as an actor was in the psychiatric division of a local hospital, where his principal duty was to press down firmly upon the knees of patients as they received charge of electricity as part of a prescribed program of electroconvulsive therapy, which is more popularly known as shock treatment. This was an intriguing surprise to me, and a line of work I had never heard of before. I did not believe him then, and I do not believe a word of it now.

On Easter morning, months later, when I had been at the Rusk Institute of Rehabilitation Medicine for a while and could handle a telephone again, Mario Puzo called to tell me:

"Joe, I gotta come clean with you. It may be a sacrilege to say so, but I really believe you've come back from the dead."

It was in the middle of that second week in intensive care that Mario, to the excruciating chagrin of us both, made his short, obligatory pilgrimage to the intensive-care unit to visit me, led there no doubt by his close friend Carol Gino, who had herself been a nurse before deciding that she would rather write books about nurses than continue working as one, and who had come there for a very long visit, one very much longer than Mario would have liked. I do not believe I am exaggerating when I state that it was as painful for me to look at Mario as it was for him to look at me. In the more than 30 years we have been friends, there has always been this scrupulous reluctance by each of us ever to impose an unwanted social duty on the other; and both of us knew that I no more expected him to come to see me in the hospital than I would have wanted to go visit him. Yet here he was, filling us both with guilt and remorse, moved by the dictates of a conscience that his intelligence told him was irrational and by at least one person he knew, Carol, who was more responsive to the amenities of proper civil behavior than either one of us.

You should have seen how sickly he looked. I don't know how he pulled through. I don't know whether it was he or Speed or Carol who first coined the phrase that Mario would rather eat a broom than visit a hospital, but I find that image extremely graphic. I do not know what it is like to eat a broom. I myself would rather *be* in a hospital than ever have to find out, although I do concede that in matters of eating there is much room for individuality.

It would be metaphorically incorrect to depict him as hanging back in the distance, for there was no distance in that confined area for him to hang back in. It would be hard, however, to conceive of his having remained farther away from me than he did, and from the moment he entered, he gave the impression of being impatient to leave.

Carol, on the other hand, breezed right up to my bedside on a bubbling crest of animation, folded her elbows on the rail, and began chatting away without inhibition, to me, to Kim Kudzin, my steady staff nurse, and to others who stopped by just out of interest for minutes at a time. Not before or since have I seen Carol so happily at home. She reminded me, I told her then, of a thirsty cowboy after roundup striding into a saloon, or more precisely, I added, of a hooker who'd made it big on the outside returning to the brothel from which she'd graduated, just to talk over old times in the setting in which she'd spent her most gladsome years. She asked and answered questions about new and old equipment and procedures and dilated freely on her own experience in hospitals and hospices. And Mario, all the while, waxed paler and paler in the background as he waited for her to finish and depart and, with an aspect of agony, ran his forefinger around inside the collar of a shirt within which his neck appeared to be shrinking with each minute that passed. I knew this much about Mario: There were no more than three restaurants he looked forward to going to on those infrequent occasions he was forced to come into Manhattan. On this occasion, he soon found himself dining in the hospital cafeteria, along with the two nurses Carol had invited for their dinner break in order to prolong as much as possible her exhilarating plunge into this orgy of reminiscence. And to let Mario know, perhaps, that she was having more fun here with the nurses than she did at the Cannes Film Festival, to which it was his habit to drag her annually.

Mel Brooks was back to see me during a very low period. He was to leave for Europe the next day, and he was greatly depressed by the steep deterioration in my physical state since he'd seen me the first time and by the ironic phenomenon that his newest movie appeared to be doing better in Europe than here. We did what we could do to cheer each other up.

This time, he arrived with two of our closest friends, and a couple of others were there with me already. The whole lousy bunch of them were going out to dinner in Chinatown without me. This was a group that normally went out to dinner together about once a week—sometimes more. The Gourmet Club really consisted of a herd of gluttonous pigs who ate Chinese food ravenously and disgustingly and among whom I, in my prime, and a very short composer named Hershy Kay, now deceased, were the outstanding performers. Mel could begin eating more viciously than any of the rest of us, but he lacked staying power and would be sighing aloud for dessert and bigger box-office receipts while Hershy and I were still mopping up what remained of the beef and spinach, roast pork, stuffed bean curd and lobster or crab in black bean sauce, maybe both. And pan-fried smelts or butterfish.

Mel is made of sterner stuff than Mario and did not shrink from coming close to touch and stare and to fire at me whatever questions were burning in his thoughts. He boasted without joy that, from the looks of me, he probably could triple whatever scores I was making on the breathing tests he watched me take, and disdained to try. He was angrily affronted, almost deeply personally insulted, that I could be suffering from pneumonia and just lie there in bed like a person who didn't have pneumonia. He fell into contemplation of my left shoulder muscle, appalled by my inability to raise the elbow from the mattress even the tiniest bit. He was glum, shaken, and he clucked his tongue.

Life hangs by a thread, was pretty much the observation he made to me in a choked voice. He promised to telephone me from the airport on his return from Europe when he changed planes—putting smiles on the faces of those of us acquainted with his compulsion to telephone everybody from any airport while he waited for his plane. Buttoning his heavy winter coat as he turned to leave, he was discoursing in brooding soliloquy on the frailty of human health, and on the fickleness of an American movie audience that was not for this latest masterpiece by the creator of the film "Springtime for Hitler" (released as "The Procedures") smashing the astounding attendance records set by his previous ones, while patrons in

Munich, Vienna and Luxembourg were charging down from the mountains and coming out of the forests in droves the size of which had never been seen in movie houses before.

Fame is fleeting, is pretty much the observation I made to him in response. The others—Speed, George, Julie Green, Joe Stein—expressed sincere and sorrowful regret at leaving me there while they went down to Chinatown. Who could believe them? Those liars, those hypocrites! They looked so eager to be going out to eat without me.

15

THE DICTATORSHIP
OF THE OVARIES

Barbara Ehrenreich and Deirdre English

This selection presents a feminist perspective on the healing experience. The authors are well known for their critical writing on social and biological issues in medicine as they relate to women. This excerpt from their book, *For Her Own Good: 150 Years of the Experts' Advice to Women*, presents some chilling examples of how, until quite recently, doctors often violated their central principle: "First, do no harm." That they did not know or admit that they were harming women hardly excuses their actions. The authors show that male doctors' assumptions about women's bodies often led them to perform needless operations and other invasive procedures. Perhaps the strongest of these assumptions was the notion that a woman's reproductive system controls her personality and behavior.

The feminist critique of male-dominated gynecological medicine has brought about important changes in the way medicine is practiced on women as well as in women's awareness of their role as patients. Far more women are becoming gynecologists and obstetricians. More women are seeking out the help of midwives and asserting their need for greater control over their own reproductive processes. Although these changes in the gender aspects of medicine in the United States are by no means complete, books like *For Her Own Good* have propelled those changes in constructive directions.

It was medicine's task to translate the evolutionary theory of women into the language of flesh and blood, tissues and organs. The result was a theory which put woman's mind, body and soul in the thrall of her all-powerful reproductive organs. "The Uterus, it must be remembered," Dr. F. Hollick wrote, "is the *controlling* organ in the female body, being the most excitable of all, and so intimately connected, by the ramifications of its numerous nerves, with every other part."[1] Professor M. L. Holbrook, addressing a medical society in 1870, observed that it seemed "as if the Almighty, in creating the female sex, *had taken the uterus and built up a woman around it*."[2] [Emphasis in original.]

To other medical theorists, it was the ovaries which occupied center stage. Dr. G. L. Austin's 1883 book of advice for "maiden, wife and mother" asserts that the ovaries "give woman all her characteristics of body and mind."[3] This passage written in 1870 by Dr. W. W. Bliss, is, if somewhat overwrought, nonetheless typical:

> Accepting, then, these views of the gigantic power and influence of the ovaries over the whole animal economy of woman,—that they are the most powerful agents in all the commotions of her system; that on them rest her intellectual standing in society, her physical perfection, and all that lends beauty to those fine and delicate contours which are constant objects of admiration, all that is great, noble and beautiful, all that is voluptuous, tender, and endearing; that her fidelity, her devotedness, her perpetual vigilance, forecast, and all those qualities of mind and disposition which inspire respect and love and fit her as the safest counsellor and friend of man, spring from the ovaries,—*what must be their influence and power over the great vocation of woman and the august purposes of her existence when these organs have become compromised through disease!*[4] [Emphasis in original.]

According to this "psychology of the ovary" woman's entire personality was directed by the ovaries, and any abnormalities, from irritability to insanity, could be traced to some ovarian disease. Dr. Bliss added, with unbecoming spitefulness, that "the influence of the ovaries over the mind is displayed in woman's artfulness and dissimulation."

It should be emphasized, before we follow the workings of the uterus and ovaries any further, that woman's total submission to the "sex function" did not make her a *sexual* being. The medical model of female nature, embodied in the "psychology of the ovary," drew a rigid distinction between reproductivity and sexuality. Women were urged by the health books and the doctors to indulge in deep preoccupation with themselves as "The Sex"; they were to devote themselves to developing their reproductive powers and their maternal instinct. Yet doctors said they had no predilection for the sex act itself. Even a woman physician, Dr. Mary Wood-Allen, wrote (perhaps from experience) that women embrace their husbands "without a particle of sex desire."[5] Hygiene manuals stated that the more cultured the woman, "the more is the sensual refined away from her nature," and warned against "any spasmodic convulsion" on a woman's part during intercourse lest it interfere with conception. Female sexuality was seen as unwomanly and possibly even detrimental to the supreme function of reproduction.

The doctors themselves never seemed entirely convinced, though, that the uterus and ovaries had successfully stamped out female sexuality. Underneath the complacent denials of female sexual feelings, there lurked the age-old male fascination with woman's "insatiable lust," which, once awakened, might turn out to be uncontrollable. Doctors dwelt on cases in which women were destroyed by their cravings; one doctor claimed to have discovered a case of "virgin nymphomania." The twenty-five-year-old British physician Robert Brudenell Carter leaves us with this tantalizing observation on his female patients:

> . . . no one who has realized the amount of moral evil wrought in girls . . . whose prurient desires have been increased by Indian hemp and partially gratified by medical manipulations, can deny that remedy is worse than disease. I have . . . seen young unmarried women, of the middle class of society, reduced by the constant use of the speculum to the mental and moral condition of prostitutes; seeking to give themselves the same indulgence by the practice of solitary vice; and asking every medical practitioner . . . to institute an examination of the sexual organs.[6]

But if the uterus and ovaries could not be counted on to suppress all sexual strivings, they were still sufficiently in control to be blamed for all possible female disorders, from headaches to sore throats and indigestion. Dr. M. E. Dirix wrote in 1869:

> Thus, women are treated for diseases of the stomach, liver, kidneys, heart, lungs, etc.; yet, in most instances, these diseases will be found on due investigation, to be, in reality, no diseases at all, but merely the sympathetic reactions or the symptoms of one disease, namely, a disease of the womb.[7]

Even tuberculosis could be traced to the capricious ovaries. When men were consumptive, doctors sought some environmental factor, such as overexposure, to explain the disease. But for women it was a result of reproductive malfunction. Dr. Azell Ames wrote in 1875:

> It being beyond doubt that consumption . . . is itself produced by the failure of the [menstrual] function in the forming girls . . . one has been the parent of the other with interchangeable priority. [Actually, as we know today, it is true that consumption may *result* in suspension of the menses.][8]

Since the reproductive organs were the source of disease, they were the obvious target in the treatment of disease. Any symptom—backaches, irritability, indigestion, etc.—could provoke a medical assault on the sexual organs. Historian Ann Douglas Wood describes the "local treatments" used in the mid-nineteenth century for almost any female complaint:

> This [local] treatment had four stages, although not every case went through all four: a manual investigation, "leeching," "injections," and "cauterization." Dewees [an American medical professor] and Bennet, a famous English gynecologist widely read

in America, both advocated placing the leeches right on the vulva or the neck of the uterus, although Bennet cautioned the doctor to count them as they dropped off when satiated, lest he "lose" some. Bennet had known adventurous leeches to advance into the cervical cavity of the uterus itself, and he noted, "I think I have scarcely ever seen more acute pain than that experienced by several of my patients under these circumstances." Less distressing to a 20th century mind, but perhaps even more senseless, were the "injections" into the uterus advocated by these doctors. The uterus became a kind of catch-all, or what one exasperated doctor referred to as a "Chinese toy shop": Water, milk and water, linseed tea, and "decoction of marshmallow . . . tepid or cold" found their way inside nervous women patients. The final step, performed at this time, one must remember, with no anesthetic but a little opium or alcohol, was cauterization, either through the application of nitrate of silver, or, in cases of more severe infection, through the use of much stronger hydrate of potassa, or even the "actual cautery," a "white-hot iron" instrument.[9]

In the second half of the century, these fumbling experiments with the female interior gave way to the more decisive technique of surgery—aimed increasingly at the control of female personality disorders. There had been a brief fad of clitoridectomy (removal of the clitoris) in the sixties, following the introduction of the operation by the English physician Isaac Baker Brown. Although most doctors frowned on the practice of removing the clitoris, they tended to agree that it might be necessary in cases of nymphomania, intractable masturbation, or "unnatural growth" of that organ. (The last clitoridectomy we know of in the United States was performed in 1948 on a child of five, as a cure for masturbation.)

The most common form of surgical intervention in the female personality was ovariotomy, removal of the ovaries—or "female castration." In 1906 a leading gynecological surgeon estimated that there were 150,000 women in the United States who had lost their ovaries under the knife. Some doctors boasted that they had removed from fifteen hundred to two thousand ovaries apiece.[10] According to historian G. J. Barker-Benfield:

> Among the indications were troublesomeness, eating like a ploughman, masturbation, attempted suicide, erotic tendencies, persecution mania, simple "cussedness," and dysmenorrhea [painful menstruation]. Most apparent in the enormous variety of symptoms doctors took to indicate castration was a strong current of sexual appetitiveness on the part of women.[11]

The rationale for the operation flowed directly from the theory of the "psychology of the ovary": since the ovaries controlled the personality, they must be responsible for any psychological disorders; conversely, psychological disorders were a sure sign of ovarian disease. Ergo, the organs must be removed.

One might think, given the all-powerful role of the ovaries, that an ovaryless woman would be like a rudderless ship—desexed and directionless. But on the contrary, the proponents of ovariotomy argued, a woman who was relieved of a diseased ovary would be a *better* woman. One 1893 advocate of the operation claimed that "patients are improved, some of them cured; . . . the moral sense of the patient is elevated . . . she becomes tractable, orderly, industrious, and cleanly."*[12] Patients

---

*It is unlikely that the operation had this effect on a woman's personality. It would have produced the symptoms of menopause, which do not include any established personality changes.

were often brought in by their husbands, who complained of their unruly behavior. Doctors also claimed that women—troublesome but still sane enough to recognize their problem—often "came to us pleading to have their ovaries removed."[13] The operation was judged successful if the woman was restored to a placid contentment with her domestic functions.

The overwhelming majority of women who had leeches or hot steel applied to their cervices, or who had their clitorises or ovaries removed, were women of the middle to upper classes, for after all, these procedures cost money. But it should not be imagined that poor women were spared the gynecologist's exotic catalog of tortures simply because they couldn't pay. The pioneering work in gynecological surgery had been performed by Marion Sims on black female slaves he kept for the sole purpose of surgical experimentation. He operated on one of them thirty times in four years, being foiled over and over by postoperative infections.[14] After moving to New York, Sims continued his experimentation on indigent Irish women in the wards of the New York Women's Hospital. So, though middle-class women suffered most from the doctors' actual practice, it was poor and black women who had suffered through the brutal period of experimentation.

NOTES

1. FREDERICK HOLLICK, M.D., *The Diseases of Women, Their Cause and Cure Familiarly Explained* (New York: T. W. Strong, 1849).
2. Quoted in ANN DOUGLAS WOOD, "The 'Fashionable Diseases': Women's Complaints and Their Treatment in Nineteenth-Century America," *Journal of Interdisciplinary History* 4, Summer 1973, p. 29.
3. Quoted in RITA ARDITTI, "Women as Objects: Science and Sexual Politics," *Science for the People,* September 1974, p. 8.
4. W. W. BLISS, *Woman and Her Thirty-Years' Pilgrimage* (Boston: B. B. Russell, 1870), p. 96.
5. Quoted in JOHN S. HALLER, Jr., and ROBIN M. HALLER, *The Physician and Sexuality in Victorian America* (Urbana, Illinois: University of Illinois Press, 1974), p. 101.
6. Quoted in ILZA VEITH, *Hysteria: The History of a Disease* (Chicago and London: The University of Chicago Press, 1965), p. 205.
7. M. E. DIRIX, M. D., *Woman's Complete Guide to Health* (New York: W. A. Townsend and Adams, 1869), pp. 23–24.
8. Quoted in RACHEL GILLETT FRUCHTER, "Women's Weakness: Consumption and Women in the 19th Century," Columbia University School of Public Health, unpublished paper, 1973.
9. WOOD, op. cit., p. 30.
10. G. J. BARKER-BENFIELD, *The Horrors of the Half-Known Life: Male Attitudes Toward Women and Sexuality in Nineteenth-Century America* (New York: Harper & Row, 1976), pp. 121–24.
11. BEN BARKER-BENFIELD, "The Spermatic Economy: A Nineteenth Century View of Sexuality," *Feminist Studies* 1, Summer 1972, pp. 45–74.
12. BARKER-BENFIELD, *Horrors of the Half-Known Life,* p. 122.
13. Ibid., p. 30.
14. Ibid., pp. 96–102.

16

ANN AND RICK

William Stockton

Dr. Richard Berkowitz heads the world-famous OBGYN clinic at Mt. Sinai Hospital in New York City. In recent years he has become widely known for his role in the development of several advanced obstetrical procedures, including the sonogram technologies and in-utero fetal blood transfusions described here. Berkowitz's clinic also treats women who are carrying more fetuses than they can possibly bring to term as healthy babies. Berkowitz is accustomed, therefore, to dealing with some of the most stressful and emotion-laden issues in modern obstetric medicine.

On the surface this account by medical researcher William Stockton describes the use of advanced medical technologies and professional knowledge to save a growing fetus. But there is another story here. In a medical emergency there is no time to lose. Decisions must be made quickly. The doctor may attempt techniques that are still in the experimental stage. But in this selection the doctor is practicing on a person who knew him before he became a doctor. During the period when Berkowitz was learning how to use innovative medical technologies to save fetuses while protecting the mother, an old friend came into his office to seek his assistance; his wife was at risk of losing their unborn child.

This selection illustrates some of the emotional aspects of medical and surgical practice, which can be especially intense when a couple's hopes of having children are at stake.

Rick is tall and broad-shouldered and exudes quiet self-confidence. I had little difficulty picturing him as an executive of a New York City pollution control company. He studied chemical engineering at Cornell, where he was regarded as a serious, hardworking student whose ambition would ultimately carry him to success. He was born in New York City, but grew up across the Hudson in New Jersey.

Ann was raised in New York City, which her voice still betrays. She is the daughter of a policeman. Ann's mother died when Ann was two years old. She spent most of her childhood and adolescence shifted around New York's boroughs, living with relatives. She went to high school in Brooklyn, married in her early twenties, and had a son, Gregory. Ann was divorced and raising Greg alone and working as a secretary at the same pollution control company where Rick came to work.

After their marriage, Ann and Rick very much wanted to have a child. What they didn't know was that their differing blood types, when combined genetically, would make having a baby the most difficult, trying experience of their lives. It would be an experience that ironically might have been prevented if Ann had given birth to Greg just one or two years later. Ann is a victim of Rh incompatibility. Her babies can die in the womb of a condition called erythroblastosis fetalis.

This disease occurs once in about every 200 pregnancies. It's not a genetic defect in which unwanted genes are passed to children. Instead, it is a condition caused by unwanted antibodies in the mother's blood that react to genetically determined factors in the baby's blood. It affects second and subsequent pregnancies. Women with the condition can usually have one normal child before the trouble begins. Women who face this problem now are given an injection within seventy-two hours of the birth of each baby or after an abortion or miscarriage. If they receive the injection, the problem won't bother them. However, there are women like Ann who had their first child before the preventive substance was developed and are still of childbearing age. If they wish more children, as Ann did after marrying Rick, they are destined to have difficulties.

In Rh disease, antibodies in the mother's blood cross the placenta and attack the red blood cells of the growing fetus, destroying the baby's blood as quickly as it is manufactured. The result is usually a spontaneous abortion, a stillborn infant, or a seriously ill child who often dies within hours or days of birth. Children who survive to birth are given transfusions to exchange all their blood. Many go on to lead normal lives.

Most women with the condition must have the progress of their pregnancy monitored closely through blood tests that chart the buildup of the antibodies that could attack the baby's blood cells. If this buildup reaches dangerous levels, doctors may attempt to transfuse blood directly into the fetus to replace the blood being destroyed. A needle is inserted through the mother's abdomen and blood is injected into the fetus' abdominal cavity, where it is absorbed into the bloodstream. The procedure is risky and uncomfortable. But it often works. That turned out to be

Ann and Rick's only hope. To receive this unusual treatment, they sought help from Yale University's high-risk obstetrical unit. . . .

Ann has a snowy complexion and a round face framed by brown hair that gives her a delicate beauty, like that of a finely crafted china doll. She is energetic and speaks rapidly and enthusiastically, using her hands to tell a story. She radiates energy, and it makes her appealing. I could understand how Rick, who is deliberate and quiet, would be attracted to her.

"After I had Greg I had several miscarriages and apparently I was building up antibodies which would affect subsequent pregnancies, but I didn't know it," she said, sitting on the floor and leaning against the couch and Rick's leg. "Then in 1975 I became pregnant and things went well until the seventh month. I was going to a local obstetrician and he did some routine tests and discovered that there was an Rh problem. So he sent me to Yale for an amniocentesis and a scanning with ultrasound. That's how we met John Hobbins. The tests indicated that the baby might be affected, but not too severely. So my local obstetrician delivered the baby.

"I had the baby by caesarian section. It was only mildly affected with Rh and they would have transfused it and everything would probably have been okay, but the baby had a herniated diaphragm. Its intestines were coming through a hole in the diaphragm. They had delivered the baby early because my antibodies were building up. And because of this there was also the possibility of a problem with immature lungs. But with the hole in the diaphragm they had to rush the baby up to Yale and Rick jumped in the car and drove up behind the ambulance. That's when he first saw the newborn special-care unit at Yale. The baby died after several hours. Poor Rick had to wait through all that.

"The problem of Rh disease gets worse with each pregnancy. But that baby turned out to be only mildly affected with Rh and John Hobbins said he thought that if we tried again the Rh might not be a problem. We also talked about adoption, but that is so long-drawn and painful and difficult. We also considered artificial insemination. But in the end we decided to try again. I would be cared for from the first by the doctors at Yale. I had become a high-risk pregnancy." . . .

About 85 percent of all people have the Rh antigens in their blood and are Rh+. The other 15 percent don't have the antigens and are Rh−. Each person's blood also has antibodies that wait to attack other types of blood. For example, if your blood type is A, your blood carries antibodies that will react against blood cells from Types B and AB blood. If you receive a transfusion of Type B blood, the antibodies against Type B blood will go into battle, causing clumping of your own Type A blood cells as well as the Type B cells you received in the transfusion. That causes a severe reaction and often death. Thus there are always antibodies to most other blood types in your blood, waiting to destroy blood cells from another type.

But such antibodies aren't present where the Rh antigens are concerned. If you are Rh− and you are transfused with Rh+ blood, nothing will happen—the first time. But after the first transfusion your immune system has been alerted. The next time you receive Rh+ blood, antibodies to the Rh+ antigens will be waiting. There will be a reaction, possibly severe.

With that knowledge, doctors finally unraveled the mysterious newborn diseases. For the problem to occur, the mother must be Rh− and the father Rh+. Because of the genetic factors at work, the fetus growing in the mother's uterus would usually be Rh+. Red blood cells are too large to pass across the placenta from the mother's circulation to the fetus'. Thus, although the mother's Rh− antigens and the fetus' Rh+ antigens would produce an immune reaction if the two bloods were mixed, that doesn't happen during the first pregnancy.

But during delivery of the first chid (during the birth of Greg, in Ann's case) some of the infant's blood enters the mother's body, probably as the placenta is removed. If the infant's blood type is different from the mother's, say Type B in a mother with Type A, then the mother's Type A antibodies immediately attack the infant's wandering Type B blood cells and destroy them. There will be no Rh problem with future pregnancies for that woman. But if the infant's Rh+ blood is of the same type—say, Type A in the mother and Type A in the infant—then the infant's blood cells won't be destroyed. They will remain. But the infant's Rh+ antigens will cause a reaction by the mother's immune system. The infant's Rh+ antigens stimulate the production of anti-Rh+ antibodies by the mother's immune system. Her immune system is now sensitized to Rh+.

During the next pregnancy, the anti-Rh+ antibodies in her blood are small enough that they *can* cross the placenta to the fetus' bloodstream. As the fetus grows, these antibodies cross over in increasing numbers, searching out and attacking the fetus' Rh+ blood cells. To compensate, the fetus' blood-forming machinery begins to work overtime, enlarging itself, but to no avail. The anti-Rh+ antibodies in the mother's blood are relentless. If they don't eventually kill the fetus, causing a miscarriage or a stillbirth, then the baby will be severely ill at birth. . . .

Ann had Type A blood and was Rh−. Her first husband was Type A and Rh+. Greg was an Rh+ baby and a few drops of his blood entered Ann's bloodstream when he was born, causing her body to form anti-Rh+ antibodies. Rick, in turn, was Rh+. All of Ann's subsequent pregnancies carried an Rh+ fetus, and her anti-Rh+ antibodies crossed the placenta and attacked the fetus' Rh+ blood. It had nothing to do with the hole in the diaphragm of the baby born in 1975. But it did account for the mild Rh disease the doctors detected in that baby before it died.

If doctors know that an Rh− mother has given birth to an Rh+ baby of the same blood type, all they need do is immunize the mother within about seventy-two hours of the first birth, thus preventing antibodies from being formed. But development of a material that could be injected to accomplish this didn't come until the early 1960s. It wasn't in widespread use until one or two years after Greg was born.

During the final weeks of her 1975 pregnancy, which produced the baby with the herniated diaphragm, Ann went to Yale every two weeks for an ultrasound scan and amniocentesis to measure the extent to which the Rh problem was affecting her growing baby. Rick would leave work to accompany her.

One day as Ann lay on the treatment table while John Hobbins was preparing to insert the amniocentesis needle into her abdomen, a white-coated doctor entered the room. Neither Rick nor Ann noticed his face. He stood with his back to them, conferring in low tones with Hobbins.

Rick studied the doctor's back. Slowly he began to realize that something was familiar. It was his build, the way he stood. Suddenly it clicked. "Is that Dick Berkowitz?" Rick blurted.

The doctor whirled. It *was* Dick Berkowitz. There followed one of those unexpected college classmate reunions filled with handshakes and exclamations of surprise, subdued somewhat by the surroundings and the medical procedure under way.

Dick Berkowitz and Rick had both belonged to Tau Delta Phi social fraternity as undergraduates at Cornell. They lived in the frat house and were friends, although not extremely close. Seeing Berkowitz at Yale was particularly startling to Rick. His fraternity friend had been a cutup who preferred parties to study, brilliant in those courses that interested him and squeaking through the rest. It seemed amazing that Dick Berkowitz had become a doctor, let alone a member of the obstetrics and gynecology faculty at Yale. In fact, Rick learned, Berkowitz was such a brilliant obstetrician that he had been invited to join the faculty and team with Hobbins in the high-risk obstetrics program.

All during the latter part of her 1975 pregnancy, Hobbins cared for Ann. A year after that baby died, Ann became pregnant again. This time, Hobbins and Berkowitz were to care for her jointly, as they do with all their patients. But when Ann's troubles began late in the summer of 1976, Hobbins was on vacation. The full responsibility for her care fell to Berkowitz, including the risky intrauterine transfusions. The fact that he had renewed his friendship with an old fraternity brother and now had exclusive responsibility for the care of his friend's wife ultimately presented the doctor with one of the more difficult ethical crises of his career and caused him considerable personal distress. . . .

When Ann had been pregnant for twenty-two weeks she went to Yale for the first amniocentesis of her new pregnancy. As expected, the levels of anti-Rh+ antibodies in her blood had been rising. It was almost certain that Hobbins and Berkowitz would find elevated bilirubin levels. The ultrasound might reveal other difficulties.

"There is some bilirubin present in the amniotic fluid of a normal pregnancy," Berkowitz said, leafing through Ann's medical records folder. "The amount is generally a function of the gestational age of the fetus. On a piece of graph paper you plot the amount of bilirubin against the number of weeks of gestation. The curve that results will fall into one of three zones—Zone 1, 2, or 3.

"Zone 1 means the baby is totally unaffected with the Rh problem or only mildly affected. Zone 2 is the transition zone. When someone moves into Zone 3, that means trouble. You have three options. First, you can do nothing and the fetus will die. Second, you can deliver the baby immediately by caesarian section. If the baby is only, say, twenty-eight or thirty weeks old, it may die of problems associated with prematurity. The third option is intrauterine transfusions."

I had read up on such transfusions. I knew they were risky for the baby and uncomfortable for the mother. A large-diameter needle is inserted into the mother's abdomen and on into the fetus' abdomen. Blood that has been carefully checked for its blood type and antigens that might cause the mother's immune system to mount an attack is injected into the fetus' peritoneal or abdominal cavity. From there it is assimilated by the fetus' blood-starved tissues.

Sometimes, when such an intrauterine-transfused baby is born, its body contains 90 percent or more transfused blood. The transfusions are a delaying tactic, a buying of time. As the pregnancy advances, the mother's anti-Rh+ antibodies grow stronger and continue to attack the fetus' blood-forming tissues. The transfusions keep the fetus growing until it is big enough to be delivered by caesarian section and has a chance of survival in the newborn special-care unit. . . .

[Ann continued.] "They started the amniocentesis taps at twenty weeks. John Hobbins was doing the taps because he'd done them in the previous pregnancy. The first two taps, the bilirubin was in low Zone 2. The baby was mildly affected, but they weren't too worried. The baby wasn't in trouble or anything.

"I went up for the third tap one morning and John Hobbins was on vacation, so Dick Berkowitz did it. It was routine and I came back home. Then in the afternoon Dick called and he was very concerned. The lab analysis of the amniotic fluid showed that I had to have an intrauterine transfusion. He wanted me to come up that night so he could do the transfusion first thing the next morning. . . .

Ann spent the night in the hospital and the next morning was taken to a treatment room equipped with an X-ray unit and an ultrasound scanner. Berkowitz used the ultrasound picture to locate the baby's abdomen. As was usually the case with Ann, the fetus was in an incorrect position and she had to get up on all fours while Berkowitz tugged and pulled at her belly, trying to move the fetus. He had no luck, so he sent her out to walk the halls. When she returned, the baby had moved and the abdomen was exposed for insertion of the needle.

Berkowitz gave Ann a local anesthetic just below the navel and inserted the first needle, using the last ultrasound image to guide his thrust. When he thought the needle was in place, he injected a small amount of opaque dye, which shows up as a dark spot on an X ray. The technician took X rays and hurried into an adjacent darkroom to develop them while everyone waited, the needle protruding from Ann's stomach. Berkowitz sighed with relief when the technician returned with the films. The needle was in the abdominal cavity—perfectly placed.

The doctor then attached an apparatus to the needle that permitted drawing blood from a bag hanging overhead, injecting it through the needle, and monitoring the buildup of pressure in the baby's abdominal cavity as more and more blood was pumped in. Through it all, the single needle protruding from Ann's abdomen danced and jiggled as the baby moved. Little is known about whether fetuses feel pain, but the assumption is that the needle does cause a sensation, perhaps painful, which causes the fetus to thrash about.

Berkowitz injected 60 cubic centimeters of blood that day, a satisfactory amount. Ann came back a week later for a routine amniocentesis to monitor bilirubin levels, which were stable, reflecting the benefits of the transfusion. A week after that, she returned for the next transfusion.

When Berkowitz ran the ultrasound scanner's transducer over Ann's belly preparatory to giving the second transfusion, the picture that flashed on the television monitor was a chilling sight. Fluid had begun to build up in the baby's tissues and the swelling was obvious on the screen. It was a sure sign of approaching heart failure, a condition called hydrops. The fetus' tiny heart wasn't beating strongly enough and couldn't push enough blood through its blood vessels to keep all the body's chemical processes in balance. Excess fluid was the result.

The fluid buildup was a grave sign. Only 15 percent of all Rh fetuses with congestive heart failure survive. Berkowitz went ahead with the transfusion, but he had to insert four needles before he finally had one in the right position. He was able to inject only 49 cc of blood, a disappointing amount.

Ann returned to her hospital room, as she did after each transfusion, and Berkowitz called Joe Warshaw. He explained the problem. "She's at twenty-nine and a half weeks," he said. "What would happen if we took the baby now? What if I did a C-section now?"

There was a pause at the other end of the line. The baby would have a 10 percent chance of survival, came the answer.

Berkowitz called a pediatric cardiologist on the Yale faculty and asked his advice. The best treatment, the cardiologist said, might be to give Ann digitalis, a heart stimulant. The drug would cross the placenta to the fetus' blood and possibly stimulate its flagging heart. The drug wouldn't have an adverse effect on Ann. But it might make it possible for the baby to make use of the newly transfused blood. Berkowitz met with Ann and Rick to outline the problem.

"I told them that we could see the fluid and what that meant, that the statistics were pretty grim. I told them we could take the baby, but that the odds were poor. I outlined the digitalis treatment and told them that was what I wanted to do. All we could do was give Ann the digitalis and wait and see.

"There's a fine line here between giving the patient all the facts and letting them help make decisions but still managing the case yourself. This kind of decision can't be an emotional thing. You hope you have the very best information possible and then you couple that with your judgment and your experience. Medicine is often more art than science, but it's an art based on experience."

The gamble paid off. When Ann came in for her third transfusion, the ultrasound showed the fluid had gone. Presumably the digitalis had stimulated the fetus' heart sufficiently.

But it was a difficult transfusion, nevertheless. Berkowitz inserted one, two, three needles, waiting each time for the X ray to come back. Each time the dye revealed that the needle wasn't on target. Ann waited, lying on the table, her discomfort and her anxiety growing with each needle, watching the needles dance and jiggle where they protruded from her belly.

"Once the first needle misses the mark, it gets tough," Berkowitz said, grimacing at the memory. "Interpreting the X rays is hard. They are two-dimensional and they show the needle and the fetus, but they don't show the angles involved. Ultrasound shows us the angles, but then you have to turn it off to actually insert the needle. If the baby moves in the meantime, then it's all changed again."

The risk to the fetus during intrauterine transfusions runs as high as 10 percent. The big danger is that a needle will hit a vital organ, the heart for example, and cause serious damage, even death. There is always a danger of an infection in the womb that could cause a spontaneous abortion.

When Berkowitz inserted the fourth needle that day, the danger that always loomed suddenly struck. When the technician hurried back into the room, the films showed the dye spreading to the fetus' bowel. He had inadvertently shoved the needle too far and pierced the intestine. He backed the needle off slightly. Concentrating intensely, sweat pouring from his forehead, he injected more dye to see if pulling the needle back had placed it correctly. When the next X rays came back, he relaxed a little. Finally, the baby had paused in its movements and the needle was on target. He began injecting the blood.

After Ann returned to her room, Berkowitz met with her and Rick and told them about piercing the bowel. He said there was no way to tell what damage, if any, had been done. He asked them to come back in two days for an ultrasound scan. It revealed that everything was fine. There had been no short-term damage. . . .

Two weeks after the fetus' bowel was pierced, Ann appeared for her fourth transfusion. Berkowitz knew that with each passing day the chances of something going wrong increased. Ann's immune system was determined to get rid of the fetus, this seeming cancer growing in her uterus. There was no chance the baby could remain in the womb for a full nine months. It was only a matter of time before heart failure would set in. The trick for Berkowitz—the melding of the science and art of medicine—was to wait until the last possible moment and then deliver the baby. The critical factor became the maturity of the fetus' lungs. If the baby was delivered and the lungs weren't ready, it would develop respiratory distress syndrome in the newborn special-care unit. That condition, combined with Rh disease, is often fatal.

Thus the amniotic fluid withdrawn every two weeks took on another importance: measurement of fatty substances that indicate lung maturity. The substances are known chemically as lipids and are named lecithin and sphingomyelin. A fetus' developing lungs produce both of these lipids. Before the thirty-fourth week of gestation there is more sphingomyelin in the amniotic fluid than lecithin. This means the lungs are still immature. At about thirty-four weeks lecithin production jumps markedly. When there is twice as much lecithin as sphingomyelin, or a ratio of 2 to 1, doctors are assured that the lungs are mature enough for delivery. There is little likelihood of the newborn child developing respiratory distress syndrome. A ratio lower than 2 to 1 often means trouble. When Ann received her fourth intrauterine transfusion at thirty-three weeks' gestation, the ratio was disturbingly low.

"It was 0.6," Berkowitz said, studying Ann's medical records. "That meant the lungs were extremely immature and it seemed certain the baby would have respiratory distress syndrome." . . .

"Then she came back a week later for another amniotic tap. The bilirubin was still high, which didn't surprise anyone. But the lecithin to sphingomyelin ratio had dropped! It should have risen but instead it had dropped to 0.4. The low L to S ratio was disappointing, but all other signs were stable. She didn't need to be transfused again for another week. So we decided to wait another week.

"A week later she came back and we tapped her again but didn't transfuse her.

We wanted to wait for the lab results on the ratio. But it was still 0.4. At this point we had to either transfuse her again or deliver the baby. We were reluctant to transfuse again because of the inherent risk to the fetus every time you do that. So we decided to give her steroids to attempt to speed up lung maturation.". . .

The decision to administer steroids was made on a Saturday in October. The next day Ann returned to Yale for an injection of steroids. She returned again Monday and Tuesday for more injections. Late Tuesday afternoon she checked into a room on the obstetrical floor of Yale–New Haven Hospital. Berkowitz and an assistant would deliver the baby the next morning. . . .

[Ann continued.] "Dick asked about my scar. What kind of scar I wanted. With the other baby I had a scar that was horizontal across my abdomen. Dick wanted to make one that would be vertical. He said I wouldn't be able to wear a bikini. I told him I didn't care one bit. Just get that baby out of there.

"Then I started to cry. I don't know why. Dick was looking at me crying. 'You shouldn't be crying now. This is a happy time,' he said. That just made me cry more. The thing that was on my mind was that the other baby never cried. He just made gurgling sounds. I never heard him cry. Then I noticed there were other people in the room, sort of standing around. They had on surgical greens. I kept wondering who they were. And then I realized it was the pediatricians from the perinatal unit. Joe Warshaw's people. They seemed to have a table in the corner and they were laying out their things. They were waiting to take the baby down to their unit.

"Then the baby came out. The first thing someone said was, 'Oh! It's a boy.' I heard Dick say, 'My, he's big.' I kept listening for him to cry. But there wasn't a sound. 'Isn't he going to cry?' I asked. 'Isn't he going to cry?' I don't know how many times I asked that. But no one said anything.". . .

"The C-section was routine," Berkowitz said. "Ann received spinal anesthesia. We draped her and washed the abdomen with a sterile solution. She was awake, so I could talk to her. She was comfortable, but she felt nothing. There was a heart monitor on her—that's standard—and it was beeping in the background. With a spinal the woman is literally paralyzed from the waist down. She doesn't do any pushing or anything to help deliver the baby. . . .

"We opened the abdomen in layers and entered the peritoneal cavity. I put in a retractor, which pulled everything back and exposed the lower segment of the uterus. Then I picked up the peritoneum, which is a tough, smooth, and colorless membrane sac that holds the abdominal organs, and snipped it open. I dissected it away and pushed it down, which pushed the bladder out of the way. Then I made an incision in the uterus and lifted the baby out.

"I was holding the baby by its legs and head. The resident clamped the umbilical cord and I turned around with it and a pediatrician was standing there with a sterile sheet draped over his arms. I literally dropped the baby into the sheet. They use a sterile sheet so I remain sterile. I still had a lot of work to do.

"It was a big baby, which surprised me. You get used to seeing these little pipsqueaks when you deliver Rh babies. There was no evidence of hydrops—the fluid buildup. The belly wasn't swollen and the placenta didn't look water-laden. And there was no evidence of any immediate acute problems.

"Ann was terribly, terribly concerned that the baby was okay. She was crying and I could see the tension in her was enormous. She was saying something about she couldn't hear him crying. They were working on him in the corner and then he began to cry. Everybody let out a sigh. Sort of a little cheer. Then the pediatricians were getting ready to zip him out of the room and someone asked if they weren't going to show him to his mother. So they held him up to Ann's face for a few seconds and then they were gone."

17

MIDWIFERY AS FEMINIST PRAXIS

Barbara Katz Rothman

In this selection award-winning medical sociologist Barbara Katz Rothman explores a subject that is on the frontiers of health care reform. Midwifery is among the oldest professions on earth, but in the United States it has been overshadowed by hospital birth. The practice began coming back into vogue among educated women during the 1960s. As noted in the earlier selection by Ehrenreich and English, the feminist critique of male-dominated medicine (and especially obstetrics) changed the way women think about their bodies and about the medical care they receive. This led to a change in attitudes toward reproduction, childbirth, and the idea of progress in medicine. Views of childbirth began to shift away from the notion of pregnancy as an illness toward the recognition of pregnancy and childbirth as natural processes that require medical intervention only in highly unusual circumstances.

Katz Rothman's rejection of the traditional illness model of childbirth in favor of a female-centered approach to procreation is one example of the continuing movement to give women greater control over their reproductive lives. The female-centered approach, based on the guiding influence of the skilled midwife, is designed to put birthing back in the social context of home and community rather than the technological context of the hospital.

Recent developments in U.S. medicine have in a sense caught up with the feminist movement and its support of midwifery, natural childbirth, and home delivery. Pressures to reduce medical costs, to shorten or eliminate hospital stays, to encourage appropriate care by paraprofessionals, and to allow greater choice in medical care all imply a shift toward the practices Katz Rothman describes and advocates. The fact that highly sophisticated hospital care is available in emergencies also contributes to the sense of security felt by women who choose to direct their own childbirth with the aid of the modern midwife.

In most of the chapters of this book, as I address issue after issue, I find myself trying to imagine woman-centered alternatives. What if, I wonder, women really controlled contraception and abortion, not in isolated, embattled feminist-run abortion clinics, and not in the ever-uneasy alliance with population-control forces, but in an ongoing, empowered way. What would abortion and contraception look like, what would our models be? It is an even greater leap of imagination to think about a woman-centered approach to infertility: how would feminists recreate the infertility clinics? And what would feminist adoption be? Try to imagine a woman-centered, feminist-run adoption agency.

But when we turn to the care of pregnant and birthing women, no such flights of imagination are required. There is an ancient, and continuing, worldwide tradition of woman-centered care: midwifery. Long before the obstetricians arrived on the scene, there was a practice and a tradition of midwifery. And that tradition continues today: with full professional autonomy (that is, the right to control itself as an occupation) in some states and underground, even illegally, in other states. I am speaking here of woman-taught and woman-controlled midwifery, and not the medically, obstetrically trained nurse-specialist programs which have incorporated the word "midwife." Some women trained as nurse-midwives are, and some are not, part of the midwifery tradition, but it is that alternative tradition, that non-medical model of procreation, which I address.

Midwifery is, I believe, feminist praxis. Marx used the word *praxis* to mean conscious physical labor directed toward transforming the material world so it will satisfy human needs. Midwifery works with the labor of women to transform, to create, the birth experience to meet the needs of women. It is a social, political activity, dialectically linking biology and society, the physical and the social experience of motherhood. The very word *midwife* means *with the woman*. That is more than a physical location: it is an ideological and political stance. Midwifery represents a rejection of the artificial dualisms of patriarchal and technological ideologies. The midwifery model of pregnancy rejects technological mind-body dualism as it rejects the patriarchal alienation of the woman from her fetus. That of course is too negative, and too self-conscious a way of putting it. Rather than rejecting dualisms, midwifery continues to see unity.

The political agenda for feminism is quite clear: we must empower the midwives, enable them to practice midwifery as a fully autonomous profession, not subject to the control of physicians.

It is very difficult, in this society at this time, to even think of pregnancy, and especially childbirth, in non-medical terms, to imagine that midwives are doing anything other than being maybe "nicer," "kinder," or more "sensitive" than obstetricians. But it is not just warmth or empathy that midwives have to offer: there are some lovely obstetricians around too. And it's not just their gender that distinguishes midwives, especially as more and more women enter obstetrics. What midwives offer us is an alternative ideological base, and consequently the potential for developing an alternative body of knowledge about procreation.

The medical model sees a vulnerable fetus caught in a woman's body (the child of man held by woman) and a woman, although stronger than the fetus, also made vulnerable by its intrusion (weakened by what the man has "done to her," what he has growing in her). The job of the obstetrician is to help effect the separation of the two, so they can "recover," so that the woman can "return to normal," and the baby can be "managed" separately. The ideologies of technology and patriarchy focus the vision and the work of obstetrics.

In such a model, the development of hospitalization for childbirth made sense, and the increasing regionalization of maternity services (locating "high-risk" services in a central large teaching hospital) is perfectly rational, even imperative. One would not expect, after all, to do the best job of auto repair in the driveway, or even in the local gas station; the most well-equipped garage is the place for the best repairs. The workman is only as good as his tools. Birth is best done, as are auto repairs, where the access to tools is best.

But there are inherent problems in limiting our vision of childbirth to its technical, medical dimension. That vision of childbirth enables us to think only in terms of morbidity and mortality rates, and not the often wrenching social and personal implications involved in childbirth management programs and technology.

Compare this situation with a very different example of technological progress, that which has occurred in transportation with the introduction of automobiles. What if we approached the history of transportation with the same narrow focus with which we approach childbirth, defining it entirely in terms of life and limb, morbidity and mortality rates, as they vary with different modes of transportation? It is obvious that the shift over time from a horse-based to an engine-based transportation system has had effects on the morbidity and mortality rates associated with transportation. We might try to figure out the effects in terms of lives lost each year in transportation accidents, or in the more sophisticated comparison of lives lost per mile traveled in each system. It would be an interesting and valuable history of transportation to consider. But would anyone claim it is *the* history of transportation, that this is the most salient, most far-reaching effect of new modes of transportation in our lives?

The introduction of new technology in transportation has had a fundamental impact on American life. It has influenced family organization, our perceptions of time and space, our vision of the world in which we live. There is a context, a social context, in which we see the meaning of technology in transportation. A medical history of transportation is interesting and important, but it is only one (rather narrow) facet of the story. And so it is with childbirth.

The medical monopoly on childbirth, its control by physicians, has meant defining birth in medical terms, and thus narrowing our scope of perception. The other equally salient, humanly meaningful aspects of childbirth are lost to us, outside our narrow range of vision. This narrowed vision has given us detailed knowledge of some of the physiology of pregnancy, childbirth, and newborns, but without context. The woman whose pregnant uterus we think we understand is located three bus fares away from the facility we have designed for her care. The newborn whose blood is so finely analyzed is placed at a distance that must be measured in more than miles from the family on whom she will ultimately depend.

What midwifery offers us is not just tossing in a few social or psychological variables, but a reconceptualization of the "facts" of procreation. A profession controls not only people—as doctors control the nurses who "follow orders," the patients who "comply"—more important, a profession controls the development of knowledge. In regard to birth, the profession of medicine determines not only who may attend a birth, or what birth attendants may do, but it controls also what we know of birth itself.

In its control over practice, the profession of medicine maintains control over research—research in its broadest sense. Data are collected, both formally and informally, to support and develop the medical body of knowledge. But the data are themselves generated by the medical practices. The methods of observation in medicine have often been criticized as not being "scientific" enough, but the more fundamental flaw is in not recognizing the social processes involved in the generation of the data, of that which is there to be observed. So it develops that in our society the obstetrical perspective on pregnancy and birth is not considered just one way of looking at it, but rather the truth, the facts, science; others may have beliefs about pregnancy, but we believe medicine has the facts. However, obstetrical knowledge, like all knowledge, comes from somewhere: it has a social, historical, and political context. Medicine does not exist as something "pure," free of culture or free of idealogy. The context in which medical knowledge develops and is used shapes that knowledge. In particular, the setting of practice is an important part of the generation of the data on which the knowledge is based.

To begin to make this point clear, I am going to draw examples from two very different worlds, different "settings of practice." I am going to contrast medical obstetrical knowledge with the knowledge of a lay midwife practicing outside of medical settings. The same physiological event, the birth of a baby, can occur in many places—women labor and babies are born in a variety of settings. But the social definitions, our ideas about what is happening, are vastly different in different settings, and these differences create new social realities. In turn, these new realities, or definitions of the situation, create new physiological reality, as the birth process itself is shaped by the settings in which it occurs. Let us begin with a simple, everyday event.

Situation 1

A woman comes to the maternity floor of a large hospital. She is upset, almost crying, holding her huge belly and leaning against her husband, who seems nearly as upset as she is. "My wife's in labor," he states, and hands over a scrap of paper with times marked off—the seven- to twelve-minute intervals they have timed between contractions. The woman is ushered into a cubicle and examined. The examination might be repeated an hour later. "No," the doctors tells her, "you're not in labor yet. You have not yet begun to dilate. This is just a false alarm, a false labor. You can go home and come back when you really are in labor."

Here we have a physiological event—the painful contractions of the uterus—defined in two different ways, as labor and as not-labor. The woman and her husband are basing their definition on her feelings, the sensations she is experiencing as she has been taught to measure them—in minutes, for example. The doctor is basing his or her definition on what he or she feels as an examiner, the degree of dilation—how much the cervix has dilated. Each definition of the situation carries with it a way of acting, a set of behavioral expectations, for the people involved. As not-labor, the doctor is finished with the woman and can turn his or her attention elsewhere. The woman is to go home and stay simply pregnant a while longer. Defined as labor, however, the situation is very different. The woman changes from her status of pregnant woman to the new status of laboring woman. She will put on the appropriate costume (change from "maternity clothes" to a "hospital gown") and become a patient. The doctor will be expected to provide examination and treatment, to begin managing her condition. Only in labor will she become the doctor's responsibility.

Situation 2

Cara (an empirical midwife): I got a call that Roberta was having heavy rushes but wasn't dilating and was having a hard time. I wanted to go see her and help. When I got there, Roberta was writhing with each rush and shaking. She just didn't have any idea how to handle the energy. Joel was sitting beside her looking worried. The whole scene was a bit grim for a baby-having. I got them kissing, hugging, and had Roberta really grab on to Joel and squeeze him. Joel is a big, strong, heavy-duty man. He and I rubbed Roberta continuously and steered in the direction of relaxed. I let her know that she was having good, strong rushes, and that if she'd relax and experience it and let it happen, her rushes would accomplish a lot and open her up. She gradually accepted the fact that there was no getting out of this except to let it happen and quit fighting it.[1]

Here we have the same physiological event, a woman experiencing the same sensations and the same lack of dilation, defined along yet other lines. First note the difference in the language being used. The empirical midwife describing this situation is not talking about "contractions," the medical word for what the uterine muscle is doing, but "rushes." This midwife lives and works on the Farm, the Tennessee commune that published *Spiritual Midwifery*. The midwives explain their language:

On the farm we've come to call these contractions of the uterine muscle "rushes" because the main sensation that happens when these muscles contract is exactly the same as the sensations of rushing while coming on to a heavy psychedelic, which feels like a whole lot of energy flowing up your back and into your head. It leaves you feeling expansive and stoned if you don't fight it.[2]

This language relies on internal or subjective cues, sensations the woman herself experiences. The medical language, in contrast, relies on external or "objective" cues, information available to the examiner—how much the woman has dilated. Thus when the subjective and objective cues are at variance, in the medical situation the subjective cues are discounted. The woman's sensations of labor are "false" and the doctor's examination is "true." In the midwifery situation, the woman's experienced reality of the rushes is acknowledged. The "problem," the variance between subjective and objective measures, is here defined as the woman's inability to cope effectively, to "let it happen." This definition, of course, also carries with it consequences for the people involved: the midwife and the husband are expected to help her cope, relax, let it happen. For the woman, one of the negative consequences of this definition of the situation is that it tells her that it is in some way her own fault that she is having a hard time. In that way the midwives are doing the same thing as the doctors: imposing their definition of the situation on the laboring woman. The doctor's responsibility is very narrowly defined: to manage only "real" labor. The midwife's responsibility, in contrast, is defined more broadly, to include "helping" or "managing"—controlling the emotional as well as the physical situation.

Thus each of these alternative definitions carries with it quite different consequences, consequences that will shape the experience of all those involved, but most dramatically of the pregnant woman. It is one thing to be a pregnant woman, and quite another to be "in labor." And it is one thing to be told that the labor that you are experiencing is "false" and yet another to be told that the rushes are real and you have to learn how to relax and stop fighting them. The meaning given the particular uterine contractions of any particular woman becomes the basis for the way the event, and thus the woman, is treated.

These scenarios, and their implications, explain why it matters, even to those of us who are not midwives, that midwives come to have professional autonomy. With professional autonomy comes the power to control the setting of birth, and ultimately to control the birthing woman. As someone who is not a midwife, I prefer midwifery control to obstetrical control because obstetrical control, the "objective" medical reality if you will, diminishes the birthing woman. It makes her an object upon whom the art and science of obstetrics are practiced. The underlying ideology is that of technology, the body as machine. This depersonalizes the birthing woman, making her a suitable candidate for being hooked up to yet other machines.

The organization of the hospital maternity floor influences this mechanistic vision of the woman. Labor rooms look more like regular nursing-care rooms; delivery rooms more like operating rooms. As the woman is transferred from one to another, there is basis for more and more narrowly defining the relevant parts of her, as she first loses full personhood to become a patient, and then in the delivery room, where all the doctor sees of the woman is the exposed perineum centered in draped linen, becomes simply a pelvis from which a fetus is removed. The alternative birth settings—homes, "birthing rooms," and the like—provide a contrasting image, in which the mother is not lying flat, and is surrounded by friends and family, tied to a full social world. Such a setting may very well encourage the awareness of the social and emotional factor in the birth. Thus "contractions" may be the salient feature when palpating the abdomen of a semiconscious woman, but "rush" may seem more appropriate when talking to a woman who is experiencing one.

Is the woman I described "really" in labor when she experiences contractions with "no progress"? Who defines? Who sets the policy about whether such a woman could or should be admitted to a particular hospital? If midwife and physician disagree, upon whose judgment will the insurance company's decision to pay for the day of hospitalization rely? And so how will we learn which definition of the situation results in the better outcome for mother and baby? Unless and until midwifery achieves professional status, it controls neither the birthing woman nor the development of an alternative body of knowledge.

In sum, for midwifery to develop an alternative body of knowledge, to reach new understandings about what is happening in birth, midwives must have control over the setting of birth. I have come to see that it is not that birth is "managed" the way it is because of what we know about birth. Rather, what we know about birth has been determined by the way it is managed. And the way childbirth has been managed has been based on the underlying assumptions, beliefs, and *ideologies* that inform medicine as a profession.

NOTES

1. INA MAY GASKIN AND THE FARM MIDWIVES, 1975, *Spiritual Midwifery* (Summertown, Tennessee: Book Publishing Company).
2. Ibid., p. 346.

18

EXCESS MORTALITY IN HARLEM

Colin McCord, M.D.,
and Harold P. Freeman, M.D.

We routinely characterize a patient as ill, and in so doing we specify the probable cause of illness, but can we also diagnose the illness of an entire community or city? The grim figures on excess death in Harlem presented in this seminal paper on community health and illness suggest that we can and must. Harlem is a world-famous community only a few subway stops from the center of Manhattan. It boasts some of New York City's most important cultural and scientific institutions, among them the Dance Theater of Harlem, City College, the Schomberg Library, Mt. Sinai Medical College and Hospital, and many others. Yet the community also suffers from devastating pathologies that shorten the lives of too many of its residents.

The excess mortality described here for Harlem made front-page news when the article was first published. The news stories emphasized the shocking comparison between death rates in Harlem and Bangladesh, the world's poorest nation. But many other inner-city communities in the United States would show the same pattern of excess death and also compare unfavorably with impoverished Bangladesh. The fault, therefore, lies not in Harlem but in the failure to adequately address the social and medical problems brought on by the persistence of poverty amid affluence. Drug addiction, alcoholism, violence, depression, lack of education, and poor health are, at the level of the community and the larger society, social consequences of long-term poverty and declining economic fortunes in inner-city communities. The reader should note well, therefore, the recommendations for emergency attention to the needs of Harlem and communities like it presented in this selection.

Abstract   *In recent decades mortality rates have declined for both white and non-white Americans, but national averages obscure the extremely high mortality rates in many inner-city communities. Using data from the 1980 census and from death certificates in 1979, 1980, and 1981, we examined mortality rates in New York City's Central Harlem health district, where 96 percent of the inhabitants are black and 41 percent live below the poverty line.*

For Harlem, the age-adjusted rate of mortality from all causes was the highest in New York City, more than double that of U.S. whites and 50 percent higher than that of U.S. blacks. Almost all the excess mortality was among those less than 65 years old. With rates for the white population as the basis for comparison, the standardized (adjusted for age) mortality ratios (SMRs) for deaths under the age of 65 in Harlem were 2.91 for male residents and 2.7 for female residents. The highest ratios were for women 25 to 34 years old (SMR, 6.13) and men 35 to 44 years old (SMR, 5.98). The chief causes of this excess mortality were cardiovascular disease (23.5 percent of the excess deaths; SMR, 2.23), cirrhosis (17.9 percent; SMR, 10.5), homicide (14.9 percent; SMR, 14.2), and neoplasms (12.6 percent; SMR, 1.77). Survival analysis showed that black men in Harlem were less likely to reach the age of 65 than men in Bangladesh. Of the 353 health areas in New York, 54 (with a total population of 650,000) had mortality rates for persons under 65 years old that were at least twice the expected rate. All but one of these areas of high mortality were predominantly black or Hispanic.

We conclude that Harlem and probably other inner-city areas with largely black populations have extremely high mortality rates that justify special consideration analogous to that given to natural-disaster areas.

Mortality rates for white and nonwhite Americans have fallen steadily and in parallel since 1930 (Fig. 1). Lower rates for nonwhites have been associated with an improved living standard, better education, and better access to health care.[1,2] These improvements, however, have not been evenly distributed. Most health indicators, including mortality rates, are worse in the impoverished areas of this country.[3–9] It is not widely recognized just how much certain inner-city areas lag behind the rest of the United States. We used census data and data from the Bureau of Health Statistics and Analysis of the New York City Health Department to estimate the amount, distribution, and causes of excess mortality in the New York City community of Harlem.

THE COMMUNITY

Harlem is a neighborhood in upper Manhattan just north of Central Park. Its population is 96 percent black and has been predominantly black since before World War I. It was the center of the Harlem Renaissance of black culture in the 1920s,

Colin McCord, M.D., and Harold P. Freeman, M.D., "Excess Mortality in Harlem," *New England Journal of Medicine* 322 (1990): 173–177.

and it continues to be a cultural center for black Americans. The median family income in Harlem, according to the 1980 census, was $6,497, as compared with $16,818 in all New York City, $21,023 in the United States, and $12,674 among all blacks in the United States. The families of 40.8 percent of the people of Harlem had incomes below the government-defined poverty line in 1980. The total population of Harlem fell from 233,000 in 1960 to 121,905 in 1980. In the same 20-year period the death rate from homicide rose from 25.3 to 90.8 per 100,000.

The neighborhood is not economically homogeneous. There is a middle-to-upper-class community of about 25,000 people living in new, private apartment complexes or houses, a less affluent group of 25,000 living in public housing projects, and a third group of about 75,000 who live in substandard housing. Most of the population loss has been in the group living in substandard housing, much of it abandoned or partially occupied buildings.

The pattern of medical care in Harlem is similar to that reported for other poor and black communities.[10,11] As compared with the per capita averages for New York City, the rate of hospital admissions is 26 percent higher, the use of emergency rooms is 73 percent higher, the use of hospital outpatient departments is 134 percent higher, and the number of primary care physicians per 1000 people is 74 percent lower.[12]

METHODS

Age-adjusted death rates for whites and nonwhites were taken from *Vital Statistics of the United States, 1980.*[13] Age-adjusted rates for nonwhites rather than blacks were used in Figure 1 because the deaths of blacks were not reported separately before 1970. Age-adjusted mortality rates for blacks in the United States have been slightly higher in recent years than those for all nonwhites (8.4 per 1000 for blacks and 7.7 per 1000 for all nonwhites in 1980). The age-adjusted mortality rates for Harlem in 1960, 1970, and 1980, as well as certain disease-specific death rates, were calculated from data supplied by the New York City Health Department. The U.S. population in 1940 was used as the reference for all the age-adjusted rates in Figure 1.

Tapes were provided by the New York City Health Department containing everything but personal identifying information from all death certificates in 1979, 1980, and 1981. Deaths were recorded by age, sex, underlying cause, health-center district, and health area. The Central Harlem Health Center District corresponds to the usual definition of the Harlem community. For our analysis, we calculated age-, sex-, and cause-specific death rates for Harlem using the recorded deaths for 1979, 1980, and 1981 and population data from the 1980 census. New York City determines the underlying cause of death by the methods proposed by the National Center for Health Statistics.[14] We used the diagnostic categories of the ninth revision of the *International Classification of Diseases.*[15] They were generally but not always grouped in the way that the New York City Bureau of Health Statistics and Analysis groups diagnoses in its annual reports of vital statistics according to health

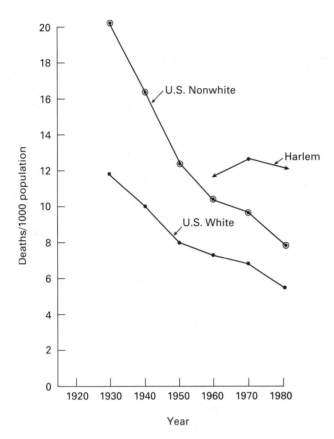

Figure 1. Age-Adjusted Death Rates in Harlem (1960–1980) and the United States (1930–1980).

areas and health-center districts. For example, "cardiovascular disease" refers to diagnostic categories 390 through 448 in the *International Classification of Diseases,* and "ill defined" refers to categories 780 through 789.

The reference death rates we used to calculate the standardized mortality ratios (SMRs) are those of the white population of the United States, as published in *Vital Statistics of the United States, 1980.*[13] To calculate the SMRs, the total number of observed deaths in 1979, 1980, and 1981 for each age group, sex, and cause was divided by the expected number of deaths, based on the population of each sex and age group and the reference death rate. Using the same methods, we calculated the SMR for deaths under the age of 65 for each health area in the city with a population of more than 3000. New York City has 353 health areas, with an average population of 21,000. Only 11 have a population of less than 3000.

The survival curves in Figure 2 were constructed with the use of life tables. The tables for Bangladesh were from a report of the Matlab study area of the International Center for Diarrheal Disease Research,[9] modified from 5-year to 10-year age intervals. Life tables for Harlem were calculated with the same formulas and for the same 10-year intervals. Life tables for the United States are from *Vital Statistics of the United States, 1980.*[13]

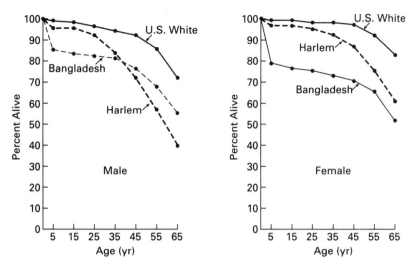

Figure 2. Survival to the age of 65 in Harlem, Bangladesh, and among U.S. Whites in 1980.

RESULTS

Since 1950, when the New York City Health Department began to keep death records according to health-center district, Central Harlem has consistently had the highest infant mortality rate and one of the highest crude death rates in the city. In 1970 and 1980, age-adjusted mortality rates for Harlem residents were the highest in New York City, much worse than the rates for nonwhites in the United States as a whole, and they had changed little since 1960 (Fig. 1). This lack of improvement in the age-adjusted death rate reflected worsening mortality rates for persons be-tween the ages of 15 and 65 that more than offset the drop in mortality among in-fants and young children (Fig. 3).

Figure 2 shows the survival curves for male and female residents of Harlem, as compared with those for whites in the United States and those for the residents of an area in rural Bangladesh. Bangladesh is categorized by the World Bank as one of the lowest-income countries in the world. The Matlab demographic-study area is thought to have somewhat lower death rates than Bangladesh as a whole, but the rates are typical for the region. Life expectancy at birth in Matlab was 56.5 years in 1980, as compared with an estimated 49 years for Bangladesh and 57 years for India in 1986.[9,16] For men, the rate of survival beyond the age of 40 is lower in Harlem than Bangladesh. For women, overall survival to the age of 65 is somewhat better in Harlem, but only because the death rate among girls under 5 is very high in Bangladesh.

The SMRs for Harlem (Table 1) were high for those of all ages below 75, but they were particularly high for those between 25 and 64 years old and for children under 4. In the three years 1979 to 1981, there were 6415 deaths in Harlem. If the

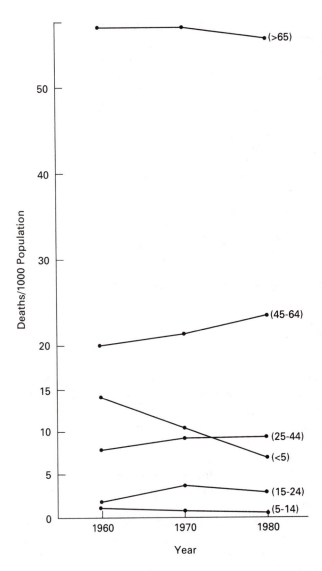

Figure 3. Age-Specific Death Rates in Harlem from 1960 to 1980. Age groups are shown in parentheses.

death rate among U.S. whites had applied to this community, there would have been 3994 deaths. Eighty-seven percent of the 2421 excess deaths were of persons under 65.

Table 2 compares the numbers of observed and expected deaths among persons under 65, according to the chief underlying causes. A large proportion of the observed excess was directly due to violence and substance abuse, but these causes did not account for most of the excess. Cirrhosis, homicide, accidents, drug dependency, and alcohol use were considered the most important underlying causes of death in 35 percent of all deaths among people under 65, and in 45 percent of the excess deaths.

Table 1. Standardized Mortality Ratios for Harlem, 1979 to 1981.*

AGE (YR)	OBSERVED DEATHS (NO.)	STANDARDIZED MORTALITY RATIO	ANNUAL EXCESS DEATHS[†]
Male			
0–4	81	2.45	462
5–14	10	1.10	4
15–24	105	2.28	214
25–34	248	5.77	911
35–44	347	5.98	1401
45–54	521	3.28	1824
55–64	783	2.10	2026
65–74	727	1.23	945
≥75	747	1.001	14
Total	3569	1.72	878
Total <65	2095	2.91	948
Female			
0–4	57	2.19	291
5–14	9	1.80	17
15–24	32	1.88	48
25–34	98	6.13	330
35–44	148	4.63	510
45–54	303	3.40	927
55–64	508	2.09	973
65–74	699	1.47	968
≥75	992	0.96	−315
Total	2846	1.47	449
Total <65	1155	2.70	445

*Reference death rates are those for U.S. whites in 1980.

[†]Per 100,000 population in each age group.

For people between the ages of 65 and 74 the SMRs in Harlem were much lower than those for people younger than 65. For residents of Harlem 75 years old or older, overall death rates were essentially the same as those for U.S. whites (Table 1). Disease-specific SMRs for people over the age of 65 were below those of younger age groups in almost every category. In several categories (notably cardio-vascular disease in Harlem residents 75 or older), they were lower than in whites. This may represent the survival of the fittest in this area of excess mortality.

To estimate the number of people in New York City whose mortality rates were similar to those of people in Harlem, SMRs for persons under the age of 65 were cal-culated for each of New York's 342 health areas with populations over 3000. There were 54 areas with SMRs of 2.0 or higher for persons under the age of 65. This means that these 54 health areas had at least twice the expected number of deaths (Fig. 4). The total population of these high-risk areas was 650,000. In 53 of them more than half the population was black or Hispanic. There was much more varia-

Table 2.   Causes of Excess Mortality in Harlem, 1979 to 1981.*

CAUSE	OBSERVED DEATHS (NO.)	STANDARDIZED MORTALITY RATIO	ANNUAL EXCESS DEATHS PER 100,000	% OF EXCESS DEATHS
Cardiovascular disease	880	2.23	157.5	23.5
Cirrhosis	410	10.49	120.4	17.9
Homicide	332	14.24	100.2	14.9
Neoplasm	604	1.77	84.9	12.6
Drug dependency	153	283.10	49.5	7.4
Diabetes	94	5.43	24.9	3.7
Alcohol use	73	11.33	21.6	3.2
Pneumonia and influenza	78	5.07	20.3	3.0
Disorders in newborns	64	7.24	17.9	2.7
Infection	65	5.60	17.3	2.6
Accident	155	1.17	7.2	1.1
Ill defined	44	2.07	7.4	1.1
Renal	26	4.54	6.6	0.9
Chronic obstructive pulmonary disease	35	1.29	2.6	0.4
Congenital anomalies	23	1.21	1.3	0.2
Suicide	33	0.81	−2.5	—
All other	181	3.13	40.0	6.0
All causes	3250	2.75	671.2	100.0

*The calculations are based on the deaths of all persons—male and female—under the age of 65. The reference death rates are those for U.S. whites in 1980.

tion in the SMRs of the health areas predominantly inhabited by members of minority groups than in the areas that were less than half nonwhite (Fig. 4). White areas were relatively narrowly clustered around a mean SMR of 0.97. The SMRs for predominantly black or Hispanic health areas ranged from 0.59 to 3.95, with a mean of 1.77. The SMRs for the 10 health areas in Harlem ranged from 2.16 to 3.95.

It is believed that recent U.S. censuses have undercounted blacks and other minority groups, particularly young men. This would lead to an increase in the age-specific mortality rates used to calculate life tables and SMRs. The Bureau of the Census has estimated the scale of undercounting in various ways—the highest figure is 19 percent for black men in the 25-to-34-year-old group.[17] Because the absolute amount of the observed excess mortality in Harlem is so great, recalculation has little effect on the data presented here, but for the calculations required for Figure 3 and Tables 1 and 2 we increased the 1980 census population in each sex and age group by an amount conforming to the largest Census Bureau estimate of the undercounting. This produced a slight increase in the percentage shown to be still living at the age of 65 in Figure 2 and a slight reduction in the SMRs in Tables 1 and 2. (With this correction the SMR for male residents under the age of 65 was 2.91 rather than 3.15.)

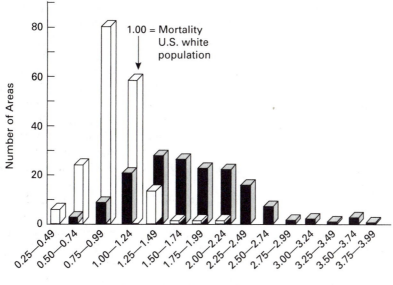

Figure 4. Standardized Mortality Ratios for Persons under 65 in 342 Health Areas in New York City, 1979 to 1981. The shaded bars denote communities more than half of whose residents are nonwhite and the open bars communities that are half or more white. Bars to the right of the arrow represent communities in which the mortality of persons under the age of 65 was higher than that of U.S. whites.

DISCUSSION

An improvement in child mortality in Harlem between 1960 and 1980 was accompanied by rising mortality rates for persons between the ages of 25 and 65. There was therefore no improvement in overall age-adjusted mortality. Death rates for those between the ages of 5 and 65 were worse in Harlem than in Bangladesh.

We have not attempted to calculate SMRs since 1981, because the 1980 census is the most recent reliable estimate of the population of New York City, but all available evidence indicates that there has been very little change since then. The total number of deaths in Harlem from 1985 through 1987 was 1.6 percent higher than from 1979 through 1981. According to the New York City Planning Department, the decline in Harlem's population stopped in 1980 and the total population has been growing at the rate of 1 percent per year since then.[18] If this estimate is accepted, there has been a slight drop in the crude death rate for Harlem since 1980, but not large enough to affect any of our conclusions. Since 1980 the number of deaths of persons 25 to 44 years of age has increased considerably (31 percent), and the acquired immunodeficiency syndrome (AIDS) has become the most common cause of death in this age group in Harlem and in all New York City. The number of deaths from AIDS is expected to continue to rise.

The situation in Harlem is extreme, but it is not an isolated phenomenon. We identified 54 health areas (of 353) in New York City, with a total population of 650,000, in which there were more than twice as many deaths among people under the age of 65 as would be expected if the death rates of U.S. whites applied. All but one of these health areas have populations more than half composed of minority members. These are areas that were left behind when the minority population of the city as a whole experienced the same improvement in life expectancy that was seen in the rest of the United States.[19] Similar pockets of high mortality have been described in other U.S. cities.[3,20] Jenkins et al. calculated SMRs for all deaths in Roxbury and adjacent areas of Boston that were almost as high in 1972–1973 as those reported here.[20] This area of highest mortality in Boston was the area with the highest proportion of minority groups.

It will be useful to know more about the circumstances surrounding premature deaths in high-risk communities to determine the relative importance of contributing factors such as poverty, inadequate housing, psychological stress, substance abuse, malnutrition, and inadequate access to medical care. But action to correct the appalling health conditions reflected in these statistics need not wait for more research. The essential first steps are to identify these pockets of high mortality and to recognize the urgent severity of the problem. Widespread poverty and inadequate housing are obvious in Harlem and demand a direct attack wherever they are present. The most important health investigations will be those designed to evaluate the effectiveness of measures to prevent and treat the causes of death already identified. The SMR for persons under 65 years of age may be a useful tool both to identify the high-mortality areas and to monitor the effect of measures to reduce mortality. This ratio is simpler to calculate than the years of productive life lost,[6] and the information obtained is similar.

Those responsible for implementing health programs must face the reality of high death rates in Harlem and the enormous burden of disease that requires treatment in the existing facilities. The health care system is overloaded with such treatment and is poorly structured to support preventive measures, detect disease early, and care for adults with chronic problems. At the same time, the population at highest risk has limited contact with the health care system except in emergencies. Brudny and Dobkyn reported that 83 percent of 181 patients discharged from Harlem Hospital with tuberculosis in 1988 were lost to follow-up and did not continue treatment.[21] New approaches must be developed to take preventive and therapeutic measures out of the hospitals, clinics, and emergency rooms and deliver them to the population at highest risk.

Intensive educational campaigns to improve nutrition and reduce the use of alcohol, drugs, and tobacco are needed and should be directed at children and adolescents, since habits are formed early and the death rates begin to rise immediately after adolescence. Education will have little effect unless it is combined with access to adequate incomes, useful employment, and decent housing for these children and their parents. Education can help in controlling epidemic drug use and associated crime only if it is combined with effective and coordinated police and public action. AIDS in Harlem is largely related to intravenous drug use and is not likely to be controlled until drugs are controlled, but effective education about this disease is also urgently needed.

Knowledge of the history of previous efforts to improve health in Harlem does not lead to optimism about the future. The Harlem Health Task Force was formed in 1976 because Harlem and the Carter administration recognized that death rates were high. An improved system of clinics, more drug-treatment centers, and active community-outreach programs were recommended. The recommendations have been implemented to varying degrees, but funding has been limited. The preventive and curative health care system is essentially unchanged today. Drug use has increased, and the proportion of the population receiving public assistance has increased. There has been no decrease in the death rates.

In 1977 Jenkins et al. pointed out that the number of excess deaths recorded each year in the areas of worst health in Boston was considerably larger than the number of deaths in places that the U.S. government had designated as natural-disaster areas. They suggested that these zones of excess mortality be declared disaster areas and that measures be implemented on this basis.[20] No such action was taken then or is planned now. If the high-mortality zones of New York City were designated a disaster area today, 650,000 people would be living in it. A major political and financial commitment will be needed to eradicate the root causes of this high mortality: vicious poverty and inadequate access to the basic health care that is the right of all Americans.

REFERENCES

1. MANTON KG, PATRICK CH, JOHNSON KW.   Health differentials between blacks and whites: recent trends in mortality and morbidity. Milbank Q 1987; 65:Suppl 1:125–99.
2. DAVIS K, LILLIE-BLANTON M, LYONS B, MULLAN F, POWE N, ROWLAND D.   Health care for black Americans: the public sector role. Milbank Q 1987; 65: Suppl 1:213–47.
3. KITAGAWA EM, HAUSER PM.   Differential mortality in the United States: a study in socioeconomic epidemiology. Cambridge, Mass.: Harvard University Press, 1973.
4. WOOLHANDLER S, HIMMELSTEIN DU, SILBER R, BADER M, HARNLY M, JONES A.   Medical care and mortality: racial differences in preventable deaths. Int J Health Serv 1985; 15:1–22.
5. SAVAGE D, LINDENBAUM J, VAN RYZIN J, STRUENING E, GARRETT TJ.   Race, poverty, and survival in multiple myeloma. Cancer 1984; 54:3085–94.
6. Black/white comparisons of premature mortality for public health program planning—District of Columbia. MMWR 1989; 38:33–7.
7. FREEMAN HP, WASFIE TJ.   Cancer of the breast in poor black women. Cancer 1989; 63:2562–9.
8. Cancer in the economically disadvantaged: a special report prepared by the subcommittee on cancer in the economically disadvantaged. New York: American Cancer Society, 1986.
9. Demographic surveillance system—Matlab. Vital events and migration tables, 1980. Scientific report no. 58. Dhaka, Bangladesh: International Centre for Diarrheal Disease Research, 1982.
10. DAVIS K, SCHOEN C.   Health and the war on poverty: a ten-year appraisal. Washington, D.C.: Brookings Institution, 1978.
11. BLENDON RJ, AIKEN LH, FREEMAN HE, COREY CR.   Access to medical care for black and white Americans: a matter of continuing concern. JAMA 1989; 261:278–81.
12. Community health atlas of New York. New York: United Hospital Fund, 1986.
13. Vital statistics of the United States 1980. Hyattsville, Md.: National Center for Health Statistics, 1985. (DHHS publication no. (PHS) 85–1101.)
14. Vital statistics: instructions for classifying the underlying cause of death, 1980. Hyattsville, Md.: National Center for Health Statistics, 1980.
15. The international classification of diseases. 9th revision, clinical modification: ICD-9-CM. 2nd ed.

Washington, D.C.: Department of Health and Human Services, 1980. (DHHS publication no. (PHS) 80–1260.)

16. The state of the world's children 1988 (UNICEF). New York: Oxford University Press, 1988.

17. FAY RE, PASSEL JS, ROBINSON JG.   Coverage of population in the 1980 census. Washington, D.C.: Bureau of the Census, 1988. (Publication no. PHC 80–E4.)

18. Community district needs, 1989. New York: Department of City Planning, 1987. (DCP publication no. 87–10.)

19. Summary of vital statistics, 1986. New York: Bureau of Health Statistics and Analysis, 1986.

20. JENKINS CD, TUTHILL RW, TANNENBAUM SI, KIRBY CR.   Zones of excess mortality in Massachusetts. N Engl J Med 1977; 296:1354–6.

21. BRUDNY K, DOBKYN J.   Poor compliance is the major obstacle in controlling the HIV-associated tuberculosis outbreak. Presented at the Fifth International Conference on Acquired Immune Deficiency Syndrome, Montreal, June 8, 1989.

19

AIDS PATIENTS

Victor Ayala

Sociologist Victor Ayala has worked among hospitalized AIDS patients for more than five years. This essay is based on his first three years of work as a counselor to AIDS patients in a large inner-city hospital, where he still works in the evenings. During the day Ayala is the director of a compensatory education program at New York Technical Institute. But AIDS, he would no doubt agree, has been the formative issue of his life. After working with the Gay Men's Health Crisis during the first few years of the epidemic, Ayala decided to apply his insights and skills to a dissertation about indigent patients on the AIDS ward of Oremus Hospital (a fictitious name for a very real institution) in a low-income section of Brooklyn.

Much has been written about the scourge of AIDS, but little attention has been paid to the plight of the growing number of indigent patients who suffer and die on the AIDS wards of public hospitals. The intent of Ayala's unusual research and activism is to show the world that even the most despised street addict is a human being in need of care. Through his efforts to understand the links between the lives of indigent, often addicted, patients outside and inside the hospital, Ayala finds ways of easing the burden of illness for both the staff and the patients on the AIDS ward.

The first day on the job I was shown the medical ward where I would spend the next twenty-two months of my life. I met five patients in various stages of HIV diagnosis and AIDS-related illness. I wondered into what kind of situation I had gotten myself. At first, the level of suffering was overwhelming. During these early days, I would have to leave the sickrooms in the middle of a counseling session in order to regain composure. There were to be many sleepless nights as my rest was invaded by the memories of the sick moaning, complaining and physically struggling with illness and death.

I didn't want to be there. I felt astonished, saddened, heartbroken at the magnitude of illness there. I hated the smell, the sight of people so distorted. They moved so slowly, and the look of death was in their eyes. Some of them would not talk to me. . . .

The initial shock dissipated and I focused more on the duties and responsibilities of the caseworker. After gathering the necessary demographic and family history information for the case record, I assessed social service needs and helped to identify the hospital discharge plan for each patient. To do this required interaction and discourse, an assessment of the patient's understanding of the diagnosis or medical condition. This was not usually an easy process. It often took much time to engage patients. My questions about personal life-style matters were often perceived as invasions of privacy and viewed with great suspicion. It became clear that I needed to find ways of establishing trust and confidence with people whose lives were often characterized by desertion, betrayal and dishonesty.

It was not uncommon, during the initial meetings, for patients to refuse to speak with me ("What the fuck do you want?" "Who are you?" "I don't want to be answering so many questions!"). Some people ignored me, simply pulling the sheets over their heads, hoping that I would just leave the room. If they spoke, it was to ask that I turn off the lights and close the door on my way out. When I reached the point where I no longer took this rejection personally, I would take a seat in the patient's room, remain silent and wait until they spoke. This might take several tries to be effective, however. Other times, I attempted to buy the patient's confidence by doing little favors for them—purchasing cigarettes, candy, or clothing or making telephone calls, sometimes taking their requests to the doctors or nurses. This would circulate among the patients and in time I cultivated a favorable reputation ("That Ayala is OK, you can talk to him, he listens . . . respects our type of people . . .").

As a caseworker I was exposed to the factors with which these, the disenfranchised of the city community, dealt on a regular basis: homelessness, drug addiction, loneliness, chaotic life-styles, and now the unfamiliar routine of hospitalization and the uncontrollable developments in their bodies. Much of the counseling time was spent encouraging the patients to speak about their lives and understanding of AIDS. It was important for me to be genuine, empathic and honest about caring for them and wanting to make their hospital experience easier. Since most were

Reprinted from *Falling Through the Cracks: AIDS and the Urban "Underclass"* (Ph.D. diss., City University of New York Graduate School, 1991), by permission of the author.

homeless, intravenous drug users, sex workers, assorted criminals or homosexuals and sometimes various combinations of these, they were unaccustomed to sharing their experiences with anyone who listened in a nonjudgmental fashion. Even if they believed that I was there to help, there was often curiosity as to my real motivations. I always revealed myself as a caseworker and sometimes as a graduate student of sociology, especially to those whose experience seemed pertinent to my research.

There is a thin line between empathy and overidentification, and being "tested" by patients readily clarified the issue. I was always at risk of being used or manipulated by patients into actions which would sometimes prove harmful to them in the long run. This was particularly true of the substance abusers who routinely tried to badger, beg or cajole me into obtaining greater and greater doses of methadone for them from the physicians. In the beginning of my hospital experience, I would rush to the nurses' station in order to accommodate the patient. Fortunately, the more experienced members of the staff and certain situations with individual patients made me realize that such patient behavior was manipulative and really a reflection of poor impulse control or pain intolerance. My lack of experience in this area created friction with the medical staff. Some of the doctors and nurses perceived my intervention on behalf of the patient as interference or an attempt to impose my judgment on theirs.

Regardless of the patient's stage of the dying process, it was difficult to cope with the emotions surrounding their fears of the illness and their mortality. The counseling sessions were often intense and physically draining and, as I was both caseworker and researcher, required a serious commitment. Being available, both physically and emotionally, to the patients and their families was challenging and a spiritual awakening. It became clear that my reflection on the issues of death and dying was necessary, indeed unavoidable, in order to facilitate the patient's dying process experiences. Crossing the line from caseworker to fellow human being and back was less mechanical each time, as it should be, although never easy. . . .

Confronted by a number of patients exceeding the ability and resources of the facility or neighborhood social services kept me in a state of continual frustration. There was a strong feeling of uselessness in the face of their deteriorating health and death. The magnitude of psycho-social, medical, financial, and political deficits brought to the landscape of my interaction a sense of powerlessness. Simply knowing that my "shift" would soon be finished was a help. At other times absenteeism was the only was I could cope with the situation or my anger and depression with it. As my tenure in this job lengthened I had to make a concerted, conscious effort to distance myself emotionally from the patient's pain in order to minimize my own. Objectivity was the only way to deliver the best possible service with the least personal cost. I wrote the following after a discussion with a fellow social worker:

> On this ward I deal with 28 patients. It's difficult. I have to document everything that I'm doing with them. Hey, we're short staffed, could you imagine trying to be on top of the histories, personal circumstances of every one of these patients? I mean, this one is homeless, that one is a drug addict, the other one has AIDS and won't face it. You have the doctors always pushing you to find housing for patients . . . they want them

OUT. So, they see you in the halls and yell, "Hey, did you find housing for so and so?" We're just so short staffed; sometimes I just can't handle this. I don't know how I do this.

Boy, so many people are dying up here . . . it's like a dying club. Sometimes I can't believe it. I just need to get out of here. I'm transferring to the ER. At least in there, the patients keep moving, they come in and move out.

Eventually it got to the point where I had to find and make a mental note of individual, specific ways in which I helped specific patients in order to feel good about this job. I focused on simply being present, listening, providing emotional support, touching them physically as concrete ways of easing their pain and transition to death. Acknowledging their lives, encouraging them to cease dwelling on the past, encouraging them to live each day as best they could was difficult but essential to their well-being and mine. I made a point of observing the demonstrations of commitment, even heroism on the part of co-workers. It was important to celebrate the fact that the "glass was half full" rather than "half empty."

Time proved to be a finite resource. I was never sure that there would be enough of it to uncover the needed research information or to adequately serve the patient's needs. It was not uncommon for the patient to become incapacitated or to die with my work unfinished. . . .

The increasing physical weariness and occasional depression forced me to dissociate myself emotionally from the job and the research from time to time. I concentrated on being more professional in the execution of my duties.

In time, I became savvy to the maneuvering of "hustlers" disguising their requests as real expressions of need. Growing to understand the background and nature of the study group enabled me to distinguish a patient participating in a bona fide methadone drug treatment program from one simply wanting the drug.

Doctors' and nurses' attitudes were, at times, condescending and felt in two directions. One was toward the patient, adopting a "blaming the victim" attitude and distancing themselves, believing that the illness was their fault ("If they didn't do what they're doing, they wouldn't have AIDS. . . . If they'd follow my directions, they'd be outta' here!"). Another direction in which poor attitudes were aimed was toward the caseworker. Such attitudes were expressed when, often to initiate an examination, the doctor would interrupt a counseling session, discounting my presence and invalidating my work, as if perhaps I were not there at all. One intern interrupted a session, telling me not to allow the patient to cry and "get out of control." He insisted I focus on helping the patient understand the medical procedure and the diagnosis. Ironically, I was doing just that, but with his clinical blinders on, he was not able to see that emotional expressions could be the vehicles to physical awareness. Another incident occurred at a time when a patient was near death. As I held her hand and connected with her to reassure her and comfort her passing through this most fearful of moments, a doctor abruptly came in to draw blood and, even in his awareness of the moment, could not separate himself from the clinical procedures even for one moment to experience the humanness of bonding with the patient.

Despite the staff's posture, I was usually able to convince them of the need for more attention for those who were truly in need. I learned how to approach the staff with extraordinary requests. I learned as well to respect the staff's work habits and accepted the fact that it is the doctor and/or nurse who decides when patients are seen and how they are medically treated.

Conversely, the physicians and nurses relied on me to identify the patient's social service needs and services. It was my function to clarify the medical issues for the patient and family, if any. I was responsible for the development and implementation of discharge plans so as to avoid unnecessarily long hospital stays. In the best of circumstances, this proved advantageous for the patient and the facility. But in too many instances the inadequate availability of appropriate housing, supportive counseling and community-based referrals, or other services would leave patients to fend for themselves once discharged from the hospital.

Discharge proved especially difficult for the undomiciled patient. Confirmed AIDS-diagnosed patients were not accepted by local shelters. Such resistance was a source of great friction between the hospital administrators and doctors and the caseworkers and neighborhood social service organizations. Battles over turf or areas of professional responsibility could easily leave the patient without adequate care. . . .

The staff was placed in the awkward position of withholding information as to HIV+ or AIDS position status from family or friends if the patient so wished. Many of the patients willingly informed friends or family of their diagnosis. But in most cases this happened only after several counseling sessions. In some instances the caseworker was requested to be present at the time of revelation. There were too many cases where wives, lovers or pregnant girlfriends could not be told the truth about a patient's status because of the latter's refusal to reveal it. Fear of rejection, embarrassment or simply irresponsibility kept the patient from sharing this information with those who had a right to know. In potentially life-threatening situations, moral suasion was applied in order to prompt the revelation. In too many instances, the news was revealed after the patient's demise. Then, the medical, nursing and social service staff was left to cope with the family's or friend's outrage.

A patient I was working with introduced me to his wife, who had recently had one child and was two months pregnant. He did not want her to know that he was HIV+ and had AIDS. During my conversation with her, she said that he had told her he had pneumonia. Despite much dialogue he resisted telling her the truth. The doctors and I confirmed that if he did not tell her, we would. Later, the wife was informed and initiated HIV antibody testing. Although pleased with this development, I was struck by how much control over the situation the husband had. . . .

Because of the limited knowledge and experience demonstrated by most patients, the medical staff readily assumed complete control of the treatment process. They saw little reason or benefit in trying to educate the patient at this "late" stage. It is unclear that this had a detrimental effect on the quality of care or the sensitivity with which services were delivered. But it was sometimes observed that patients, no matter how poorly informed, received better, more extensive care when concerned family or friends were regularly present at the hospital. Such family members were able to intervene as patient advocates, questioning medical services and negotiating better results.

The "clash" of cultures also impacted the staff/patient relationships and medical care delivered. As noted, most of the patients were of Hispanic, African or Caribbean origin. Sometimes English was not their primary language. This was not the case for the facility's care givers, who were of East Indian, Middle Eastern, African or Hispanic origin with varying degrees of English language proficiency. Cultural biases, conflicting perceptions, misunderstandings, even the need to simply wait for translators all served to postpone, delay and hamper the quality of care given to these people. So, in their effort to simply deliver medical care, there is little interest in moving beyond the culture and language barriers. The health care provider moves on, . . . and the patients withdraw a little more, knowing they are not understood.

Fear of contagion was a subtle and sometimes obvious impediment to treatment. Doctors, nurses, administrators and others as well as the researcher worked with trepidation in this regard. The principal concern was about being accidentally pricked by needles used to make injections in HIV status unknown or HIV+ patients. When such accidents occurred, the hospital workers had to deal with the apprehension and anger about infection and the routine of being tested every six months until they felt safe again. The following comments, obtained during conversation with a surgery resident, are representative:

> I'm afraid, scared during surgery. . . . Do you know how many needle "sticks" I've had? I've even had an eye wash of HIV juice! I was doing surgery and it flew into my eye. . . . Everybody should be tested. It's not right for me to face this risk. HIV test should be pre-operation. Hey, I'd like to see my 22-month-old son grow up.

From discussion with a surgery intern:

> Hey, we have a right to refuse treatment of a patient, especially if it's not for an acute medical distress—something life threatening. If the person refuses HIV testing, why should I have to treat them? Why do I have to be put at risk? AIDS should at least be treated like other communicable diseases. . . . There must be mandatory testing! . . .

I was able to contain my fear of exposure by keeping in mind the information circulated by the CDC about HIV transmission modes. My concerns were more about susceptibility to live, "airborne" bacteria expelled by patients with rare, more or less contagious diseases such as salmonella, tuberculosis, meningitis, chicken pox and herpes simplex. Complicating the issue further was the observation that neither the patients nor hospital staff always abided by established, published precautionary guidelines. I began to fear contagion from less than vigilant co-workers. I took precautions, but the longer the research project lasted, the more concerned I grew that the statistical odds of infection were increasing.

Interestingly, the need to continue overshadowed the fear of contagion. These people needed someone, some connection between their desolate existence and those who can provide some comfort in these times of stress and pain. Even the health care workers, entrenched in medical procedures and detailed relationships, continued to serve. Perhaps one can assume it was to support their own existence, to maintain their livelihood. But when pregnant nurses came in day after day and donned protective clothing, caring for patient after patient, one cannot dismiss that perhaps even they felt the pangs of humanity and did their jobs because they felt the need and the rewards of merging medical treatment with human understanding. . . .

At the demise of a patient the staff assumes a purely utilitarian function. When the physician pronounces death, a team of nurses' aides (two or more) prepare themselves outside the room, donning masks, gowns and latex gloves. I have been granted permission to observe the process, so I don similar protective garb.

The room is just as I had left it. The machinery is still there and the room is in disarray. There is dried blood on the floor. David's motionless body rests on its back, the bloodstained gauze pads scattered about the bed where they had fallen when he last struggled to breathe.

First, the life support machine(s), if any, are disconnected. They are very careful. It is important to avoid any body fluids which might ooze from points where catheters or other tubes had been inserted. Such tubes and other disposable machine parts are discarded in a red plastic bag. This color is an indication to all staff persons that hazardous infectious waste is contained therein.

One of the nurses began to remove the IV tube from his upper arm, then the ING tube from his nose. She pulled back the top hospital sheet and removed the catheter from his penis, saying, "Hey, you got to be careful with how you remove these tubes . . . this stuff is dangerous [a prick with the tip of a tube or catheter might expose one to the highly infectious body fluids]. The tubes were disposed of in the specially marked bags.

Together, we pushed David's body forward so that one of us could remove the sheet from beneath him. Next, his hands were crossed, secured with surgical tape and placed on his chest. The ankles were similarly secured.

The team is careful to guide me, the novice in the handling of the body. "Just do it this way, we won't have no seepage. . . . We got to be careful with body fluids. . . . Just do as I tell you. . . . Stop being so nervous! Let's just get it done."

We rolled his body to the right-hand corner of the bed and rolled a new sheet under the midsection of his body. A similar move to the left was completed to spread the sheet completely under the corpse. A mortuary tag is tied to the toe and beginning at the head the torso is wrapped in gauze. Next, the body is neatly wrapped in the sheet. All is ready for the next staff person, who will take his body to the morgue.

There is something bitter and ironic about death in a hospital. The mission of the facility and endeavors of the staff are directed toward recuperation and the extension of life. Despite all the training, experience and resources, death happens. It occurs at random. Some patients will die under circumstances from which others recover. The inevitability of death is an occupational nuisance; the joker in the card deck to be drawn at any time. Yet the staff tries to beat the odds. . . .

When a patient is near death and the staff has decided not to artificially prolong life, there are visible cues which are observed by the other patients. The sight of patients dying unattended is traumatic for the others. Their situations are so similar that they believe their death will be the same. Toward the end, fear is a constant companion. Consider the case of Canute, recorded in my field notes:

> A few days later, Canute began what would later be called the "final stages." He floats in and out of consciousness. There is no one to cut his hair and the beard has grown long and unmanageable. His face is distorted by pain; one eye is nearly closed. He cries incessantly and often yells for help. He had to be restrained.
>
> Over the next few days, he grows weaker. In a barely audible voice, he complains about the pain. It was difficult to watch Canute's slow descent into death. We'd sit quietly together for awhile, then he'd ask, "What do you think is happening?" As I responded, he would close his eyes as if he did not really want to know.
>
> The obvious physical decline and pain was not enough to initiate a confrontation of his dying. The fear of death prevented him from talking with me about his feelings. There were few questions or comments about his perceptions.
>
> The routine of the hospital went on all around him seemingly oblivious to his dying. During the last few days I stopped by his darkened, silent room to find him lying in the unlaundered sheets, staring blankly at the ceiling, his face unshaven, hair uncombed and meal trays untouched.

Alone and in pain, the dying patients are at the most vulnerable and helpless point of their lives. The fear and hurt are difficult to express, especially since there were so few people who listened to them in life. Isolation is intensified by the fact that most of this population have very strained if not broken family ties. Relatives had little reason to contact them when they were in good health. There is little incentive to be supportive now at the dawn of death. Since a large portion of the population studied were homeless, they had few if any friends in the community who could offer support. In general this population is alone and unsupported at their death. Canute, for example, resisted the hospital chaplain's visit because he felt that it was not "time yet." There was no one to hear his struggle. He was left alone, except at meal and medication time. . . .

The singularity, aloneness and isolation of the AIDS patient continues even after death. Often unclaimed bodies remain in the hospital morgue for days or weeks until relatives are found and come to claim them. Others are simply interred in municipal paupers' graves. In Canute's case no one came to claim the body. Attempts to reach the family were in vain. The body lay in the morgue for some time. He was eventually buried, probably in Potter's Field. . . .

Waiting to die is a very difficult thing to do, especially when they have so few opportunities for distraction or resources to increase understanding. Escape from the hospital is a familiar theme. Most want to live as they were accustomed to until "their time comes." The medical ward is often viewed as a prison death row. They express feelings that might be expected from a convict who has exhausted the last appeal. Reprieve has been denied. They must simply endure the pain and discomfort until it is time.

> Anne is typical: For the most part, she appears resigned to her demise. "I know all about it [AIDS]. I'll leave it in God's hands. I know I don't have much time. I know

what's happening. I know I'm going to get sicker. . . . I'm a fighter, I'm a Cancer. I leave it in God's hands. If it ain't my time. I'm not going nowhere."

Days later Anne remains on the respirator. The edema has worsened. The doctors expect renal failure. We spend time together quietly. When I hold her hand her eyes open and she winks at me. She struggles to breathe even on the respirator. The doctor thinks she may need to be suctioned "but perhaps this is it."

She tries to raise herself from the bed, which angers the doctor. She's terribly afraid and I tell her it's okay to let go if she wishes. I wiped the tears from her eyes. She winked again and clasped my hand. Moments later, she died.

In contrast to Anne, Delores reverted to denial of the dying process, wishing to leave the hospital so that she could resume her "life." She refused to see that her "days were numbered." The hospital staff related to her as if it were business as usual. The doctors treated each symptom separately as the occasion arose; "treat the acute medical condition." Their aim was her eventual discharge. The issue of her death was never really discussed with her. Toward the end, the last two weeks of her life, Delores was surrounded by other AIDS patients in various stages of demise. She believed there was time to live before she went through the same things. . . .

Under "normal" circumstances (advanced age, premature birth, accident), death is understandable. The death of an AIDS patient is perceived as tragic, yet it is also something "they brought on themselves" [deserved] or asked for by way of "inappropriate behavior." In addition, the generally working or middle-class hospital administration most often views the AIDS patients as long since doomed to self-destruction by their dysfunctional behavior patterns. The fact that they were drug users, prostitutes, gay, illiterate, homeless means, in the abstract, that there is little reason to go beyond basic care in addressing their medical conditions. There is an undercurrent of "blaming the victim," and it is manifest in the wording and tone of official documents as well as staff-patient interaction. As Canute put it:

I don't hardly leave my room anymore. Most of my friends left or died. That's why you see me laying down. I feel sad. I say it this way, we all going to die. But let the man prove himself. We don't need to be treated like dogs. Some of the people [staff] in here ignore us. The doctors, nurses don't really care. At least they should let us die like human beings. They should listen to us once in awhile, that's all. That's all my friends wanted.

You feel lonely in here, it's damn boring and depressing in here. I think it's important that people listen to us. . . .

In addition, the underclass status of the population implies that they are a drain on hospital resources. Without a doubt, when they are released there will be others to fill the bed.

As it is, these patients are left to cope with the disease(s) and their mortality by themselves. Here, they flounder and the sight is pitiful. They are anguished and their cries just to be heard go unheeded. Again Canute:

They're all going to leave me, I can't blame nobody, when it's your time, it's your time . . . [but] I hope it's later, I don't want to die here. This [hospital] is a motherfucker, these people leave you in your room and shit, they don't pay attention to you. Yeah, they bring the medication and food, but that's it. . . . After I die, I don't care what happens.

This is not to say that the nurses or physicians are unfeeling or careless. In fact, I witnessed many herculean efforts to circumvent death. I also observed much compassion in those serving the people. But, in the end, the patient is left alone to die quietly. There are situations when the patients could be revived, their lives extended or their passing made easier. But physicians and nurses have the discretion to use or withhold these measures.

As the "end" approaches, people avoid the patient's room. There is less and less staff-patient interaction. The doors remain closed, lights turned off. It is important that the staff apportion its efforts among those patients who can potentially be saved.

The application of modern technologies to prolong life was not regular. Some physicians hesitated to initiate such protocols on behalf of intravenous drug users and/or homeless AIDS patients who were expected to die soon. At times a "why bother" attitude was evident. At other times I would walk onto the medical ward and find that two or three people with AIDS were intubated (breathing assisted by a respirator). In these cases the physicians had chosen to aggressively prolong life in the face of a terminal illness. Some of these intibated patients "bounced back"; their lives were temporarily extended. Others expired despite the effort.

While working at Oremus Hospital I noticed that the "do not resuscitate" (DNR) policy and the related use of cardiopulmonary resuscitation (CPR) were sensitive, complicated issues. In general, the communication between patient and physician regarding this matter was quite limited. It seemed difficult for the doctors to speak of this procedure with the patients. Since many patients were in a state of denial or had some misunderstanding or misinterpretation of the diagnosis, they were reluctant to discuss this issue with their physicians. Planning or preparing for death was not something they seemed ready to handle. Most often, the institution of such a policy was a decision left to the house and/or attending physician. . . .

The professional staff shortage also affects the extent of life-prolonging measures exacted on behalf of these patients. Sometimes there may be four or five respirators running in a 28-bed ward attended by two nurses and three aides during a specific shift. The extent of emergency care provided under those conditions is necessarily limited. . . .

Patients who resist or argue with the prescribed treatments in ways that are deemed antisocial or ignorant by the staff find their wishes or requests denied or ignored. At worst, an unacceptable manner widens the gap between health care worker and patient so that actual services decline or diminish in quality. There are now fewer opportunities for the patient to be educated, for understanding and acceptance to be enhanced. Ultimately they are penalized for this behavior by being denied access to specifics or avoided by the system. I think the great demand for medical attention results in an overload of cases beyond the limit that can be served by the staff. In such a situation, they simply have no time to spare and perhaps little patience for the client who creates "unnecessary" behavioral problems.

The staff may also have difficulty dealing with the people who struggle to live. As Dr. Kübler-Ross points out, the health care staff "can do this only when [they] have faced [their] own fears of death, . . . destructive wishes and become aware of . . . [their] own defenses which may interfere with . . . patient care." The achievement of such empathy or compassion would be a monumental one, for most of the staff seem so overwhelmed with the nature of these terminal cases that they erect psychological barriers to block the horrors, thus stifling most chances for real introspection. Yet the staff is given no supportive service to help them cope with their own fears of death or the routinely or occasionally difficult patient.

Perhaps more than any other social class of terminally ill people, the population studied needs much professional assistance in coping with the inevitability of death. But there is no significant help for them. In Oremus Hospital the medical staff are too overwhelmed by the sheer numbers and the facility too burdened by the cost of care to provide the necessary psycho-social counseling. In the best-case scenario the medical staff, too, would receive counseling and guidance in coping with their own fears of dying and their perceptions of the population served, thus reinforcing the emotional support provided to the patients. . . .

20

MISS FRUMKIN

Susan Sheehan

Susan Sheehan's book *Is There No Place on Earth for Me?* is widely regarded by social scientists as one of the best descriptions of schizophrenic patients and how the treatment of schizophrenia has changed in the past forty years. An accomplished journalist with a well-developed sociological imagination, Sheehan specializes in social documentary. She skillfully weaves descriptions of the patient, Sylvia Frumkin, with accounts of the suffering she endures (and also sometimes causes to the nurses and orderlies assigned to her care). This excerpt follows Miss Frumkin through a brief period when her medication was not working well and she was hallucinating quite severely. Unfortunately, such periods were quite frequent in Miss Frumkin's life.

The development of psychotropic drugs like Thorazine, which is used to ease hallucinations, brought about vast changes in the treatment of severe mental illness. The availability of these drugs led state mental hospitals to discharge thousands of patients on the assumption that they would be cared for in their communities. Unfortunately, severely disabled patients like Miss Frumkin often cannot carry out a treatment program requiring self-administration of drugs. Changes in their condition (such as those brought on by stress) require that their medication be adjusted, a process that demands continual surveillance by trained clinicians.

This situation, in turn, helps explain the "revolving door" condition of much contemporary treatment of severely mentally ill people. Moreover, although in principle Miss Frumkin could be cared for in a community-based treatment program, such programs often are not available owing to lack of funding and "not in my backyard" protests against the presence of former mental patients. In practice, therefore, patients like Miss Frumkin often spend much time in psychiatric emergency rooms and temporary care situations, which explains the title Sheehan chose for her book about Sylvia Frumkin's life of raging desperation.

It was after eleven o'clock in the morning on Friday, June 16, by the time Miss Frumkin had been screened for admission by Dr. Sun, had changed into state clothes, and had taken a chair in the women's dayhall. After shooing Paulette Finestone away, she remained seated for a while, seemingly oblivious of everything and everyone around her. But not for long. Soon she was on her feet, hurrying over to the nurse on duty. She demanded to use the telephone. When the nurse told her she would have to wait until another patient had finished making a call, Miss Frumkin screamed at her. The nurse escorted her to the telephone a few minutes later. Miss Frumkin dialed the extension of Dr. Werner, Creedmoor's director. She tried to tell Dr. Werner's secretary her troubles, but became incoherent. The nurse and a therapy aide had to struggle with her to get her to put the telephone down. The nurse, who had been at the admission screening, then led Miss Frumkin to the treatment room and tried to give her the injection of Thorazine that Dr. Sun had ordered that she be given immediately for agitation. Miss Frumkin refused the injection. She said she would take Thorazine orally instead. The nurse poured Thorazine into a paper cup and handed it to Miss Frumkin, breaking a rule that requires written permission from a doctor to substitute one form of a drug for another. Rules were broken hundreds of times a week in the Clearview unit. This knowledge didn't sit easily with Mrs. Plotnick, who is a perfectionist, but there was little she could do except to rail periodically against the difference between the way things were at Creedmoor and the way she thought they ought to be. Between sips of the bad-tasting Thorazine, Miss Frumkin called the nurse a jerk, a slut, and a dodo. After Miss Frumkin's insults became threats and she started to hit the nurse, the nurse went to Dr. Sun, caught him just as he was leaving, and got him to write out a seclusion order, which went into effect at twelve-fifteen. Once Miss Frumkin had been put in the seclusion room, she flopped down on the mattress as if she were relieved to be there. A few minutes later, a therapy aide brought her lunch on a tray. Miss Frumkin, who had been mumbling unintelligibly, took the tray, wolfed down the food, and handed the tray back. She soon lay down and dozed off. When the seclusion order expired, at two-fifteen, the door to the room was opened. Miss Frumkin was asleep. She was left in the room to sleep, with the door open.

Miss Frumkin awakened shortly before four, but she appeared content to stay in the quiet room. Around five o'clock, she felt hungry, got up, and walked into the dayhall. When the door to the dining-room corridor was opened, she went into the corridor and stood in line with the other patients, whispering to herself. Dinner at Clearview was usually served at five-twenty. Like breakfast and lunch, the meal was served cafeteria-style. Each patient took a tray, a plate, and eating utensils, and walked past a counter. Food-service workers positioned behind the counter doled out portions of some foods; patients helped themselves to others.

The dining room that served the patients on Clearview's admissions side was a bright, buff-colored room with tables for four. There were containers filled with plastic flowers on the tables. The dining room was a moderately attractive place when it was empty. It was not an attractive place at mealtimes. Many of the patients—Miss Frumkin was one of them—ate sloppily and in great haste. A few patients were so dejected that they ate little or nothing. Therapy aides helped those who could not feed themselves. Sometimes there were forks, knives, and spoons in the dining room; sometimes (after a patient had used forks and knives as weapons) there were just spoons. The food was what one might expect at a state institution with a computerized food plan (pot roast was on the menu fifty-two times a year, not fifty-one or fifty-three times) and a food budget of a dollar and sixty-seven cents per patient per day. Vegetables that were considered "expensive and exotic"—asparagus, cauliflower, Brussels sprouts, broccoli—were never served. "Extended" (casserole-type) dishes were served often: They were inexpensive and filling. The menu was nutritious, starchy, easy to gain weight on, and inflexible. Diabetic patients could get tea and coffee without sugar, but no patient could get coffee without milk, no matter how much he or she desired black coffee. Half an hour was allotted for each meal. Most patients spent ten minutes in the dining room. Some years earlier, an attempt had been made to slow the meals down—to prolong them from half an hour to an hour—so that patients could relax and chat more. The attempt had been a failure. Instead of chatting more when they were made to sit together longer, they had fought more. Clearview's patients appeared glad to eat and run, and the dining-room employees, many of whom were grouchy, appeared glad to have them do so—especially at dinnertime, so that they could go home early.

After shoveling into her mouth three helpings of everything served at dinner on June 16, Miss Frumkin returned to the dayhall, settled into an easy chair, and watched television quietly. At nine o'clock, she took the fifty milligrams of Moban that Dr. Khanna had prescribed for her. A therapy aide on the evening shift let her watch TV until ten-thirty before taking her into the dormitory, where the other women were already asleep. She assigned Miss Frumkin an empty bed next to a window. Clearview's beds had foam-rubber mattresses. Two-thirds of the mattress rested on unspringy lattice springs; the remaining third rested on two storage drawers built into the foot of the bed. Neither these drawers nor the wardrobes in each cubicle had locks; many patients slept clutching their pocketbooks. The pillows were covered with a water-repellent material rather than with soft ticking, and were unpleasantly hard. Although Miss Frumkin had had little sleep in the last thirty-six hours, she wasn't tired. She got into bed without taking her clothes off and lay quietly under the sheets and under the bedspread, which the therapy aide had forgotten to remove.

A few minutes after the night shift came on duty, Miss Frumkin got out of bed. She walked hurriedly down the long corridor from the dormitory to the dayhall. She then headed back toward the dormitory, but stopped at the employees' lunchroom when she saw a short, stocky black woman named Bernice Parrott sitting there. Mrs. Parrott was one of the 12:00-to-8:30 therapy aides assigned to 043 and 044. Miss Frumkin told her that there was some water on the floor of the dayhall and asked her if she had a mop. When Mrs. Parrott replied that she didn't, Miss Frumkin warned her that if she didn't mop up the water she would report her to the night supervisor. Mrs. Parrott asked Miss Frumkin to go back to bed, and said she would take care of the water. Mrs. Parrott went into the dayhall, found a puddle of urine on the floor, and went to the utility room to get a mop. When she returned to the dayhall carrying the mop, she found Miss Frumkin standing a few feet from the puddle. Miss Frumkin ordered Mrs. Parrott, at the top of her voice, to clean up the dayhall. Before Mrs. Parrott could clean anything, Miss Frumkin ran over to her and demanded the mop. Mrs. Parrott held on to the mop with all her strength, fearful of what Miss Frumkin would do with it if she got her hands on it. Miss Frumkin grabbed Mrs. Parrot's dress, struck her several times on the head with her fist, kicked her, and tried to bite her, screaming "Nigger, I'll nix you!" as she fought to gain possession of the mop. Mrs. Parrot was in pain, but she whirled around, pinned Miss Frumkin against a wall, pried herself loose, and ran to the nearest telephone, which was in the ward office. She hurled the mop through an open door to the employees' toilet, in the far corner of the office, picked up the telephone, and called the night supervisor, who was in the secretaries' office in the central corridor watching some members of the night shift sign in. Meanwhile, with her free hand Mrs. Parrott continued to fend off Mis Frumkin, who had followed her into the office and was still after the mop. Mrs. Parrott and Miss Frumkin wrestled; Mrs. Parrott succeeded in bringing Miss Frumkin to the floor and was able to hold her until the night supervisor came to her assistance.

Because there were no registered nurses on duty at Clearview or in Creedmoor's other geographical units during the evening and night shifts, one or two nurses, members of Creedmoor's "nurse management team," responded to calls for help from the units between four o'clock in the afternoon and eight in the morning. When the night supervisor saw Mrs. Parrott and Miss Frumkin engaged in combat, she telephoned the nurse management team. While the night supervisor was on the telephone, Miss Frumkin managed to struggle to her feet. She tried unsuccessfully to snatch the telephone away from the night supervisor. By the time the registered nurse arrived, within a few minutes of being called, Mrs. Parrott and the night supervisor had put Miss Frumkin into an empty seclusion room. Miss Frumkin was banging furiously on the door of the seclusion room. The nurse telephoned the doctor on night duty (the resident who handled night admissions was the only doctor on call for all the geographical units at Creedmoor from four-thirty in the afternoon to eight in the morning), and he gave her a verbal order to put Miss Frumkin in seclusion for two hours. Mrs. Parrott and the night supervisor helped the nurse hold Miss Frumkin down so that the nurse could give her the Thorazine injection for agitation, as Dr. Sun had ordered. The nurse was supposed to take Miss Frumkin's vital signs before giving her the injection—if a patient's blood pressure is low, an injection can cause hypotensive shock—but Miss Frumkin was so agitated that the nurse couldn't take her vital signs. Miss Frumkin remained agitated all night. The doctor renewed her seclusion order three times. When the day shift reported to work, she was still agitated, and so received another injection of Thorazine. . . .

Miss Frumkin was let out of seclusion at eight-forty-five, after receiving her Thorazine injection. She spent most of Saturday, June 17, in the dayhall, sometimes snoozing, sometimes screaming at the therapy aides and the patients. She took the Moban tablets she was given without protesting. They didn't seem to have any effect on her. She became upset again on Saturday evening. She took her clothes off, refused to go to bed, banged on many of the doors in the ward, kept the other patients awake, and insisted that she needed a blood test, because she might be pregnant. At eleven o'clock, she was given an injection of Thorazine and was put into seclusion. The nurse management team was called over twice to help with her; the doctor on night duty renewed the seclusion order twice. Miss Frumkin spent the night singing, laughing, and talking to herself.

On Sunday morning, Miss Frumkin was again let out into the dayhall. She was quiet for a few hours and then became disruptive. She took her clothes off in the men's dayhall. Irving Frumkin came to visit but soon left, because his daughter refused to pay any attention to him. She required injections of Thorazine at five o'clock and at eleven-fifteen, and spent another noisy night in seclusion, banging on the locked door.

After Miss Frumkin was let out of seclusion on Monday morning, June 19, she ate a substantial breakfast, swallowed her morning Moban tablets complacently, and bounded into the dayhall. She was wearing the green T-shirt and green pants she had been wearing since Friday morning, but no shoes and no bra. The soles of her feet were black. Within a few minutes of entering the dayhall, she had borrowed four hair curlers and a tube of bright-red lipstick from two other patients. She spent a long time rolling a few strands of the hair in the center of her head around each of the four curlers. She applied the lipstick to her face until every inch of it was covered except her eyes. Some of the patients stared at her and laughed; others stared and gave no sign of having seen anything out of the ordinary. Then Miss Frumkin talked for an hour, nonstop, to some of the other patients, to some of their visitors, to the therapy aides, to the cleaner, to laundry workers and dining-room employees and other people who passed through the ward, and to herself. One of her soliloquies, delivered at Indianapolis 500 speed, was peppered with the names of actors, television stars, pop and rock singers, and past and present historical and political figures, as well as with brand names. It began like this: "Hitler did a good job. He cleaned up the streets. He invented the Volkswagon. I love Darth Vader. I am Darth Vader. I figured out that Mayor Koch is Charles Nelson Reilly. Adolf Hitler is forgiven. He invented methadone and the Mercedes-Benz. It was all a price war. I'm Tania and I have the biggest house in the country. Bess Myerson was originally the Statue of Liberty. I married Neil Diamond a long time ago." She grabbed the shirts of two male patients standing near her. "Elvis Presley, this is John Travolta. I've been married to Geraldo Rivera for fifteen years. The ultimate doll is Ronald Dahl. Dahl. Dahl. Dahl." Sometimes Miss Frumkin got stuck on a word or a cluster of words, like a needle on a scratched phonograph record. "As I was saying, as I was saying, Dahl, Dahl, Dahl," she repeated until she slipped into the next groove. This time, she retrieved the word *ultimate*. It got her going again in third gear. "I have the ultimate question: Are we going to bring back the Edsel?" She walked over to the TV, where a few people were watching a quiz show. "Ultimate television set, is that the Thanksgiving Parade?" She stood in front of a woman who was watching TV, blocking her view of the quiz show. "Are you wearing Ultima makeup by Revlon? The man who gave me this beautiful haircut is Jason. He's the ultimate hairdresser, trust me. Dahl was the ultimate television host." Miss Frumkin walked over to a therapy aide. "How do you like my new hairstyle?" she asked.

The therapy aide shook her head in dismay as she looked at the four hair curlers and the red-lipstick war paint. "Why'd you put that stuff on your face, honey?" she asked.

"Because I wanted to look like you," Miss Frumkin answered.

The therapy aide went off and returned with some cold cream and some absorbent cotton. She stood next to Miss Frumkin and wiped a little bit of lipstick off one cheek. "I went to high school with you, but I didn't know it at the time," Miss Frumkin said, backing out of face-cleaning range with considerable agility. She recited a poem:

> Mary had a little watch.
> She swallowed it, it's gone.
> Now everywhere that Mary goes
> Time marches on.

Vainly pursuing her with the cotton and the cream, the therapy aide said, "Sylvia, did you make that up?"

Miss Frumkin's expression became quizzical. "I don't know if I made it up or if I read it in a greeting card," she said, and she scurried off, her pretty gray eyes still surrounded by an expanse of lipstick.

For the next five minutes, Miss Frumkin was a perpetual-motion machine, marching, pacing, jogging, and trotting all over the ward. She ran down the long corridor from the women's dayhall to the men's dayhall and then ran back. She occasionally stopped to ask a patient if she looked like him or her today. Most of the patients—Travolta and Presley among them—ignored her or walked away as she approached them. Sometimes a patient shouted "Stop staring at me," or "Don't look at me like that!" at her. One patient told Miss Frumkin that she was the greatest show on earth. A visitor said to the patient she was visiting, "You may be sick, but you're not sick enough to be locked up with people like that. Get yourself together so you can get out of this snake pit." Miss Frumkin grabbed one patient's hand and said, "I'm scared." The patient's hand went limp until she let go of it. She kissed a male patient on the mouth and elicited no response. She took her T-shirt off, revealing ponderous breasts. She called the therapy aide who eventually came over to put her T-shirt back on "Miss Priss." She sprinted out to the porch, where a patient was writing in a diary and two visitors were chatting with another patient. She grabbed the diarist's fountain pen, getting an ink blotch on one of the visitors' dresses in the process. She didn't apologize to the woman for staining her dress; she didn't seem to have even noticed the ink stain. She asked the other visitor for a pencil, accepted it without thanks, and tossed the pen and the pencil out through the bars of the porch. "There," she said, with satisfaction. "I've planted a pen-and-pencil tree." She went back into the dayhall, bummed a cigarette from a patient who appeared afraid not to let her have it, lit it with a lighted cigarette she had pulled out of another patient's mouth, put the cigarette back in the other patient's

mouth, and started to smoke. "The moon is made of cigarettes," she said. "A tobacco leaf just jumped out of my hair." She took five puffs on the cigarette and
threw it on the dayhall floor. Two other patients swooped down to pick it up and
started to fight over it. Miss Frumkin walked across the dayhall, threw her arms
around a rabbi, who was visiting a patient, and begged a half-empty paper cup of
Coca-Cola from another patient. As she sipped it, she said that it was an egg cream.
She wandered around the porch and the dayhall picking cigarette butts up off the
floor. She put the cigarette butts in the little bit of Coke remaining. "This is the ultimate drink," she said. "It's vodka. It's schnapps. Cigarette water is chicken soup."
She drank it down. Barbara Herbert, who had been watching Miss Frumkin, told
her she was disgusting. The two women exchanged insults.

"I'm Brigitte Bardot!" Mrs. Herbert shouted at Miss Frumkin after apparently
running out of all the barnyard epithets she knew.

"No, you're not!" Miss Frumkin shouted back.

"God is my father!" Mrs. Herbert yelled.

"I am my mother!" Miss Frumkin screamed, and she marched off stiffly, like a
toy soldier that had just been wound up.

After a short period of parading, Miss Frumkin headed for an aqua chair in
which a timid-looking elderly woman was sitting. "Excuse me," she said, lifting the
frail old lady out of the chair and setting her down on the lap of a patient seated on
a nearby sofa. She made herself comfortable in the aqua chair. At one o'clock, after
lunch, a therapy aide handed Miss Frumkin two twenty-five-milligram Moban tablets.
She swallowed the pills, saying they were eyedrops, and then said, "I was a Buddhist
and a born-again Christian, and now I'm trying to get back to my own religion."

Paulette Finestone, who was seated in an adjacent orange chair, said, "Sylvia,
you're Jewish, just like me."

Miss Frumkin shrugged, gave Miss Finestone a recipe for mayonnaise in Yid-
dish, and said that JE 333 was God's phone number. Then, in a strong, clear voice,
she sang, "We three kings of Orient are, raising prices of fueling your car." Then
she said "Praise the Lord," and, temporarily spent, sprawled sidewise across the aqua
chair. A while later, she put the words of what she said was the Thirty-seventh Psalm
to the tune of "Desiderata." The words were one part Twenty-third Psalm and three
parts gibberish. She then embarked on what sounded like an autobiographical
odyssey: "I was born in Brooklyn, where the tree grows. Everyone who is anyone was
born in Brooklyn. A tree grows in Brooklyn, so saith Bugs Bunny. If you don't believe me, ask, ask, ask . . . The trouble is, we all moved from Brooklyn to Queens
when I was nine. My grandmother may have invented the potato pancake, but I invented the egg cream. I went to the High School of Music and Art. Music and Art
became a furniture store, so I went to a private school. My sister Joyce is older than
me by—well, if I was born on May 5, 1948, and she was born on September 29, 1942,
it must be six years and eight months, no, five years and eight months. Well, whatever, five years, six years, eight years, eight months. I once got an eight on a math
test. I even had to wear Joyce's old gym suits and how low can you get? Joyce went
to an almost Ivy League college. She's a big shot. Jimmy and Rosalynn are always
inviting her to the White House. I've lost a lot of weight at Weight Watchers. I want

a lifetime subscription to *Weight Watchers* magazine. Grandma came and lived with us. After Grandma died, four weeks after I turned eighteen, Aunt Lottie came and lived with us. I also had an Aunt Goldie. Doesn't every Jewish family have an Aunt Goldie? Uncle Simon threw me into the water at the University Settlement Camp. The first thing I ever said as a kid was 'See my skinny bones,' because I was Claude Kirchner. I didn't want to play the Wizard of Oz when I was Bob Keeshan. You know what the trouble was? Our cat Gingersnap died. I tortured Gingersnap. I killed the cat. Gingersnap was a middle-aged unicorn." As Miss Frumkin said the word *unicorn,* she paused, got up, and walked toward the mural on the dayhall wall until she was only a few inches away from it—a distance from which she could see it without her glasses. "Is this a nuthouse?" she asked the unicorn in the mural. "Do elephants like peanuts? I fell into the gap. I don't want to come out. I've been married five times. You want Ringo, I want Paul, and the prince wants me. Elton John is John Yarrow. One thing about Creedmoor, it's like a rainbow. When I leave here, I'm going on a long vacation. Transitional can borrow me, but I always come back. I own the place. My father built it." Stepping over a woman who was sleeping on the floor, she sat down on a vacant chair and said, "I'm the one loser."

While Miss Frumkin was singing her version of "We Three Kings of Orient Are," Transitional Services' clinical coordinator, Peter Orenstein, and a nurse from Transitional Services were listening to her. They had come to the ward to visit Miss Frumkin. She had ignored them. After watching part of her performance in the dayhall, they were troubled by what they had seen, and asked Stephanie Fulton, the treatment-team leader for 043 and 044, to let them read Miss Frumkin's chart. When they had read it, the nurse said sadly to Dr. Sun, who was in the chart room, "She's so out of contact. She's so out of control. How could we have lost so much ground in three days?" Orenstein asked Miss Fulton to please keep him informed about Miss Frumkin's progress. He said that Transitional Services would try to hold her place for a while, in the hope that she would soon be over this crisis. The nurse wrote a note about their visit on Miss Frumkin's record at Transitional Services. "Sylvia appears to be having an acute schizophrenic episode," the note read. "She was extremely bizarre and inappropriate in appearance and her conversation. She made frequent reference to her sister 'Joyce and her White House invitations.' The face was covered with lipstick and her attention span was very short. She apparently is prone to agitated behavior, because there had been numerous seclusion orders written on her chart."

That afternoon, Dr. Sun wrote out an order to discontinue the Moban tablets. Moban wasn't of any use to a patient as agitated as Miss Frumkin, he said later. He prescribed 400 milligrams of Thorazine liquid for Miss Frumkin, to be taken twice a day in 200-milligram doses. He increased the dosage of the Thorazine injections she was to be given as needed for severe agitation, from 50 milligrams every four hours to 75 milligrams every two hours. And he put down on her chart that she should have another skull X ray, an electroencephalogram, and a neurological consultation in Building 40. This order was apparently overlooked: Months went by and Miss Frumkin didn't go to Building 40 for the skull X ray, the EEG, or the neurological consultation.

Later that afternoon, Miss Frumkin had another hostile exchange of words with Barbara Herbert and a fight with Paulette Finestone after she had grabbed a Bible that Miss Finestone was quietly reading; she sang "Big Wide Wonderful World" in a loud voice; and she outtalked everyone else in the ward. "I created the Muppets," she said just before dinner. "I'm the first woman mayor of Hollywood. I lost more weight than anyone else at Weight Watchers. My cat's name was Strawberry Butterscotch McLean. Strawberry is my favorite flavor. I like strawberry ice cream, strawberry shortcake, strawberry anything. Senior day is drawing to a close. I'm going to marry John Travolta." Miss Frumkin splattered a substantial amount of the food she intended to eat for dinner over her already stained clothes. She was distraught early in the evening, but quieted down for a couple of hours after swallowing her 200 milligrams of Thorazine and went to bed. She didn't sleep well. During the night of the nineteenth, the nurse management team was called twice, Miss Frumkin was given two injections of Thorazine, and she spent a good part of the night in the seclusion room, yelling, banging on the door, and keeping the patients in the dormitory awake.

21

DISSATISFACTION GUARANTEED

Robert L. Kane and Rosalie A. Kane

These excerpts capture the frustrations and some of the problems involved in the delivery of health care to Native Americans. Written a generation ago, it describes the condition of health services for the Navajo Nation in Arizona during the 1970s. Unfortunately, not much has changed in the ensuing years. Here and there, there have been some improvements, and efforts have been made to decentralize the federal Indian Health Service. But most of the basic sociological obstacles to progress remain.

Poverty, alcoholism, chronic unemployment, and persistent racism help maintain the reservation system as a neocolonial system within the larger society. While many of the professionals in the Indian Health Service are highly dedicated and spend much time traveling through the vast reservations to bring higher-quality medical care to local facilities, the system has always been underfunded. Cuts in federally funded social programs in the 1980s made significant improvements impossible. Efforts to create a synthesis of traditional and scientific medicine, as described in this selection, will require a social movement led by Native Americans, one that demands greater autonomy and decentralization of Indian health services.

On June 25, 1970, the Redding (Calif.) *Record Searchlight* carried an unusual piece of medical news:

> Richard Oakes' fever hit 106. His pulse was irregular. The 28-year-old Mohawk's body shook on his hospital bed in San Francisco.
>
> Then, as skeptical doctors stood by, Mad Bear placed an ancient and secret Indian medicine in the tube that fed the young activist.
>
> Oakes responded within five minutes and within an hour, says Mad Bear, his temperature was normal, his pulse regular and his body relaxed.
>
> Doctors at San Francisco General Hospital admit there was a positive response Monday to the Indian medicine.
>
> Mad Bear, a smile playing on his massive, creased face, recalled that doctors felt the trio was "just fooling around" when they asked permission to treat Oakes. They were allowed to administer the medicine, he said, because Oakes' condition was such that, "what harm could we do?" The doctors say it was Oakes' religious right to be administered the Indian "herbs."
>
> Mad Bear refuses to say what was placed in the teaspoon of medicine placed in the intravenous tube.

Richard Oakes' illness, which kept him hovering on the brink of death during two weeks of coma, was as dramatic in onset as in cure. Mr. Oakes, a leader of the Alcatraz Indian Movement, is also a leader of the Pit River Indians, who are pressing claims for the return of stolen California land. Because of his activities in the second capacity, he was attacked and almost beaten to death with a pool cue in a bar in San Francisco.

Richard Oakes was injured in an Indian cause and, appropriately, his recovery was brought about by an Indian medicine.

Fortunately, the physicians in charge were willing to cede the patient's "religious right" to the medicine. Perhaps they were also aware that medicine men are often skilled in the use of curing herbs. This instance is a clear-cut example of a happy blending of white and Indian medical practices. The intravenous tube of the modern hospital was used to convey the secret, potent drug to the patient!

In the usual, less dramatic course of events, particularly on Indian reservations, sick Indians receive treatment from Indian Health Service physicians in Indian Health Service facilities. In such settings one might expect a synthesis of white and Indian medicine on a routine basis. Unfortunately, the end product would probably not be claimed by either culture as a credit to its medical systems. Too many health problems are unsolved and, worse, almost unattacked. And too many patients have bitter feelings about their dealings with the Indian Health Service. . . .

If one set out to design a health system which would be assured of failure, what might be the prime ingredients?

1. The medical care should be offered in a form which is not highly valued by the consumer.
2. The providers and the consumers should be unable to communicate.

3. The providers should represent a system which has a history of unjust and inconsistent dealings with the consumers.
4. The providers should remain with the consumers for no more than a few years lest they become too familiar with their ways.
5. The administration of the medical care system should rest as much as possible at a centralized level away from the scene of delivery. It should stress uniformity of procedure despite local differences in need.
6. Funding should not be related to local needs and conditions but rather should encourage maximum volume of services regardless of quality.

The Indian Health Service, which renders health care to the Navajo, contains all of these elements. Some of the factors are a legacy of history, in which case the Indian Health Service is not responsible for the condition but is faced with the challenge of minimizing it. Other factors are a direct result of PHS administrative structure. Taken together, they describe a health system with built-in obstacles.

First, the medical care is offered in a form which is not highly valued by the consumer. Traditional Navajo medicine classifies the practices of the white physician at the lowest level.

The Navajo religion is a closed system based on mythology into which all phases of life are incorporated. Harmony is the ultimate good, and health or well-being requires a preservation of the prescribed order. Sickness is any disruption of the state of harmony, be it physical, mental, social or environmental in nature. Disharmony is created in two ways: 1) transgression of prescribed behavior, that is violation of a taboo, or 2) witchcraft. Treatment of the symptom or its etiology must be sought from the appropriate practitioner among the hierarchy.

The Singer is the high priest in the Navajo religion. He alone has the ability to cure illness, that is, to restore the individual to a state of harmony. He does not deign to provide symptomatic treatment, nor to set bones or attend women at childbirth. Through elaborate and obsessively precise ceremony, the Singer rectifies the transgression or removes the spell. The ceremonies are long (often more than a week), involving intense interactions between the practitioner and the patient. No history is taken and no physical examination is performed. Often the patient's family and friends are active participants. The fees are quite high (as befits a practitioner who has studied over five years to learn his skill), and in addition the patient must bear the attendant costs of feeding and housing guests.

The second-ranking practitioner in the Navajo hierarchy is the diagnostician. Since the Singer does not make a diagnosis, the diagnostician must ascertain the etiology of the disease in order to recommend the appropriate specialist. In contrast to the Singer, the diagnostician undergoes no extended apprenticeship. Instead he relies on psychic gifts supplemented by prayer and ceremony to arrive at his conclusions. Commonly these practitioners employ hand-trembling, stargazing, or crystal-gazing as diagnostic techniques. Here, too, no history or physical examination is included. A fee is charged for the service, although considerably less than the fee of the Singer.

For those who lack the means to afford the services of the Singer and diagnostician, symptomatic treatment is available from the lowest of Navajo practitioners, the herbalist. Symptomatic relief, however, is not equated with cure and by no means eliminates the need for a Sing when resources permit. Herbal remedies are used in times of pain, but are considered temporary relief for a still unresolved problem. Indeed the Navajo is likely to try any source of relief available to him at the time, be it herbalist, Hopi medicine man, Christian faith healer, or even PHS physician.

The PHS physician is perceived by the traditional Navajo as something on the order of (or possibly less than) the herbalist. The typical interaction between the patient and PHS clinician certainly differs from the ideal relationship between Singer and patient. The doctor spends very little time with the patient, and much of that is spent in asking questions, poking, and probing. The family is usually excluded from the treatment, either because of distance from the hospital or at the physician's request. And the physician relies on a wide range of medicinal preparations for oral, parenteral, and intravenous use.

Moreover, the symptomatic treatment offered by PHS cannot have been worthwhile, because the doctor did not charge for it. We have noted that fees are an integral part of the traditional Navajo system. Somewhat like a modern psychiatrist who believes a successful treatment may not be free, the Singer prefers charges even to members of his own family. Navajos who can afford the bills may prefer to visit a physician in private practice in an off-reservation town rather than accept free medicine.

A second built-in problem is that the physicians and the practitioners cannot communicate properly. The Navajo language, a derivative of the Athabascan tongue, is particularly difficult for unfamiliar ears. Its complexity was put to good use in World War II, when Navajos speaking in their native tongue conveyed information that no Japanese could decipher. It is said that no white man can ever hope to speak Navajo well. Personal experience leads us to doubt that anyone could use it for communication without many years of exposure. . . .

Indian people working in their own communities form the backbone of the organization and provide the potential for its ultimate success. Ironically these are the persons most dependent on the system and least likely to make any efforts to change it. Too often they mutely accept policies inflicted by others, bending with prevailing trends but unconfident that they represent a permanent improvement. . . .

Navajo patients make their own judgments about white man's medicine and the form in which they receive it. We have collected some reactions of patients within the Shiprock Service Unit. Translated from Navajo, the words constitute an eloquent indictment of the PHS system.

> *"Seventy miles to PHS is too far—especially when you are on foot and sick."* (Female, age 27)

> *"I waited too long for the doctor—waiting in line, lobby, hallway, in office, and for medicine. Just waiting all the way."* (Female, age 50)

> *"Us elders, we have to pay $15 to get to Shiprock from here. Mostly we have to sit in the back of a truck."* (Male, age 81) . . .

Since the questions were asked in Navajo by persons not directly identified with the delivery of care, the replies were frank and vigorous. The patients' deep resentment over what they considered impolite or unkind behavior on the part of hospital personnel is clearly expressed:

> *"Well, while being hospitalized I feel like I am hated by all the nurses because I call for help every time I need assistance. I wish there were nurses who can be more friendly."*

> *"We need a good doctor just like they have in town because lots of these doctors at Shiprock were not very good and not kind to the Indian people especially the older people."*

> *"We like doctors and nurses be enthusiasm in their patients and know how to encourage them and not discourage the patient and make them feel sicker."*

Not only white employees came in for censure. Indeed the bitterness is even greater against Navajo employees, who are often met in their capacity as interpreters:

> *"Nurses aide did not interpret what my problem really was to the doctor. She was mean to me."*

> *"Navajo women employees in O.B. too rough with the new mother."*

> *"Usually some Navajo employees do not use their manners or respect."*

> *"Interpreter do not cooperate with me. One time one of the nurses told me wash my own son."*

It was eye-opening for the hospital staff to realize the extent to which they were silently condemned by an apparently stoical group. As in other studies, this data shows more anger over the manner of care than the ability or inability to cure. . . .

Yardsticks to measure community health are hard to find. Clearly concentration on end results is more difficult than counting heads and procedures. Good health is a commodity which is hard to define, let alone measure. Usually we fall back on measurements of disease, and even then we have difficulties. Mortality figures are the most obvious index of community health—such measurements as life expectancy and infant mortality are fairly accurate throughout the whole country. When these crude indices are used to look at our Shiprock community, it is apparent that the health effort is not designed to combat one of the leading causes of death, namely, accidents.

When we try to measure other signs of ill-health which are less decisive than death we run into more difficulty. We cannot measure the incidence of ill-health in a community by counting hospitalizations or visits to a doctor; many factors influence whether an illness is treated, including the personal beliefs of the sick person and the accessibility of treatment. Sometimes the most serious symptoms are not brought to medical attention. Another way of measuring health status is to look at the level of functioning among adults in a community in terms of employment levels and utilization of sick leave. A region such as the Navajo reservation, however, does not offer full employment even to its healthy residents. Furthermore, the Navajo culture does not place the same positive value on work as does the Anglo culture. . . .

End-result evaluation becomes even more crucial in considering the effectiveness of treatment of patients with chronic problems. We suspect that, in many instances, expectations of the medical care system will have to be narrowed to the alleviation of discomfort and the improvement of function. This goal does not diminish the importance of the health professionals. Rather it engages them in the very difficult task of refining techniques of producing behavioral changes, of ensuring that patients are motivated to follow medical regimens, and of involving the patient as an active participant in the preservation of his own health. As a starting point, health professionals need to break down the components of medical intervention that do satisfy the patient and make a positive impact on his physical or mental well-being.

Part of the data for analyzing the doctor-patient relationships and their actual effectiveness in promoting physical or mental health must come from the patients themselves. End-result evaluation cannot confine itself to the activities in the doctor's office or the hospital ward. . . . [Earlier] we reported an opinion survey of Navajo patients in the Shiprock Area. Some of the responses suggested that a visit to the hospital left the patient anxious or humiliated. Other responses indicated that certain patients who tired of waiting at the clinic simply left without the medicines required for maintenance of their health status. Unlike laboratory data, this kind of human response information is hard to collect, hard to analyze, and hard to utilize, but it is, nonetheless, important in considering the effectiveness of the medical care which is offered.

22

IDEOLOGY AND HOLISTIC ALTERNATIVES

Kathleen Deierlein

Alternative medical practices, including faith healing, indigenous medicine, and holistic medicine, are among the fastest-growing forms of medical treatment in the United States. They account for many billions of dollars in private health care expenditures, especially since they are not often covered under insurance plans. What are the sociological explanations for the increased popularity of forms of healing that are not generally considered scientific? What does the proliferation of such alternatives tell us about problems of conventional medicine? These are some of the issues addressed by medical sociologist Kathleen Deierlein's study of holistic medicine. In this selection several of the patients included in her study offer their versions of why they turned to holistic medicine.

From a broader social perspective, we know that the triumphs of scientific medicine in this century have left some proportion of patients unsatisfied. These patients have rejected modern medicine in favor of nonscientific practices. Although they constitute a small proportion of the total population, they are numerous enough to provide thriving practices for many alternative practitioners—and their numbers are augmented by others who wish to hedge their bets by consulting both scientific and alternative healers. Indeed, part of the popularity of alternative practices stems from the human desire to cheat death, no matter how slight the odds of success.

Many alternative medical practices harness the autonomic nervous system and the mysterious influences of the emotions to effect changes in physical symptoms. The power of these influences reinforces the patients' distrust of scientific rationalism. These and other themes are touched upon by Deierlein's informants as they explain why they chose holistic healing. By carefully listening to these patients' accounts of their experiences with illness and holistic medicine, one can learn much about the problems of scientific medicine as developed in many of the essays in this book.

Given the dominance of biomedicine as the conventional healing system, what is it that motivates people to leave behind the security of their culturally common faith in regular medicine and pursue the uncertain path of helpseeking from a faith healer, shaman, or otherwise uncredentialled health provider?

While much evidence shows the increasing availability and widespread use of alternative and holistic health care practitioners, little empirical research in sociology has been done on this phenomenon. A study of 27 people who used holistic medical and nonmedical healers found, not surprisingly, that the majority had become dissatisfied with conventional medicine's inability to cure them of some particular illness. But the study also showed that a small group of users, including health professionals such as nurses and doctors, experienced a cognitive shift away from conventional medicine and toward holistic alternatives because their in-depth knowledge of biomedicine gave them a heightened awareness of its shortcomings. Although individuals in the latter group are far fewer in number than those in the former, it is because of them that we recognize desensitization, and not merely dissatisfaction, as the precondition to continued use of holistic medical alternatives.

Desensitization was the first stage in a three-stage career path (Becker 1963) common to all users; at this stage users became desensitized to the explanations for health and illness offered by the conventional medical framework. They experienced a gradual but explicit detachment from the biomedical ideology which was accompanied by a loss of faith in the physician as an adequate provider of medical care.

This stage paved the way for the second stage, when a crucial experience and/or a referral person became pivotal in each user's initial decision to try holistic medicine. At the third stage, users became socialized to alternative medical beliefs from having a continuous, significant relationship with a holistic practitioner in which they learned the language and adopted the norms, attitudes and values of the new ideology.

CRUCIAL EXPERIENCE OR TRANSITION PERSON

Every respondent in the study came to try holistic medicine because they had had a crucial experience involving medical care, or because a holistic health center or practitioner* was recommended by a friend or acquaintance.

The crucial experience of a medical emergency was a turning point for ten respondents. Four of these reported a serious injury (automobile accident, a fall, sports injury and hip injury) where they ended up in a conventional medical setting with a physical therapist who recommended they seek out a holistic practitioner. The other

*The types of practitioner first sought by these 27 respondents were: acupuncturist (in 4 cases); acupressurist (8); chiropractor (3); physician using holistic therapies (7); and spiritual or psychic healer (5).

Reprinted from *The Role of Ideology in the Use of Holistic Medical Alternatives* (Ph.D. diss., City University of New York Graduate School, 1992), by permission of the author.

six experienced a sudden worsening of a chronic illness or a diagnosis of imminent surgery, which functioned as the final impetus for pushing them "over the edge" and into a holistic practitioner's office, attempting to find an alternative way to treat the problem. Four of these six had the crucial experience *combined with* a friend who suggested a particular holistic practitioner during the crisis or shortly afterward.

The suggestion of a lay referral agent (Freidson 1960, 1961) such as a friend, acquaintance or family member was enough in and of itself for 10 cases, and a psychotherapist or spiritual counselor was the referral agent for three of these ten cases. (13 cases were in or had ever been in psychotherapy.) This key "transition" person or sponsor was someone who knew of or used a holistic healer and encouraged the respondent to try holistic medicine for their medical problem.

SOCIALIZATION TO THE BELIEFS AND LANGUAGE

Respondents in this study who spoke at length about their conversion to holistic beliefs described the importance of their relationship with a healer in devotional terms. Concentrated learning of holistic principles seemed to occur in this type of relationship; other less intense healer-client relationships were described, but less frequently. The relationship relies on the patient's complete faith in the healer's abilities and recommendations. Three people—all clients of the same healer—expressed so strong an attachment to her that they were reluctant to move out of the geographic area and were dismayed at the thought of being without her. One said:

> I'm sure I'm coming across as being totally anti-doctors. There is a place for doctors, but I choose if there's any other option available, to not go to a doctor because I'm afraid of what they're going to do to me. I would always select a holistic practitioner. Every now and then I think "what if I were to move away?" And the major, major reason why I don't want to leave this area is because of [the healer]. [She does not] practice anywhere other than down in Florida. And that would be the only other place I would want to live, and I don't really want to live there. Because I would hate to sever my ties with [her].

When asked if she would be inclined to try another holistic center, she replied:

> Well, I would, yes, because I would be away from the one I trust completely. There are different kinds of holistic medicine. It's not all the same. Different kinds of modalities. I believe very strongly in the ones I have experienced that I know work.

Another respondent explained that healing was assisted by her trust and confidence in the healer. She had been sexually abused as a child, and came to holistic medicine because of chronic bladder infections which disrupted her life. Through her relationship with the healer, she came to see a connection between her specific illness and the repression of sexual emotions. When asked whether it was the acupressure or talking which released the emotions, she said:

I think it's a combination. I've come out of [acupressure] feeling very happy at times, I've come out feeling very angry; it depends on what we were talking about. I came out where I cried hysterically for an hour, sometimes I've come home and gone to sleep, I was just wiped out. It depends—it's both. They don't like to separate the physical from the emotional. So while they're treating you, they're talking to you. To me, I can't separate it. Whether it's [the acupressure] that's releasing the emotions as opposed to just talking. I can't say it's all from the talking.

Although the respondent had previously considered going to a nearby women's crisis center for therapy, it was not until the healer suggested it that she made the decision to go. . . . Her willingness to begin therapy at the crisis center was directly related to her feelings of self-responsibility, which like other parts of the ideology, she learned from working with the healer. She said:

[With this healer and therapy] the person helps you but you have to do a lot for yourself. It's not like "you heal me." You have to take responsibility for yourself and help heal yourself.

American people go to the doctor, they say "heal me, but I'm not going to do anything for me. You take the responsibility for making me better, but I won't. And the only thing I'm doing for my responsibility is going to you. It's your job."

The following expresses the essence of her relationship with the healer:

I have seen other [healers] but she's the one I prefer. Because she knows my history. I have a bond with her. . . . She understands what I'm talking about. Not that the others don't, but when I go to someone else, I don't tell them what's bothering me. I'll talk to them about things in general, but I can't really tell them, just because I prefer telling [my healer so that] I don't have to get into everything again. So it works better that way.

The data in this study do not support the existence of a genre of "true believers" prior to trying holistic medicine, but show that individuals who start out as novices may *move toward* "true believing," and that a commitment to the healer-client relationship makes likely the continued commitment to the ideology.

Users move toward the "holistic user" identity by learning the language of the holistic ideology, and this occurs most frequently in the context of a healer-client relationship, a finding which lends support for more general theories about the importance of the doctor-patient relationship.

A Change of Views: Users Compare Their Health Beliefs with Others'

Most respondents in this study felt that their new health beliefs were more reasonable or accurate than those of the general population. Paradoxically, most respondents saw a growing trend toward greater health awareness in the population, but *all* expressed the belief that the general population is ignorant about what makes for "true" health. One said:

I think I am ahead of them. See, the average person does think of their health sometimes, but they do nothing about it. Like, they'll think about it but they'll go on and
smoke. They know that it's no good for them, I'm sure they know that. And they know
what they're eating is not good. But they'll go right out and eat fried food or they'll
continue smoking, but I don't. Once I read something . . . I might have done it before,
but if I go and read something on it tomorrow, that'll be *out*.

Another said:

I think I'm in a minority. Most people want to be responsible, in general to be responsible for their own lives. [But] they avoid taking responsibility, they avoid issues in
their own lives, of seeing "how I have allowed this to happen to myself." They would
rather look outside of themselves to place blame somewhere . . . "he made me do this"
or "my boss is making me sick" or "I was exposed to a virus on the subway, someone was
sneezing." People want to look outside of themselves rather than take responsibility.

Comparing her beliefs to those held by the rest of the population, one woman
said:

Opposite ends of the spectrum. I believe if you're eating healthy, you'll feel better.
And if you're dieting, I mean it all goes hand in hand. I have these people at [work],
for example, that are very fat. They're very heavy, and they can't breathe. So they
smoke. And they do all this stuff. And my eyes sometimes roll. And they'll ask me
[about my health food lunch] and then say, "Oh no, I don't want to do that. It's too
much work." Or they'll ask me "Oh, could I try that? How much was that ?"
   [If it's] $5 a pound for this sauce I bought from the health food store, they say "Too
expensive. I'll just eat what I have." In other words, [I think to myself] "so you eat the
garbage, and you pay less money for the garbage, and I'll pay more money." They
make fun sometimes, I take out all my little [containers]. I don't have time for a lot of
cooking. The health food stuff takes a lot of chopping and cutting, so I go and I buy
everything for lunch. And they say "What's that you're eating? Oh, God, what is *that*?"
   Meanwhile, I'm not sick. And they have breast cancer and ulcers and they can't
breathe, and high blood pressure, and obese; and she has varicose veins, the other
one, that are popping in her legs. So, lady, "if this what you want . . . "

The centrality of good diet and nutrition was mentioned repeatedly, and
often these concerns were voiced in conjunction with the topics of stress and environmental pollution—a pessimism about staying healthy without taking a more active health stance. One said:

I'm in the minority in what I think about health. For example, on [vacation recently]
there were no people who would know about holistic medicine. There aren't a lot of
people who follow good nutritional pathways where they eat only fish and chicken.
There's a consciousness of good eating but most people eat the same stuff they always
have. I'm in the minority on the kinds of foods I eat, like no sugar, additives, no prepared
foods. I eat small fish which have less chance of mercury poisoning, and chicken . . .

Or another:

I think more and more people are reaching out and saying there's got to be a better
way. Well, the whole ecological, you know, way we're living. The environment, now, ev-

erybody's suffering. People don't breathe outside. The air is so polluted. Well, we've got to do something about it. So at this point, I think I'm not in a majority. But I think we are, as the years go on, we're going to have to be—this [health action] has to be the way it will be, to live a better life.

A Change of Views: Users Identify a Shift in Health Beliefs

Respondents did not necessarily attribute a shift in their views to their work with the healer, but all expressed an awareness that their views were different now than before using holistic medicine. One said:

> Since I'm coming here, everybody says "You look so good!" I'm not a health nut now, but I've become more health conscious about being healthy, as far as eating. And my insides feel good—my inner being or whatever they call it? Feels good.
>
> I like the place. And I know this is a better way of life, using holistic medicine. Health—if you see some of their ideas, I agree with them more than anything else I have ever heard.
>
> My views have changed. It used to be, if I was ill, it was a bother. I was never ill, so I didn't think about it. Now, I think of illness as the absence of health. If you don't take care of yourself mentally, physically, spiritually, you could have an absence of health. If you're too stressed, that could cause it. If you don't eat right, that could. If you don't stay positive. . . . It's a general feeling. Healthwise, I would rate myself as a ten . . .

Another said:

> Illness is . . . a lesson to be learned, and the illness brings it to your attention. That's definitely my view. Pain and some illness. I wouldn't presume to talk about all illness because I don't know. [These views] definitely came to me as a result of [my] experiences . . .

She refers here to two experiences. First, she was:

> in and out of hospitals all during my childhood for testing and diagnosis . . . from infancy on. I think that the fact that I had a lot of negative experiences in the hospital system as a kid predisposed me to look elsewhere . . . [for help with my health].

She was desensitized by conventional medicine's inability to heal her during her childhood. Then, a second crucial experience came later when her terminally ill husband and she sought help from a physician who agreed to use alternative therapies (while simultaneously treating the patient with conventional medicine), not to reverse his cancer but to relieve his pain and make him more comfortable toward the end of his life. She witnessed horrific treatment of patients while spending extended periods of time at the hospital bedside. Her socialization to holistic medicine continues; at the time of the interview she had just completed her first year of training in acupuncture.

A Change of Health Behaviors and Practices

All respondents described, in detail, behavioral changes they had made and views they had taken on about diet and dealing with stress. One said:

In other words, if he said, smoking is unhealthy and smoking is poisonous, and I explored it and reasoned it out that nicotine or cigarettes are poisonous, then I could no longer do it. Not that I would become perfect. I didn't smoke at the time. Oh, I did smoke very lightly in high school and college. I gave that up. It was a very small amount. I quit a few times. I made up my mind to quit. That was before karate. If I hadn't quit, once I started karate I would have given it up then.

The point is, if you know something is untrue—like "this is unhealthy"—then you'd be untrue to yourself to continue to do it. The question is evaluating information on what a healthy lifestyle is, and living in accord with that.

Many expressed an attitude which can be described as health optimism or even health elitism. When queried about why some people might be more health conscious than others, respondents consistently placed themselves above others in terms of self-discipline with respect to health behaviors. One said:

It's horrendous what most people eat and live with, and their view of things is extremely limited and narrow. And they keep it that way, being threatened at the possibility of having to change or doing anything. And they look at that as a deprivation; they couldn't have their pizza or their other things which I love but I don't eat, because I feel better without it.

I want the optimum physical performance for my body. And also I want to feel good and be healthy. If I know [eating dairy is] more burden than good, aside from momentary taste bud stimulation, I won't do it. People look at having to give something up like that with an attitude of deprivation, they feel threatened and they don't want to give that up. Most of it is attitudinal and psychological. They'll keep that narrow view.

One respondent, who was preparing for graduation from a massage therapy training program, said:

I think a lot of it is, we are trained for the quick fix. I think that's part of the mentality in health right now and what needs to change and what is changing. People are into going to the doctor, [and saying] "Give me medicine, make it better. Fix me up." So it's very much working with the symptoms.

Whereas the work I do, and a lot of the alternative stuff, works toward getting to the root cause. What are the patterns that are making you have this back pain? A lot of the work I do, the work is very individual. It changes very much from person to person, in terms of how you work or what comes up because it's everybody's individual process. You are going to come in with one type of back pain, I'm going to come in with another type of back pain, they're going to be from different reasons.

A CHANGE OF LANGUAGE

It is through language that we learn about the group we are part of. Language unifies, socializes and standardizes us. Not only does language make social interaction possible and easier, but having a common language is a prerequisite for expressing common interests and establishing social solidarity among those who speak it. A group of people held together by a common interest "tends to develop peculiarities of speech which . . . function (to) distinguish the group from the larger group"

(Sapir, 1974: 53–54). Our language connects us to other members of our group, and if a subculture takes on a different language, it sets itself apart from the larger culture. Thus, subcultures and countercultures develop languages of their own. The use of a vernacular identifies the speaker as part of a "speech community," and makes the group, as well as membership in it, psychologically real. Sapir says:

> The extraordinary importance of linguistic differences for the symbolization of psychologically real as contrasted with politically or sociologically official groups is intuitively felt by most people. . . . He [or she] talks like us is equivalent to saying, "he [or she] is one of us."

One way in which users learned the ideology is through language: acquiring a set of *symbolic* phrases and jargon and buzz words to express the ideals worth focusing on in order to change their behavior. In this analysis, Geertz' (1973) view of ideology as symbolic and metaphorical will be relied upon. The data show that metaphor is one device by which we construct and most importantly, communicate the new ideology.

Self-Help and the Notion of Control

The self-help ideology as a *therapeutic* resource (Suler 1984) provides an individual with coping strategies that can be integrated into their everyday life. The language of self-help is one which encourages people to overcome powerlessness, by feeling and using their own strength to resolve problems. Suler (1984:30) says: "Personal experiences are restructured within a cognitive framework . . . so that events which may be anxiety-provoking and unfamiliar may be *translated* into a more familiar and understandable form" (emphasis mine).

The Twelve Step programs, which originated from a societal need to address the problems of alcohol addiction, use a *disease metaphor* to link together addictive behaviors with illness: alcoholism, spending, gambling, overeating, drug abuse, compulsive sex, and others. The Twelve Step model explains these behaviors as *symptoms of a progressive disease* which have made the addict's life "unmanageable," and which can never be cured but only arrested through abstinence. An individual must get group support to change the "insanity" which results from the unwanted behaviors. In addition to the group membership, one must work the "steps" of the program in order to "recover." By definition, this requires the individual to "come to believe that a power greater than ourselves" will restore that person to "sanity."

The Twelve Step programs, all based on the parent A.A. model, are referred to as spiritual programs. Only by turning his or her will over to a "higher power" can an individual begin the process of recovery. The program "promises" that one's life will take a turn for the better when one gives up trying to control the situation and "turns it over" to the protective higher power which oversees one's fate. Whereas the term "higher power" is essential, the term "God" is seldom used, because the notion of God as a loving, caring father doesn't square with members' images of their alcoholic fathers. The ideology of this type of self-help program consists of *beliefs* that define the nature and causes of the problem ('addiction is a disease for which there is no cure') and the *values* that specify goals to be striven for (Suler 1984): one's recovery is only possible through a higher power.

Holistic Language Compared

There are several similarities between the Twelve Step and holistic medical ideologies; both appear to be gaining popularity; both rely on ideal visions of what a problem-free life could be like to goal-orient their followers; both contain numerous suggestions for behavioral change; and both use a self-help language that speaks to people's needs for empowerment in the face of disease.

The major difference between the two ideologies lies in the empowerment/control factor; rather than *giving up* the willingness to control one's life (as in A.A.) the holistic language is about *taking back* the control for one's life. Whereas both languages speak of empowerment, the Twelve Steps speak about empowerment from without—"turning one's will over to a power greater"—whereas holistic ideology speaks of power from within.

Power from Within

The terminology used in the "formal" ideology (from books, pamphlets, and brochures) illustrates the holistic notion of taking control of one's health. This connects with notions of patient responsibility which are central within the holistic ideology. Pamphlets and brochures communicate norms about the role responsibilities between healer and client: phrases like "medical treatment and self-help" enforce the expectations "based on . . . a cogent philosophy that acknowledges the *patient as participant.*" Norms governing the healer's behavior include a concern for the well-being of the patient, beyond the normal levels of human concern, yet "the healer should develop the skill of 'concern without detachment'." The "exceptional patient" is one who responds to the crisis of illness by assuming control of their lives, developing a fighting spirit, achieving peace of mind, and actively participating in the doctor-patient relationship.

One booklet reports that:

> To work on one's own health, additional information and instruction is needed beyond what is provided during medical consultations. To meet such needs, staff assist clients in choosing classes and seminars on holistic health and personal growth topics.[1]

Another brochure describes biofeedback as "available as an introduction to introspection and self-directed change,"[2] the emphasis always on what one can do

---

[1]Center for Holistic Medicine, New York, NY.

[2]Ron Dushkin, M.D., "Wholistic Medicine: Caring for the Whole Person" (Lenox, MA: Kripalu Center).

to make oneself well. One brochure suggests that "the practice of creative imagery assists you in contacting your 'inner healer/guide'."[3]

The value placed on individualism and self-healing is high, and patients would ideally learn to: rely on their "inner reality," "intuitive voice," "voice within," or "the healer within"; tap their "inner resources of healing"; look to "inner guidance for the healing process," "the silence of (their) intuitive heart," "the inner teacher—that part that already knows how healing happens," and meditation as "the bridge to look within."

While these phrases hint at spirituality, there is no *mandatory* relationship with a caring, providing, overseeing God. Unlike some self-help languages which rely on notions of individualism, the holistic language is not about turning control over to anyone, a higher spiritual power or otherwise. It is about taking back and using control, by tapping into one's inner "resources."

This language does not place a value on leaving the outcome up to anything or anybody else but on taking responsibility, taking charge, and taking over. Words suggesting empowerment are central to the holistic language.

SUMMARY: LEARNED POWERFULNESS?

Very often, an experience of powerlessness from a frustrating medical experience or crucial diagnosis is followed by new notions of power and control, which become important motivators to holistic users. Loss of faith in one medical model is a precondition so that when a crucial experience or sudden worsening of illness occurs, respondents do not accept, as fate, the information they received in the doctor's office. Thus, they seek solutions elsewhere. New notions of power and control are embedded in a language which influences beliefs and behaviors, socializing holistic users to a faith in a new medical model.

Seligman et al. (1968) found that dogs placed in an experimental situation where they could not avoid receiving shocks would not try to escape the shocks once the escape barriers were removed. About the relationship between fear and learning, the researchers applied their theory to humans, suggesting that people "learn" to become helpless when faced with insurmountable obstacles, and remain so even when the obstacles are removed. Helplessness sets in when one feels out of control, or that control of a situation has been taken away. Seligman also suggested that a person who experiences helplessness in one situation may be more likely to act helplessly in other situations. . . . Respondents in this study saw holistic medicine as a way out, or a way to make sense of a previously senseless situation. At some point, they rejected a loss of control over their medical decisions, and "detoured" toward what they perceived as greater mastery in decision making.

Kobasa (1982) found that among business executives and lawyers, those with a great deal of stress protected themselves from illness by attitudes that make up the "hardy personality." One of these attitudes is of control, the opposite of helpless-

[3]Center for Holistic Medicine, New York, NY.

ness. Respondents in that study believed they had influence over the events in their life; theirs was an attitude of competence, mastery, and agency. They did not see themselves as victims of circumstance; in short, they rejected the role of victim.

The prerequisite for inclusion in this study was that the respondent had used a holistic healer *at some point* in their lives. Consequently, reasons they gave for first using holistic medicine were more likely to be out of medical necessity. But this study shows that the majority of users were only minimally aware or not aware of holistic medicine until they gradually learned about it from the healer, and suggests that such a relationship played a significant part in their continued use, as well as their learning and espousing more of the ideology.

In general, the "use" of holistic medicine can encompass a whole range of activities; some see a practitioner because they seek personal growth and greater self-awareness; some go to holistic health spas for rest and relaxation or a vacation; some go to holistic centers for health paraprofessional training (such as acupuncture or massage therapy); and some go to holistic education centers for exercise classes where they practice tai chi chuan or yoga. But while the majority engage in these health maintenance activities now, these types of activities *were not* the ways by which respondents in this study came to their initial encounter with holistic medicine. Many people learn about holistic medicine from books, television shows, and magazines, but their continued involvement with holistic medicine is sustained by an understanding of and conversion to the ideology, facilitated by a change of language.

NOTES

BECKER, HOWARD S. 1963. *Outsiders*. New York: Free Press.

FREIDSON, ELIOT. 1960. "Client Control and Medical Practice." *American Journal of Sociology* 65:374–382.

FREIDSON, ELIOT. 1961. *Patients' Views of Medical Practice*. New York: Russell Sage.

GEERTZ, CLIFFORD. 1973. *The Interpretation of Cultures*. New York: Basic Books.

KOBASA, S. R. MADDI, and S. KAHN. 1982. "Hardiness and health: a prospective study." *Journal of Personality and Social Psychology* 42, 1:168–177.

SAPIR, EDWARD. 1974. In Ben Blount, ed., *Language, Culture and Society*. Cambridge, MA: Winthrop.

SELIGMAN, MARTIN, S. F. MAIER, and J. H. GEER. 1968. "Alleviation of learned helplessness in the dog." *Journal of Abnormal Psychology* 73, 3:256–262.

SULER, JOHN. 1984. "The Role of Ideology in Self-Help Groups." *Social Policy* 14 (Winter):29–36.

23

APPLYING MORAL PRINCIPLES

Ruth Macklin

Ruth Macklin is one of the nation's leading medical ethicists. Not only is she an internationally recognized expert on the philosophical study of medical ethics, but she is also routinely called in for consultation in difficult cases confronting medical professionals, patients, and their families in the nation's hospitals. The very idea of a medical ethicist was almost unheard of twenty years ago. Health professionals have always faced agonizing ethical problems, but as life-prolonging technologies have become more successful, the social control of life and death has given rise to previously unimagined quandaries. Life-support systems for people in comas, life-prolonging procedures for people with terminal illnesses, heroic measures to keep dying patients alive—these and similar technologies are routinely employed by medical professionals, but the norms for dealing with the dilemmas they create are not yet fully established.

Medical professionals, immersed in the immediate crisis and confronted with distraught family members, often cannot resolve the moral ambiguities of the situation, as Macklin shows in some of the examples she presents. She offers some guidelines for dealing with the basic issues raised by life-prolonging technologies. Age, quality of life, personal autonomy, and consciousness are among the considerations introduced in this essay.

In the future, when doctors and hospital administrators have fully resolved the ethical issues raised by the new technologies, there may no longer be a need for specially trained medical ethicists. In that ideal future, medical and nursing schools will have incorporated the study of ethics into clinical practice. Hospital procedures will reflect broad knowledge about how to deal with the vexing moral questions that now require the help of outside experts. Unfortunately, this ideal future will not arrive any time soon. New diseases and new medical technologies will continually test the medical profession and are likely to make the role of the medical ethicist even more prominent.

Mr. DiS., an eighty-two-year-old man who had been in good health all his life, was admitted to the hospital with unusual symptoms. His wife and middle-aged daughter accompanied him to the hospital and visited him regularly. After a full workup and numerous tests, cancer was discovered in the bowel. When Mrs. DiS. and her daughter were informed of the diagnosis, they were adamant in maintaining that the patient not be told. The daughter was insistent to the point of becoming strident, and she threatened the physicians with a lawsuit if they revealed the diagnosis to the patient. Since surgery to remove the cancerous portion of the bowel was a possibility, the doctors told the family that the patient would have to be informed so that he could grant consent for the surgery. To which the daughter replied that it wouldn't be necessary at all. She would grant consent for the surgery if physicians recommended that course of treatment, so her father needn't be informed about his condition, nor need he be troubled with having to sign a form to authorize the surgery.

Although that plan of action was entirely unacceptable to the physicians, as they recognized the moral and legal requirement that adult, mentally competent patients must grant informed consent to their own treatment, the recommendation for surgery was not yet definite. Intimidated by the patient's daughter, the young doctor in charge of the case was uncertain how to proceed. His encounters with Mr. DiS. became increasingly uncomfortable. Although the patient had never asked directly what was wrong with him, he became less communicative with the medical staff and with his family, and soon appeared depressed. The family, meanwhile, continued to visit regularly but sat in silence for hours in the patient's room. Conversation became stilted and forced, and the daughter remained adamant that her father not be told of his diagnosis.

The doctor asked himself whether he nonetheless had an obligation to disclose the diagnosis to Mr. DiS. Or did he owe a duty to the family to honor their wishes? More generally, he wondered, do patients have a right to know their diagnosis and prognosis, even when they do not ask explicitly? The doctor was pondering substantive moral questions, questions about rights, duties, and obligations in the medical setting. If clear answers can be given to these questions, the procedural issues raised by the daughter could not even arise.

Although it might be unwise, on rare occasions, to disclose a diagnosis to an alert, competent patient, in the majority of cases patients have a right to be told that information and physicians have a duty to inform them. Those rare occasions include situations in which patients themselves have given an unequivocal message that they do not want to be told bad news about their condition. They also encompass the unlikely combination of circumstances in which disclosing the diagnosis to a patient is significantly likely to worsen his medical condition. An example might be a massive heart attack, after which the patient is not yet stabilized, and is known by his physician to be a profound worrier. It might jeopardize the patient's recovery to disclose bleak news about the extent of the damage to his heart in the immediate aftermath of his attack.

But it is rare that disclosure of information itself is likely to worsen a patient's medical condition. It is usually in response to their own discomfort, or to the demands of family members, that physicians choose not to inform patients of their diagnosis or prognosis. The justification is almost always that the patient is not being told "for his own good." This is a classic instance of *paternalism* in the medical setting.

Put simply, paternalism is the denial of autonomy. It is direct interference with an individual's exercise of self-rule, through either coercion or deception. A key element in paternalism is the reason given for the coercion or deception: it is alleged to be for the welfare or in the best interest of the person being coerced or deceived. Whether acts of paternalism can ever be morally justified, and if so, under what conditions, is a general substantive question on which reasonable people disagree. Specific cases are analyzed by examining the facts and applying an appropriate moral principle to those facts.

If any issue in bioethics is now settled, it is that only patients themselves, when they are alert and competent, may grant informed consent for medical or surgical interventions. So the answer to the procedural question—May the daughter of a patient grant consent for her father's surgery?—is "Certainly not!" Procedural questions about informed consent on behalf of marginally competent patients, or those who clearly lack the capacity to participate in their own treatment decisions, remain thorny. Even more preposterous than her offer to consent to her father's surgery was the daughter's threat to sue the physician who sought to disclose to the patient his diagnosis of cancer of the bowel. So intimidated are physicians by the ever-present threat of a lawsuit that they sometimes take such threats seriously and refrain from acting in ways they know to be morally right. To his credit, the young doctor in this case continued to explore his obligation to his patient.

One day, when communication between Mr. DiS. and his family had reached a low ebb, the patient turned to the physician and asked, "Can't you tell me what's wrong with me?" Seeing no chance to wriggle out, and feeling certain the patient should know what was wrong with him, the doctor told Mr. DiS. gently but clearly that he had cancer. The patient, much relieved, said, "Thank you. I thought so." and the discussion then turned to prognosis, treatment options, and what should be done next. The physician dreaded his encounter with the family, but knew he had to admit at once that he had disclosed the information to the patient. Communication between Mr. DiS. and his family improved immediately and dramatically. The patient's depression melted away. With no need to hide anything any longer, and having begun to discuss matters openly, everyone was in better spirits. When the daughter did confront the physician who had disclosed the information, she apologized for her earlier behavior, thanked him for his patience and dedication, and acknowledged that it had been best, after all, to tell her father the details of his condition.

———————

Mrs. F. was a ninety-four-year-old woman with a history of heart disease, brought to the emergency room complaining of shortness of breath. She responded well to the treatment given in the emergency room, but was still admitted as an inpatient so her condition could be monitored. After three days on a regular hospital floor, she again had trouble breathing and was found to be lethargic. Nurses called for a resuscitation, which resulted in tubes being inserted in Mrs. F., and again she responded well. After another three days in the hospital, the same series of events recurred. Although the patient again recovered heart and lung functions, this time she lapsed into a coma and was transferred to the intensive-care unit, where she remained comatose and showed no response to pain. After two days in the ICU, a fever developed and a urinary-tract infection was treated with antibiotics, given intravenously. Her condition remained unchanged for several days, and Mrs. F.'s niece was consulted in order to set a policy for future resuscitative efforts. The niece asked that her aunt not be resuscitated if the need arose again. On her twelfth day in the ICU, the patient was found to be unresponsive. In accord with the earlier decision, no resuscitative effort was made and Mrs. F. died.

Clara M. was an eighty-four-year-old diabetic woman with a history of heart failure. She came to the emergency room one day complaining of chest pains. She was admitted to the intensive-care unit with orders to "rule out MI," which means to monitor her closely in order to rule out the probability that she had suffered a myocardial infarction, or heart attack. The next morning a bed was needed in the ICU for another patient. Clara M. was asked if she minded being moved, and when she said she did not, was moved to a regular floor. There she was put in a bed with no cardiac monitor, where she remained despite test results that indicated she had suffered a myocardial infarction. At one point she tried to get out of bed to go to the bathroom, fell, and was put back in her bed. Later that day she suffered a cardiac arrest and was resuscitated. She died in the hospital two days later.

Mr. R. is a forty-nine-year-old man who has undergone both conventional and experimental treatment for leukemia over the last nine months. On this hospital admission he has decided to refuse all further treatment, including "supportive measures"—antibiotics, blood transfusions, and other elements of routine care. When asked, Mr. R. said he did not want to be resuscitated in the event of cardiac arrest. His only request was that he be made comfortable and "sleepy." His family, on the other hand—especially his daughter—could not accept this decision. They continued to pressure both Mr. R. and the physicians and nurses caring for him. Mr. R. signed a statement in the medical record confirming the requests he had made orally. His wife and daughter told the staff they must resuscitate him if he suffered a cardiac arrest. With reluctance and misgivings because of the family's demands for continued treatment, the physician respected the patient's wish and wrote an order to administer an intravenous morphine drip until the patient becomes lethargic.

How aggressive should medical treatment be? This question comes up in a hospital more often than any other. Case after case in rounds and conferences recounts situations in which physicians and other decision-makers must determine an appropriate level of care for a patient. Although it is true that no general answer can be given to this question, the reason is often misstated. It is common for doctors to assert, "Every case is unique," or, "You can't generalize about treatments." There is a core of truth in these observations, but it would be a mistake to conclude that therefore no general principles could be found to guide decision-making.

The rejection of those ethical perspectives that seek to apply general moral principles to medical cases is known as "situation ethics."[1] A reaction against dogmatic forms of morality, especially those derived from rigid religious teachings, this approach argues that each situation is different and that recognizing the uniqueness of every situation demands that decision-makers abandon doctrinaire rules and inflexible principles. What is required is to seek a "loving and humane solution" in every situation that poses an ethical dilemma. This view has its roots in the Christian ethics of love, and thus does not reject religion altogether. It does, however, seek a methodology for ethical decision-making that does not rely on moral rules or universal principles.

Although situation ethics has the virtue of being nondogmatic in its approach to ethical dilemmas, it fails to give clear guidance to the individual perplexed about the morally right thing to do. To tell the pediatrician who is in a quandary about how aggressively to treat an infant born with several birth defects to "choose the most loving and humane solution" is simply to restate the problem the physician faces. The pediatrician is agonizing over just which is the more loving and humane solution: to artificially prolong the infant's poor-quality life or to "let nature take its course."

If situation ethics requires the abandonment of all general principles, on what basis can one make a decision? Does one appeal to moral intuition? Is it by looking very hard at each case that a person comes to a flash of ethical insight? Does the "loving and humane solution" present itself when the decision-maker introspects, consulting inner moral feelings? None of these methods provides a useful guide to action. Nor does this approach lend itself to informed discussion and the ability to provide a moral justification for a preferred course of action. Situation ethics is little more than an affirmation of the subjective biases of the decision-maker: whatever feels right *is* morally right. That stance is at best unhelpful and at worst morally dangerous. The more situation ethics acknowledges the need to call on some principle or other to guide decision-making, the more it resembles perspectives derived from traditional ethical theories.

The proposition that every situation is unique is true, but its truth is almost trivial. The correct conclusion to draw is not that *no* general principles can be found, but rather that it is necessary to choose from among a variety of potentially applicable principles the one that best applies to the case at hand, given its individual features. Even so, no simple or automatic procedure exists for choosing the most applicable principle. This is partly because a number of different, perhaps conflicting, principles can be simultaneous candidates. It is also because procedural considerations enter the picture and sometimes override a substantive moral principle in the process of decision-making. A look at the similarities and differences between the three cases described earlier will illustrate these somewhat abstract points.

All three cases involve patients with life-threatening conditions. All require decisions about an appropriate level of care, and questions were raised in each situation about whether the patient should be resuscitated in the event of a cardiac arrest. Medical and nursing personnel inquired whether it was acceptable to omit some medical treatments while administering others. They also asked what counts as "aggressive" care, and what should be considered "routine."

Obvious differences exist among the three cases, despite these similarities. Mr. R. is still in the prime of life, far from having lived out a normal life span. Mrs. F. had already lived well beyond that statistical life span, while Clara M. was old but not very old. Is the age of the patient a morally relevant factor in seeking to determine the appropriate level of care? Is it morally relevant in deciding whether a patient should be placed in the ICU, where beds are always scarce?

Another difference in the cases is the role played by family. Clara M. entered the hospital with no family present, and apparently none could be found. Mrs. F. also came in without any family, but a niece was later contacted to assist in decision-making. Mr. R., in contrast, was accompanied by a devoted wife and daughter whose demands for aggressive treatment were unceasing. Should the presence or requests of family members be a factor in the level of care delivered to patients?

An ethical analysis begins by identifying the morally relevant factors. For any medical case the most important feature is the patient's prognosis. That should be determined at the outset and reassessed continually. Is the illness terminal? Are there several concurrent diseases, any one of which could worsen and threaten the patient's life? Is the patient's medical condition so poor that aggressive treatments could only prolong the dying process? The answers to these questions rest on objective facts. Although medical science contains many uncertainties, it also relies on an understanding of the natural history of diseases, the efficacy of standard treatments, and published data in the literature about similar cases.

Of the three cases, Mr. R.'s situation provides physicians with the clearest objective evidence about prognosis. The patient is suffering from the advanced stages of a terminal illness. He has undergone the complete course of conventional and experimental therapies for leukemia, and death is now imminent. Mrs. F. came into the hospital with a less certain prognosis, but during the course of her stay, the evidence mounted in support of a bleak prognosis. Having responded to initial therapy, the patient deteriorated, suffering multiple cardiac arrests and lapsing into a coma. Experience with patients such as this convinces the doctors that death from one cause or another is likely, even if efforts are made to prolong the patient's life. In the case of Clara M., however, the prognosis is neither as poor nor as certain as in the other two cases. The patient entered the hospital with a history of heart failure, complaining of chest pains. While her status was still being evaluated, she was moved out of the intensive-care unit to a place in the hospital where only less-aggressive care could be administered. It was not known whether Clara M.'s condition was terminal, so reliable information about her prognosis was yet to be confirmed.

Despite the uncertainties involved in making predictions about the future course of a patient's illness, the task is nevertheless based on objective medical information. From a moral point of view, it is more problematic to determine a patient's quality of life. Judgments about quality of life contain a subjective element, one that differs from person to person, and may even vary for a particular person from one time to another.

The distinction between subjective and objective should not be confused with the problem of uncertainty in making a diagnosis or prognosis. Objective considerations rest on observations and the known data of medical science. All scientific matters contain some uncertainty, which is why their truths are said to be probabilistic rather than absolute. But their lack of certainty does not make such matters any less objective. Subjective considerations, on the other hand, are based on the perceptions, feelings, and values of individual persons. The problem involved when one person seeks to determine another person's quality of life is entirely different from the difficulty of making judgments when uncertainty about the facts complicates a decision. A quality of life that for one person is unendurable may be acceptable for another. To base a treatment decision on the patient's quality of life is, therefore, more ethically problematic than to base it on objective facts about the patient's prognosis.

There is a world of difference between situations in which quality-of-life judgments are made by patients themselves and those in which family or medical caregivers make the assessment. In general, the one most qualified to judge quality of life is the person whose life it is. There is little doubt that Mr. R. was the best judge of his own quality of life. Both his disease and the side effects of months of chemotherapy left him ravaged by pain and discomfort. Nearing death, he requested only that he be made as comfortable as possible. His wife and daughter, quite understandably, were not yet ready to let him go. It is not so much that they assessed his quality of life as better than Mr. R. himself judged it to be. Rather, desperate in their hope for a last-minute reprieve, a miracle of remission, they demanded that physicians continue to treat the patient as aggressively as possible. But do they have the right to make that demand? The answer is a clear no when, like Mr. R., the patient is awake, alert, and oriented. Only when a patient lacks the capacity to speak for himself may family members become the primary decision-makers about medical care.

NOTE

1. JOSEPH FLETCHER, *Situation Ethics: The New Morality* (Philadelphia: Westminster Press, 1966).

24

FROM EXPLOSION
TO IMPLOSION:
TRANSFORMING HEALTHCARE

Daniel Callahan

Daniel Callahan is a veteran medical sociologist and medical policy analyst. For many years he has been a vice president of the Hastings Institute, a private foundation devoted to research on medical ethics and health care policies. In this essay he explores the causes of the health care crisis in the United States.

This selection begins with a vignette from the controversial Oregon State medical system. "Rationing" of health care procedures, as practiced in Oregon or elsewhere, is always bound to present agonizing medical dilemmas and impossible choices. The Oregon example has been at the forefront of thinking about medical reform at the national level because it represents some daring choices about limiting health care options. This essay therefore continues some of the themes developed in the earlier selection by Ruth Macklin, but at a higher level of societal complexity. Macklin was dealing with the choices faced by individual doctors or hospitals as they struggle with the gray areas of medical ethics. Callahan deals with the social-structural origins of these dilemmas in the interaction between the American individualist culture and the explosion of life-prolonging medical technologies.

Medical science will always outstrip society's ability to allow everyone to benefit from life-prolonging technologies and procedures. When medical emergencies strike, individuals and their loved ones are most concerned about personal issues of illness and care. However, the cost of heroic efforts to keep one person alive often needs to be balanced against the need for measures that will improve the health of all. Weighing these alternatives, Callahan becomes an advocate for limiting the use of costly life-prolonging technologies in favor of the investment of more resources in a community-based approach to prevention and care.

Early in December of 1987, Adam Jacoby "Coby" Howard of Rockwood, Oregon, died of leukemia. His death came in the midst of a campaign by his family, friends, and teachers to raise $100,000 for a bone-marrow transplant. The campaign still had $30,000 to go at the time of his death. A year earlier there would have been no need for such an effort. The state of Oregon would have paid for the transplant. But Coby had the misfortune of being the first victim of a new, 1987 policy set by the Oregon legislature: to stop all organ transplantation for welfare recipients and spend the money instead on prenatal care. His aunt, Susan McGree, said, "We spent precious time fiddling around trying to raise money for the operation while Coby was dying . . . Coby himself spent some of his last days going around helping collect the donation cans."[1]

What was remarkable about this event was not that a child died because he had failed to get government support for a transplant. That had happened before, but usually before the states had mandated coverage for organ transplants, when they were still classified as experimental forms of therapy. Nor was it remarkable that there had been a rationing of medical resources. Millions of Americans have long been denied critical care if they lacked money to pay for it. What was new was the openness of the decision, and the clear visibility of its victims. Instead of the kind of soft, covert rationing that has long been part of the American scene—either by the impersonal forces of the market or by the quiet, hidden way of parsimonious bureaucrats—there was a hard and open setting of priorities. Those denied treatment had faces.

The money needed for transplants, it was decided and publicly announced, would go to expectant mothers. That priority would be, so the argument went, a better investment of scarce funds. Many more of them could be helped, some 1,500 in all, compared with a handful of likely organ recipients. It was not, on the face of it, a casual or thoughtless decision. On the contrary, since the voters of Oregon had decidedly insisted that there be a strict and tough limit on state expenditures, there was no choice but for some difficult decisions to be made. A new and disturbing chapter had been opened in American healthcare. As Dr. John Kitzhaber, president of the Oregon Senate (and a physician, as it happens), noted, "Medical technology has outstripped, and will continue to outstrip, our ability to pay for it. . . . The cold reality is that . . . we must limit the money we spend on health care."[2]

Was Dr. Kitzhaber right? Many would say no. They could point out that there was a $200 million surplus in the Oregon state budget at the time. The transplant crisis was provoked by a voter-inspired expenditure limit that need not have happened and could be reversed in the future. They could in addition point out that millions of dollars are wasted, in Oregon and elsewhere, on cosmetics, expensive automobiles, VCRs, high-priced restaurants, and wasteful government programs. They could, moreover, note that just to the north, in the state of Washington, transplants remained available to welfare recipients. Even farther north, in Canada, they were available as well, and in a country that provides decent healthcare coverage for all of its citizens, regardless of their ability to pay. Its citizens can have both prenatal treatment and organ transplants. As if to rub it in, the Canadians make such treatment available while spending only 8.5 percent of their GDP (equivalent to our GNP) in 1986 on healthcare, compared with the 11.1 percent spent in the United States during the same year—and up to 11.5 percent now. That seems to underscore all the more the seemingly needless tragedy of the Oregon situation. Coby might not have had to die.

I suspect that is true, but to come to that conclusion is to choose the smaller, more poignant truth over the larger, more penetrating one. The larger truth lies with Dr. Kitzhaber's observation: We will not indefinitely continue to have the ability to pay for an expanding healthcare system, or for those endlessly emerging marvels of technology that promise to extend life. Some places will feel the pinch before others, and some will find temporary solutions better than others. Yet even if we can continue for a time to find the money to pay for organ transplants, or other yet-to-be-devised technologies, there is every reason to think that time is running out on the expansive, and expensive, enterprise of contemporary medicine. To talk about our "ability to pay" is itself misleading. If we are prepared to sacrifice other things necessary for a good society, if we want to spend most of what we have on health, then we can no doubt continue expanding indefinitely.

Yet if we begin to ask about the wisdom of that kind of unending medical progress, about the proper place of health among our whole range of social needs, and about the most responsible way to invest our money in the future, we may, and should, hesitate. In too many of our cities the hospital is the newest, best-equipped building, while the public school is the oldest, worst-equipped. Is that a good way to the future? Is that the right way to distribute our resources? We know and pity the hypochondriac, ever fearful of illness and death, ever willing to become absorbed to the point of obsession in a concern for health. We have yet to learn how to note the same characteristics in a society, one that has perhaps come to give a damaging priority to health needs, both real and imaginary. What should we think of the reported trend of Americans to feel sicker when their health is actually improving? What are we to make of the fact that contemporary Americans, the healthiest people in the history of the human race, are reported to believe that good health is the most important goal in their lives?[3] Ought that to be the most important goal for a life?

As we begin asking these larger questions, we will soon find ourselves moving uncomfortably in two realms. There is the intimate realm of individual people with names and faces, one of whom was called "Coby," and there is the larger, more impersonal and statistical realm of all of us together. As individuals we have come to need expensive organ transplants to make it through childhood, or costly bypass surgery to give us a few more years as elderly people. In our common life together as a society, however, we need those things that make for a public good: schools, highways, housing, parks, good police and fire protection. We are only now beginning to see that we cannot have it all. We cannot pursue medical advances wherever they lead us. We cannot give each individual what he or she may want or need to live some version of optimal health and longevity and, at the same time, have everything else needed to make a good society.

LOOKING FOR A WAY OUT

Our first impulse is likely to be a rejection of what will seem a stark and tragic choice. We will say that we have simply failed to manage our more than ample resources well enough, or that we are as taxpayers too selfish, or that we do not value the life of individual persons as much as we should. We will invoke the glories of greater efficiency as a way out, and whenever there is a claim that too much is being spent on healthcare, we will seek (and probably find) some other sector which appears just as profligate. We can, then, find ways to continue business as usual. If we are liberals, we can lay the blame at the feet of those unwilling to support an equitable national healthcare system. If we are of a more conservative bent, we can always claim that government regulation has hindered the market from delivering the quality and equality of which it is so splendidly capable. . . .

The power of medical progress feeds off of a potent dynamic, by now well recognized. There is the increasing weight of an aging society, one that sees the elderly as the fastest-growing age group, and with that growth a sharp upward curve through intensified treatment in meeting healthcare pressures. There is the force of technological advancement, ever ingenious in finding new ways to improve and extend life, many of them as attractive as they are expensive. There is, most of all, the power of public demand, which has come to expect medicine to improve not only health but life more generally, and which has come to see a longer and better life as not simply a benefit but as a deep and basic right.

The combined force of that dynamic has resulted in an explosion of healthcare costs; it is a force that shows no sign of abating in this country and it will probably come to threaten the healthcare systems of other, better managed countries as well. That force is intensified by some important collateral forces. Among them are the great profitability of the American healthcare system for many thousands of people, where doing good and doing well have become synonymous; the individualism of our culture, which stimulates a steady escalation of need and desire; and the drive for equality, which, though fitful, wants to extend to all the benefits enjoyed at first by a few. It is an explosion that has behind it extraordinarily potent values, habits, and desires. . . .

Of course we must find a way to manage costs. But something more is required. The financial crisis facing the healthcare system provides a superb, if probably painful, occasion to ask some basic questions once again about health and human life. Where are we going? Where *should* we be going? We have tried for some years to treat the growing problems as technical, subject to bureaucratic fixes. That has not worked. We have tried also to think about the individual's right and entitlement to healthcare. That has not proved altogether illuminating. What we have not done is to examine the very goals and ideals of contemporary medicine and healthcare. . . .

I have before my mind's eye a future healthcare system that seeks not to constantly conquer all disease and extend all life, but which seeks instead to enhance the quality of life; which seeks not always to overcome the failings and decline of the body, but helps people better accept and cope with them; which tries to keep in view that health is a means to a decent life, not a value in its own right; which works to help society curb its appetite for ever higher quality and constant improvements in healthcare. It is a system that aims to intensify inward, seeking not the endless conquests of all new frontiers, but only those that promise a more coherent individual life within a more coherent societal life. Implosion must replace explosion.

Our toughest problem is not that of a need to ration healthcare, though that will be necessary. It is that we have failed, in our understandable eagerness to vanquish illness and disability, to accept the implications of an insight available to all: We are bounded and finite beings, ineluctably subject to aging, decline, and death. We have tried to put that truth out of mind in designing a modern healthcare system, one that wants to conquer all diseases and stay the hand of death. We can score some victories in that battle, but we cannot ultimately win it. Yet we have created a system that works with the conceit that we can, and we have devised a way of life to go with that system which hides from our eyes what we are about. It is our vision of health itself, and many of our cherished ideals, that must be changed.

COPING WITH MEDICAL SUCCESS

Medicine and healthcare have, for one thing, entered a new stage of their history, one where the successes of medicine and not its failures are—in the way they interact with our values—the main source of our problems. That success has raised expectations beyond a sustainable point, addicted the system to an unending search for new and usually expensive technological solutions (many of them occasioned by earlier technological solutions), and guaranteed marginal gains for ever higher costs. Scientific medicine once thought itself standing on an open frontier, cheap to prospect, easy to plow, and endlessly rich in its great reward—better health and longer lives. But that frontier is, and must be, forever ragged and ultimately unconquerable. It takes, ironically, money and success to discover fully this truth, and we are now doing so.

A consequence of this insight is that affluent nations must ration healthcare more firmly and sternly than poor nations. The rich must make choices that the poor do not have. A common view of rationing is that it is necessary only when there is an absolute shortage of some good and that nothing can be done to improve the situation. A crowded lifeboat with finite supplies is the popular image. A better image of rationing in our situation is that of the wealthy individual or corporation on the verge of bankruptcy, their liabilities beginning to exceed their assets. In many cases, one reason is inefficiency and sheer wastefulness. Addressing these problems is where most efforts to avoid bankruptcy begin. But a second reason is much more difficult to deal with: A whole way of life, previously free of any constraints, must be radically changed.

The deepest moral problems in the provision of decent healthcare are those of the relationship between health and individual happiness (or well-being) and between health and the common good. The working assumption behind biomedical research and its clinical application is that there is a direct correlation between better health, a longer life, and enhanced human happiness. But that correlation is by no means clear. The fact that many individuals crippled, burdened, or disabled by illness are able to adapt well enough to their lives is one piece of suggestive evidence. Something other than their health determines their happiness. Still another suggestive item is the long struggle that has been waged to determine when to stop life-saving medical treatment. A longer life is not necessarily a more tolerable life.

If the deepest part of the problem of healthcare is that of the relationship between health and human happiness, any meaningful proposed solution must be integrated into an understanding of a whole way of life. We can to some extent define "health" and suggest some minimal standards for achieving it, and we can say a few things about the conditions and meaning of human happiness. Yet such efforts, however imperative, will always have about them an air of generality and abstraction. They can only take on full meaning within the setting of actual societies, and be given flesh only as part of some coherent pattern of social meaning, behavior, and institutional practice. What we make of disease and illness, the meaning we attribute to them, is not fixed. That will be a function of the place we give them in our lives, the kind of significance assigned them by society, and the way we communally interpret suffering, disability, decline, and death.

The most potent social impact of medical advancement is the way it reshapes our notions of what it is to live a life. The prospect of a longer and healthier old age, for instance, leads us to think about that phase of life differently than did our ancestors. The greatest attraction of technological innovation is its promise of first breaking the barriers of natural, biological constraints and then moving on to a dismantling of the cultural attitudes and institutions designed to live within those barriers. The impact of effective contraception on ideas and ideals of family life and family size is a good example of that phenomenon. But that process, so ingrained now as part of the lore of desirable social change, is full of hazards. We must determine whether the new possibilities—always rosy and full of promised benefits—will actually be better than the old ways. If we decide that the answer to that question is yes, then the question is: What kinds of new institutions, and with them what new barriers, should be created? The centrality of health to human life, and the social and economic power of the healthcare system in our political and moral life, can only mean that we must devise a full way of life—attitudes, practices, expectations, mores—to go with, and to shape, our healthcare system and the values that underlie it. . . .

Consider some questions that we, as a society, might ask but rarely do. What is the meaning of human health, and what is the source of that meaning? Where and how should health fit into our understanding of human life? What should medicine, and the science behind it, seek in the long run? What place and importance should be given to healthcare in managing our political and social systems? How much and what kind of illness is compatible with happiness and satisfaction in life? What kind of a life is it appropriate to expect medicine to help us achieve? What kind of medicine is best for a good society? What kind of society is best to deploy, and control, the power of medicine to shape and modify human life? How much and what kind of health does a society need in order to be a good society? What is a "good society" such that we can ask such questions?

CAN WE FIND ANSWERS?

A common objection to questions of this kind is that they seem to admit of no final answers and are resistant to public consensus. That is not necessarily true, though the answers may be long in coming and only partially articulated. They are, in any case, central and vital. The impact of health upon our personal lives, the power of the healthcare system to influence almost every other aspect of our common life, and the economic implications of the way we provide it should force us to seek common answers. We rarely do. They intimidate us with their difficulty. They befuddle us in the absence of a shared language of morality and values. They offer the possibility of threatening our pluralistic peace. They get in the way of the pragmatic incrementalism preferred in the political arena. They are just plain trouble. They also happen to be the right and unavoidable questions.

Our understanding of health and illness, death and disease, will stem from our more general way of understanding the meaning and contours of our life within our society, our way of life as a whole. That understanding will in turn help at the political level to shape our convictions about our individual and collective entitlements to good health and healthcare: Who is to provide it, pay for it, and take responsibility for it? At still another level, the way we put those convictions into practice will finally be by means of various technical and bureaucratic arrangements. . . .

There is a powerful tendency either to deny that there is a serious allocation and rationing problem or to evade the pain of difficult choices. The denial frequently takes the form of invoking some as-yet-unseen medical breakthrough to counter the massive growth of healthcare costs for the elderly or those suffering from some common diseases. More research, we are told, will save us. But there are no simple or inexpensive cures over the next horizon for cancer, heart disease, Alzheimer's, or stroke, those great killers and cripplers of the elderly and many younger people as well. The medical history of the human body, in any event, suggests that some other diseases will quickly come along to take their place even if we could dispose of them. Who had heard of AIDS a decade ago? If it is unlikely that there will be medical miracles to rescue us, it is just as unlikely that there will be bureaucratic miracles. There is a widespread belief that we can find some managerial fix, some wonderful incentive scheme to get doctors to use only proven treatments based on parsimonious diagnostic procedures, for instance. That belief is matched in fervor only by the hope that we can find some entitlement fix, some scheme that reduces government expenditures while leaving patients satisfied with their nicely calibrated out-of-pocket expenses. Those are forms of denial also. They can be combatted only by some hard work at the first level, that of our values and way of life. That is the key to everything else.

I come to the notion of a "way of life" with a particular conviction. We will not, I believe, be able to work out the problems of our healthcare system unless we shift our priorities and bias from an individual-centered to a community-centered view of health and human welfare. We cannot and ought not give up a respect for individual needs and dignity, but we can place them within a social perspective and allow that to color our understanding. We can, for instance, ask as our first questions: How much and what kind of health do we need for the common good, and what will collectively and communally help and improve us as a society? At present we ordinarily begin by asking just what it is that individuals need for their good health; if there are communal concerns, they are put in a subordinate position. I want to reverse that priority—to begin with the communal needs and to put individual needs, rights, and interests in the subordinate position. It is the latter that must act as restraint upon the former, not the other way around as at present. . . . The present system expands outwardly, so to speak; it must now turn inward, enhancing life, not always trying to save and extend it.

NOTES

1. WEBB RUBLE, "Rockwood Boy, 7, Loses Battle with Leukemia," *The Oregonian* (December 3, 1987), pp. A1 and A24.
2. JOHN KITZHABER, "Who'll Live, Who'll Die?" *The Sunday Oregonian* (November 29, 1987), p. B1.
3. LOUIS HARRIS, *Inside America* (New York: Vintage Books, 1987), p. 40.

25

BUILDING A HOSPICE:
A PERSONAL VIEWPOINT

Wade K. Smith, M.D.

Modern medicine is slowly adapting to the public's demand for more humane and pragmatic approaches to death and dying. Heavily invested in fighting illness and preventing death at almost any cost, medical practitioners are often reluctant to anticipate and plan for the death of their patients. Nor have medical professionals adequately accommodated the healing that goes on, or should go on, within the patient's social world of friends and family with the awareness of the impending death of a loved one. For these and other reasons, the hospice movement in U.S. medicine is producing the kinds of change in medical institutions described here.

This selection is a personal account by Wade K. Smith, M.D., director of the Comprehensive Cancer Center, Hunter Holmes McGuire VAMC, in Richmond, Virginia. In it Smith describes how a group of health care administrators and practitioners planned, developed, and organized one of the first hospices to be built from the ground up in the Veterans Administration hospital system. He provides a glimpse of some of the joys and frustrations of creating a hospice within a system that was not originally designed to accommodate the needs of dying patients and their families.

The care of dying patients, especially those with cancer and other chronic, often painful diseases, requires an emphasis on relieving pain and suffering, honestly communicating possible outcomes and treatment results, nourishing and sustaining relationships with family and friends, reaffirming the value of the life of the dying person, allowing them to reassume control of the fundamental decisions affecting their lives, avoiding inappropriate and futile medical treatments, and providing support for their family and friends during bereavement after the patient's death. Hospitals have performed well in improving the outcome of acute episodes of illness, but the health care system generally has not met the needs of dying patients and their families. However, hospice, a term used to describe both the institution and the concept of palliative care, has developed rapidly to meet this need. A hospice program "is a centrally administered program of palliative and supportive services which provides physical, psychological, social and spiritual care for dying persons and their families" (National Hospice Organization, Standards of a Hospice Program of Care, Washington, D.C., 1979). What follows is a personal view of one hospice program's beginnings and challenges.

Eric Cassel (1982) reminds us that suffering is caused not only by physical pain but by the perception that the integrity of the person is threatened. Persons are complex, and "all the aspects of personhood—the lived past, the family's lived past, culture and society, roles, the instrumental dimension, associations and relationships, the body, the unconscious mind, the political being, the secret life, the perceived future, and the transcendent dimension—are susceptible to damage and loss. Injuries to the integrity of the person may be expressed by sadness, anger, loneliness, depression, grief, unhappiness, melancholy, rage, withdrawal, or yearning. . . . We know little about the nature of the injuries themselves, and what we know has been learned largely from literature, not medicine. . . . If the injury is sufficient, the person suffers. The only way to learn what damage is sufficient to cause suffering, or whether suffering is present, is to ask the sufferer."

For the physician, nurse, chaplain, social worker, psychologist, or administrator used to functioning in an acute or chronic care facility, hospice care requires a fundamental shift in one's frame of reference. Caring not cure, symptom relief not reversal of the underlying disease process become the concern and goal. Previously the relationship of physician and patients was but part of the cure; now it becomes the principal healing force available to the physician; the relationship of the family and friends with the patient becomes more important; and the quality, not the duration of life is the measure of successful care.

On November 8, 1991, the Comprehensive Cancer Center at the Hunter Holmes McGuire VAMC in Richmond, Virginia, dedicated a new wing housing a twelve-bed inpatient hospice service, a home hospice service serving veterans within a fifty-mile radius and consultative services to inpatient units and outpatient clinics at our 816-bed tertiary care facility. All of us involved felt that we had travelled a long road. Beginning in 1974 the Medical College of Virginia, with which we have

The views expressed here are those of the author and do not necessarily represent the policy of the U.S. Department of Veterans Affairs. Reprinted by permission of the author.

been affiliated (as a Dean's Committee Veterans Administration Medical Center) since the 1940s, established Cancer Rehabilitation and Continuing Care Teams to provide comprehensive, coordinated, and continuous care for cancer patients in the hospital and at home, from diagnosis to death or rehabilitation. Many of us at McGuire also worked at the University Hospital and knew the value of hospice home care services. When I was asked to develop a Hematology and Medical Oncology program at McGuire in 1981, I began to explore the possibility of providing hospice care. My colleagues in medicine, surgery, radiation therapy, oncology nursing, social work, psychology, psychiatry, clinical pharmacy, and administration all saw the need and enthusiastically invested their time, advice, effort, and support.

The process seemed endless! In 1978 a Joint Subcommittee of the Senate and General Assembly of the Commonwealth of Virginia had met and recommended regulations for hospice care which were subsequently adopted. About 1981 an outstanding hospice program was developed at the Hampton Virginia VAMC only a hundred miles away. Home hospice and a few inpatient programs were developed in the community and interest at our facility was high. The time appeared ripe. In 1983 the first of two planning committees at McGuire recommended establishment of a combined inpatient and home hospice program, but funding could not be secured. Then in 1985 the provision of hospice programs was addressed by the Veterans Administration Central Office and standards establishing hospice/palliative care as a component of Comprehensive Cancer Center programs were developed. In 1988 a Comprehensive Cancer Center at McGuire was formed to provide tertiary level cancer care for the five Veterans Medical Centers serving most of Virginia and West Virginia. In 1987 a second planning committee again recommended a combined home and inpatient hospice program and proposed several sites for the building. This time funding was available and our work began in earnest. The committee planned the current facility and program, lobbied everyone in sight, and met with the contractors bidding on the job.

We asked a great deal from the hospital staff and service chiefs. To my amazement and delight, everyone responded. Hospice strikes a very personal note in the lives of most people, and the commitment of the entire medical center was and is heartfelt and effective. We broke ground in a cold rain on Veterans Day in 1989.

In January 1991 Denise Coleman, R.N., M.S.N., who had extensive administrative and clinical oncology experience, was chosen as coordinator and immediately began to develop and run the program. Using positions shared with Medicine, Social Work, and Chaplain Service, we operate 6 beds and see about 4 to 8 home patients as well as providing hands-on assistance to acute and chronic care inpatient units. A class of volunteers was trained and works actively with staff. We have evaluated several hundred veterans, accepted over a hundred as inpatients or for home care, and consulted on more. A bereavement group has been formed to assist the families of deceased patients. The group, made up of friends and surviving family members, meets weekly to discuss the problems—financial, emotional, and medical—encountered after the loss of a loved one. A chaplain, a social worker, and a psychologist participate in the meetings.

In short, we are providing a badly needed service which has been very well received by staff, patients, families, and administration. All Department of Veterans Affairs Medical Centers are now under mandate to provide hospice services within the next few years. We are gratified at the acceptance of the program but realize that the integration of hospice into an overall program of cancer control and treatment will require our continuing effort for years to come.

There remain challenges. From the vantage point of a year and a half of operation, it is clear that we underestimated the problems of integrating the hospice concept into a large bureaucratic institution. Hospice care is quantitatively as well as qualitatively different from both the acute and extended care models familiar to American physicians. The modern hospice movement in the United States arose in response to the failure of the clinic, office, and hospital to meet the full needs of terminally ill patients and their families. Indeed, in some areas—provision of adequate regular pain medication, integration of the family into the care of the patient, maintenance of a homelike setting—these same institutions often stood in the way of palliating the patient's suffering. Moreover, the unit of care is the family—a marked change in the focus of care in the VA system, which is authorized by Congress to provide care only for eligible veterans.

There continue to be severe problems obtaining funding for staff in a time of governmental cutbacks. At present we do not have funding to staff our full twelve-bed inpatient and supporting home care program, adding to the stress inherent in hospice work. We are saddened to have a waiting list and to have patients dying before we can admit them to our program.

Continuity of care by the patient's physician is an essential feature of successful hospice programs—yet academic training programs are usually discontinuous and short term; we share faculty, houseofficers, and students with our parent university hospital, usually by monthly rotations between wards at one of the other locations. We have deliberately chosen to require that physicians referring patients to our hospice program continue to care for them rather than turn them over to a full-time hospice physician in the program. Some physicians have been eager to do so, others feel poorly equipped to do so, and many are not available to do so because of our system of rotating schedules.

We have yet to fully integrate our institutional educational mission into the hospice. While we clearly need to train health care professionals in the care of the dying, surprisingly little was written about the role of the hospice in the training of health care professionals until recently. As a major clinical and research affiliate of a large academic medical center, teaching a variety of health care students at varying stages of training is an important facet of our mission. In fact, at the national level the VA system is a significant source of training funds as well as a major site for undergraduate and postgraduate medical and nursing education. Thus, our ability to train health care practitioners to care for the dying patient in a hospice program will be increasingly important.

Integration of hospice experience into the curriculum is difficult for a number of reasons outlined by Scott and MacDonald (1993), including a philosophical focus on the diagnosis, investigation, and cure of disease (and pathophysiology, I would add) rather than relief of symptoms and suffering; failure to emphasize the development of communication and interpersonal skills along with knowledge of disease; lack of stature as an independent academic discipline with its own political clout; lack of visible role models in most teaching centers; and lack of curriculum time. It is very encouraging that the need to teach palliative care principles and skills at all levels of health care education is increasingly recognized and has begun to be seriously addressed. A 16-hour clinical rotation, later expanded to 24 hours, at the St. Anthony's Hospice and Life Enrichment Program in Amarillo, Texas, was established for medical students at Texas Tech University Health Sciences Center in 1986 (Knight et al.). Programs for training of physicians at the undergraduate level in Canada and postgraduate levels in Australia, Great Britain, and the United States, post-basic course training of nurses, seminary courses, and programs in some schools of Social Work are in place and appear to be increasing in number (Corner, 1993; Sheldon, 1993; Murray, 1993). However, most health care practitioners are exposed to hospice care through articles, short courses, seminars, lectures and "on-the-job training programs."

Not surprisingly, the group of trainees we have been most successful in integrating into the care of our patients has been our hematology/medical oncology fellows—the group of post-graduate medical trainees who have completed their undergraduate medical education (4 years) and their postgraduate training in internal medicine (3–4 years), and are now engaged in caring for cancer patients over a period of three to four years of fellowship. They wish to manage their dying patients in hospice, are familiar with the hospice concept, expect to work with hospice professionals once they finish training, and often have had the experience of seeing first hand the disastrous effects that uncontrolled pain or poor psychosocial support has on the dying patient and his or her family.

Finally, our major challenge is the acceptance of death as a natural part of life, by ourselves, by our patients, by families, and by our culture. In his marvelous oration to the Massachusetts Medical Society in 1976 on caring for the cancer patient, the eminent surgeon J. Englebert Dunphy noted the equanimity achieved by many dying individuals and quotes the Harvard microbiologist Hans Zinser who, after learning he had cancer, wrote this:

> Now is death merciful. He calls me hence
> Gently, with friendly soothing of my fears
> Of ugly age and feeble impotence
> And cruel disintegration of slow years.
> Nor does he leap upon me unaware
> Like some wild beast that hungers for its prey,
> But gives me kindly warning to prepare:
> Before I go, to kiss the tears away.
> How sweet the summer! And the autumn shone
> Like warmth within our hearts as in the sky,
> Ripening rich harvests that our love had sown.
> How good that 'ere the winter comes, I die!
> Then, ageless, in your heart I'll come to rest
> Serene and proud, as when you loved me best.*

*Abstracted from information appearing in *NEJM:* Poem by Hans Zinser, in J. Englebert Dunphy, "Annual Discourse—On Caring for the Patient with Cancer," *New England Journal of Medicine,* 1976 (295):313–319.

We built our hospice to ameliorate pain and suffering, as a place where patients could transcend the threats to their persons and live until the moment of death as fully as possible. While hospice does indeed affirm life, it also places our cancer program and our medical center in perspective. It is all right to lose a patient to death. It is not our failure or their failure or their families' and friends' failure. We all are now a little bit more free and a little bit more human.

NOTES

CASSEL, E. J.   1982. The Nature of Suffering and the Goals of Medicine. *N. Engl. J. Med.* 306:639–645.

CORNER, J.   The Nursing Perspective. In Doyle, D., Hanks, G. W. C., and MacDonald, N. (ed.)., *Oxford Textbook of Palliative Medicine,* Oxford University Press, New York, 1993, 781–790.

DUNPHY, J. E.   1976. Annual Discourse—On Caring for the Patient with Cancer. *N. Engl. J. Med.* 295:313–319.

KNIGHT, C. F., KNIGHT, P. F., GELLULA, M. H., and HOLMAN, G. H.   Training Our Future Physicians: A Hospice Rotation for Medical Students. *Amer. J. Hospice and Palliative Care,* 1992, 9:23–28.

MURRAY, D. B.   Education and Training of Clergy in Palliative Care. In Doyle, D., Hanks, G. W. C., and MacDonald, N. (ed.)., *Oxford Textbook of Palliative Medicine,* Oxford University Press, New York, 1993, 795–799.

SCOTT, J. F., and MACDONALD, N.   Education in Palliative Medicine. In Doyle, D., Hanks, G. W. C., and MacDonald, N. (ed.)., *Oxford Textbook of Palliative Medicine,* Oxford University Press, New York, 1993, 761–780.

SHELDON, F.   Education and Training for Social Workers in Palliative Care. In Doyle, D., Hanks, G. W. C., and MacDonald, N. (ed.), *Oxford Textbook of Palliative Medicine,* Oxford University Press, New York, 1993, 791–795.

26

REFORMING OUR HEALTH CARE SYSTEM: A PHYSICIAN'S PERSPECTIVE

Arnold S. Relman, M.D.

The need for major changes in the American system of funding and organizing health care will be debated for at least the first half of the 1990s. Most likely the U.S. government will develop strategies for reducing the number of Americans who lack health insurance, limiting the cost of health care, and promoting comprehensive health maintenance organizations (HMOs). Given the diversity of interests involved and their intense lobbying efforts, it is unlikely that the United States will soon develop a single-payer system like the highly successful Canadian system. In consequence, inequalities in access to health care are likely to continue. But not all of those inequalities will be due to the system of care alone. Many health care problems stem from the widespread tendency of Americans to neglect their health in a variety of ways, including smoking, drug use, poor diet, and failure to make use of available medical care.

As we attempt to follow the complex debate about reform of the U.S. health care system, the plain speaking of expert but objective health professionals is of great value. An example is this overview of health care problems and possible solutions by Arnold S. Relman, M.D., a professor of medicine and social medicine at Harvard Medical School and former editor-in-chief of the prestigious *New England Journal of Medicine,* and an astute observer of the health care controversy. Although the solutions he proposes are somewhat closer to the Canadian single-payer model than those proposed by the Clinton administration, many of the points he raises in this dispassionate review of the issues are at the center of the debate over health care reform.

As almost everyone knows by now, we Americans spend huge sums of money on health care. This year we will spend about $800 billion (more than $3,000 per capita), and the cost of rising at about 8 or 9 percent per year—a rate that simply cannot be sustained. Our outlay for health is nearly one-quarter higher than Sweden's or Canada's, two-thirds more than Japan's, and almost twice as much as Britain's. About 13 percent of our entire economy is devoted to health care.

Despite this enormous expenditure, we do not seem to be getting our money's worth. We cannot provide health insurance for about 15 percent of our population, and an equal number of Americans are insured only part of the time. Most people who do have health insurance are inadequately protected against serious long-term illness or disability.

Furthermore, as judged by conventional measures of public health we don't fare very well. Infant mortality in 1990 (number of deaths under one year of age per 1,000 births) was 10.4 in the United States, compared with 7.3 in Canada and Britain, 5.9 in Sweden, and 4.5 in Japan. Life expectancy was 75.6 years in the United States, compared with 79.3 in Japan, 79.2 in Canada, 77.7 in Sweden, and 76.3 in Britain. In the United States, only 70 percent of one-year-old children are fully immunized against diphtheria, measles, and poliomyelitis; the comparable figure in Sweden is 97 percent; in Canada, 85 percent; in Japan, 84 percent; and in Britain, 78 percent.

If all the money we now spend on health care isn't buying us adequate insurance coverage or such important health benefits as longer life expectancy, lower infant mortality, and better infant immunization, what does it buy?

Before answering that question, I should say something about the relation of public health to medical care because there is widespread misunderstanding of this point. The general level of public health in a country, as measured by such things as life expectancy and infant mortality, is not a good indicator of the effectiveness of its medical care system. The public's health depends much more on genetic and cultural characteristics and environmental factors than on the quality of its medical care. In the United States, unhealthy life-styles and widespread drug abuse, violence, teenage pregnancy, and other manifestations of social pathology damage the health of many people, and these problems are not much affected by medical treatment.

Physicians can diagnose disease and sometimes save or prolong life, particularly when the problem is acute. They can comfort and reassure patients and can relieve symptoms, thereby improving the quality of life. But none of these services, valuable as they may be, is likely to affect the general level of the public's health as much as measures aimed at improving the social environment and behavior of people. To improve general life expectancy and infant mortality significantly, we need to improve the housing, education, and economic condition of our urban and rural poor. That task is beyond the reach of medicine.

Arnold S. Relman, M.D., "Reforming Our Health Care System: A Physician's Perspective," *The Key Reporter* (Autumn 1992), pp. 1–5.

AN ASSESSMENT OF OUR SYSTEM

What then does all the money spent on health care really buy? The short answer is that it buys what modern medicine has to offer—but with the encumbrances of a system that wastes enormous amounts of money on marginal, duplicative, and unnecessary services and on nonessential overhead costs. And because of this waste and inefficiency, we cannot afford to provide even basic essential services to all our people.

At its best, the quality of specialized medical care in the United States is unexcelled. The sophistication of our medical technology and the competence of our specialists are the envy of the world. For people who can afford it, the United States offers the best of highly specialized (tertiary) care and an abundance of facilities and personnel. We have more cardiac surgery, bone-marrow transplantation, joint replacement, and MRI (magnetic resonance imaging) units per capita than any other country, and we have no waiting lines for these or other technologically advanced services—provided, of course, that the patients or their insurers are able to pay. But most poor and uninsured people have little or no access to this expensive kind of tertiary care.

An even more serious deficiency in our present system is inadequate access to relatively low cost general (primary) care from family physicians, general internists, and general pediatricians. Everyone should have a primary-care physician who establishes an ongoing relationship with patients, handles most ordinary medical complaints, and advises on the need for consultation with specialists. Without oversight by a primary physician, medical care is often fragmented and uncoordinated. Lack of primary care is a problem for everyone in the United States, not just the poor, because our medical care system is now dominated by specialists, and generalists are in short supply. The number of practicing physicians has increased in the past 20 years from 153 to more than 220 per 100,000 population, but the great majority of the new doctors are specialists. About three-quarters of all physicians in this country now limit their practices to a specialty.

There are many reasons why specialty practice has so greatly overshadowed primary care in the United States, but two of the most important are the greater number of graduate specialty programs in our teaching hospitals and the more attractive economic rewards available to specialists. In most other countries, at least half the physicians are generalists, and specialists are usually seen only through referral. A system like ours, which for the most part does not require or encourage patients to see a generalist before going to a specialist, uses far more tertiary services and therefore is far more costly than systems in other countries (such as Canada, Germany, and Britain) that emphasize primary care and encourage the training of primary-care physicians.

The huge costs of U.S. health care can be attributed to many factors in addition to its domination by specialists. Probably the most important of these is our payment system. The prevalence of open-ended funding through indemnity insurance and fee-for-service reimbursement of doctors and hospitals is a powerful stimulus to provide extra services of all kinds, including many that are of marginal benefit. Although a growing number of Americans (about 40 million) get their health care through prepaid contracts with health maintenance organizations (HMOs), most people are still covered by insurance that pays the bills submitted by hospitals and doctors on a piecework basis. Discounting of bills and management of medical services through various kinds of utilization-review programs are becoming increasingly common as third-party payers struggle to contain their costs, but the fact remains that the majority of insured Americans are still covered for whatever services their physicians choose to provide, without much limitation of total cost.

Increasing competition for patients whose insurance pays on a fee-for-service basis leads practitioners to promote their services like businesses in a competitive commercial market. The continued increase in the number of physicians per capita serves only to magnify this problem. Given the economic incentives favoring specialty practice and the use of expensive tests and procedures, the growth of the physician population inevitably increases expenditures for medical care. Advertising and marketing are now accepted practices, not only among physicians but among hospitals and ambulatory-care facilities as well. Hospitals, overbuilt in many areas of the country, also feel pressures to increase their volume of services in order to remain financially solvent in a hostile and competitive marketplace. Managers of not-for-profit voluntary hospitals now tend to regard themselves as chief executive officers of struggling businesses, and they often pay more attention to their bottom line than to their responsibilities as stewards of community-based social service institutions.

Also contributing greatly to this change in the orientation of medical care is another uniquely American phenomenon that first appeared in the late 1960s and is now a pervasive, highly influential feature of our system. Investor-owned facilities—chains of hospitals and nursing homes—first arose in response to the opportunities for profit created by Medicare, Medicaid, and the spread of employer-financed health insurance coverage. More recently, as acute-care hospitals have felt the growing pressures from third-party payers, investor-owned corporations have turned to psychiatric care, HMOs, free-standing diagnostic facilities, and a great variety of ambulatory services, where profits are easier to find.

There are no accurate data, but I estimate that at least one-quarter, and perhaps one-third or more, of all the money spent on medical care now goes to investor-owned facilities. Like any business, these organizations seek to enhance their revenues by promoting the use of their profitable services and products. They use all the marketing and advertising techniques employed in ordinary commerce, and they solicit the cooperation of practicing physicians by offering joint ventures and special favors. Not-for-profit hospitals, feeling the competition, do likewise. Doctors sense this transformation, and they recognize the threat posed by a growing physician population and the constraints applied by third-party payers. They are therefore increasingly willing to exploit the opportunities for commercial profit in the goods, services, and facilities they use or recommend for their patients—something that was generally considered unethical a generation ago.

In short, our health-care system, formerly a social service that was the responsibility of dedicated professionals and not-for-profit facilities, has become a vast, profit-oriented industry. The revenue of this industry constitutes the country's health-care costs. As in any other industry, providers constantly strive to increase their profitable sales, but unlike other industries, consumers exercise little control over their consumption of products and services. It should not be surprising that such a system is afflicted not only with relentless inflation but also with neglect of the needs of the uninsured and with failure to promote the use of valuable but unprofitable health services.

Other factors combine with these economic forces to increase the volume and intensity of services and thereby to raise costs. Uncertainty about the effectiveness of many tests, drugs, and treatments leaves much room for individual professional opinion. This situation makes it easier for physicians to follow their own habits and preferences instead of generally accepted professional guidelines derived from rigorous clinical trials and careful technology assessment. There is a dearth of reliable information about the effectiveness of many kinds of medical technology. New drugs, tests, devices, and procedures are introduced far more rapidly than they can be critically evaluated and compared with existing technology. As a result, the use of tests and procedures varies greatly from place to place, without any clear relationship to medical need. In addition, fear of malpractice suits often impels physicians to order extra diagnostic tests simply to protect themselves against possible future litigation. Many doctors also feel pressured by the expectations and demands of patients who have been led to believe that modern medicine can perform miracles and who therefore expect that no effort will be spared, even when the best professional judgment would suggest a conservative approach.

Whenever the issue has been examined by panels of experts, it appears that between 15 and 30 percent of all tests and procedures performed in this country are not medically indicated, and a similar proportion are only marginally justifiable. How much all this contributes to the cost of care is hard to quantify, but we do know that increasing volume and intensity of services account for about half of the annual rate of expansion of medical costs after correction for general inflation.

The other half of the increase is due to rising medical (as opposed to general) prices, which reflect the inefficiency and high overhead costs of our medical system. Far more than in any other country, health-care providers and insurers in the United States spend huge sums on the handling and review of claims; on marketing, advertising, management, and financial services; and on general corporate overhead. At least 12 to 15 percent of the premiums paid to our 1,200 competing private medical insurance companies is used for these kinds of expenses. The typical office-based, practicing physician spends 40 to 45 percent of gross revenue on office expenses, particularly billing and collecting and malpractice premiums.

Adding the estimated costs of all this overhead to the costs of unnecessary, marginal, and duplicated services leads me to the following conclusion: At least a third of all the money we now spend on medical care in this country could be saved in a rational and better-organized system without loss of medical effectiveness—and quite possibly with substantial overall benefit to patients. The money saved would probably be enough to provide essential care for all those people now not insured and to insure everyone against the costs of long-term care. The primary need is not more money but a better system.

I believe that the key to controlling costs and providing universal coverage is to change the medical care delivery system, while simplifying and consolidating the insurance system. To achieve the latter, I favor some form of single-payer arrangement administered by quasi-public agencies in each state or economic region. These agencies initially could pool funds from all present sources (government, employers, private insurance companies, and individuals), and each could act as the sole paymaster in its region. Ultimately, all funding should come from tax revenue, but that arrangement would have to evolve gradually, after experience with the system had allowed some better estimates of costs and further public discussion of the best ways to distribute them. Federal regulation would set a fixed per capita payment for a defined range of comprehensive services, with appropriate adjustments for regional differences in cost of living. All citizens would be covered, regardless of age, employment, or health status. Medicare and Medicaid would disappear, to be folded into the total federal and state government contributions for the elderly, the poor, and the uninsured.

Increased expenditures would be initially required to cover people who now lack insurance. In such a reformed delivery system the additional cost would probably be $40 to $50 billion. How the expense would be divided between government and employers would be a political decision, but in any case a new, efficient system would produce big future savings for all payers.

The providers would be federally qualified group-model HMOs. They would compete for members, but not on the basis of price, because the price would be fixed for each region by the single payer. To qualify, the HMOs would have to be not-for-profit and owned by a board elected by the members. Physicians would be organized into self-managed multispecialty groups that would negotiate for their budget with the HMO board. Within the allotted budget, physicians would be paid salaries as determined by their own peer management. They would participate in the assessment of technology and would keep standardized records to be used in the evaluation of outcomes. Physicians would receive no bonuses or other financial incentives that might influence their advice to patients.

Any net revenue earned by the HMO would be used at the board's discretion for the improvement of facilities. The business management of the HMO, like the physician group, would be accountable to the board. The board, the business management, and the physician group would work together to provide high-quality care that would attract new members and maintain their loyalty. Members would be free to move at specified intervals to any other qualified HMO in the region. All HMOs in the region would have to operate within the same fixed total budget, but each would be free to decide on the allocation of its funds.

The payment received by the HMOs would include the cost of hospitalization, for which the HMOs would be responsible. Each HMO would either own its own hospital or contract with local hospitals on a per diem basis. In any case, there would be a strong incentive for hospitals and HMOs to work together to control hospital costs. Indeed, many new HMOs would probably form around existing community hospitals, with the hospital medical staff making up the nucleus of the medical group.

The medical groups would employ an approximately equal number of generalists and specialists, because this mix has been found optimal in the largest and most successful group-model HMOs and in countries with comprehensive universal insurance plans. Although salary differences among the different specialists would remain, these would be less than the income differences in private practice. Competitive salaries plus attractive fringe benefits, opportunities for continuing education, protection against malpractice litigation, and the opportunity to concentrate on the practice of medicine without worrying about the problems of setting up and managing a private office would undoubtedly appeal to many young physicians.

The development of many new HMOs of this kind would require assistance from the federal government. Low-interest loans to pay for start-up costs and a reinsurance system to protect against unusual medical risks would be needed; antitrust regulation would have to be modified to allow arrangements that might otherwise be viewed as restraint of trade. With federal assistance, state health-care systems based on these principles could be established on a trial basis before being implemented nationwide.

The economic effect on physicians would probably be fairly benign because the total amount of net income received by physicians would not change significantly, although there would certainly be some redistribution among the specialties. The most important change in life-style for doctors would be an exchange of their traditional independence as solo practitioners for a new career in group practice in which they would be subject to continuous peer review by their colleagues. Of course, some doctors might still prefer to continue solo practice in the fee-for-service mode. They should be allowed that choice, but they would have to find enough patients who could afford to pay them on that basis. Because such patients would become increasingly hard to find, I suspect that relatively few physicians would choose independent practice in the future. There already is evidence that growing numbers of new physicians are opting for group practice arrangements.

The success of these medical groups would depend not only on how well they satisfied the professional needs of their physicians, but also on whether they provided cost-effective medical care. As judged by patient satisfaction, professional morale, and cost control, many existing HMOs are successful, and there is no basic reason why their example could not be widely copied in the future.

Would most patients be satisfied with their care in the system I envision? The answer depends on how well the HMOs would be managed and how sensitive they would be to patients' needs and desires. If HMOs had to compete for patients not on price but on quality, and if they were controlled by boards representing the members, patient satisfaction would probably be high. Even so, some patients undoubtedly would want occasionally to consult specialists or to obtain services not available in their HMO. They should be allowed this so-called point-of-service option if they are willing to pay the additional costs. Some patients might not wish to join an HMO, preferring instead to pay for their own indemnity insurance plan. That option also should be available, although the expense would probably deter all but a small fraction of the population.

I see no reason to object to this kind of "two-tiered" system provided most people used the reformed and subsidized part of the system, thereby ensuring that its quality would be protected by the common interest of the public and the medical profession. Our present multitiered system provides inadequate care, or no care at all, for a large segment of our society.

BENEFITS OF THE NEW SYSTEM

A system of the kind I have proposed is not guaranteed to contain costs, but there are many reasons to believe that it would. All the unnecessary expenditures in our present system, which I outlined earlier, would be eliminated or greatly reduced. Covering the vast majority of Americans under a fixed per capita payment system would for the first time put a virtual cap on total health-care spending and its rate of increase. Any spending beyond this cap would be the result of consumers' exercising their point-of-service option within the HMO system or choosing alternative or supplementary indemnification insurance. These additional costs would be directly paid by consumers with their own resources rather than by third-party payers. There would be no further drain on public monies or on the resources of private businesses, and therefore no further exacerbation of the cost crisis.

This system would promote a much more prudent use of medical services; useless or very marginal tests and procedures would be minimized. Appropriate assessment of promising but unproven technology would be much easier to carry out and could be required before the technology could be introduced into general use. Clinical practice would be continually improved by the systematic collection of outcome results, which would help physicians make better decisions and patients make more informed choices. Fear of malpractice suits, which often leads physicians to order excessive tests, would be reduced because of the protection afforded by peer review and the assumption of legal responsibility by the HMOs.

I believe that the savings in such a system, when fully realized, would be large enough to allow the use of all services that good physicians might recommend and well-informed patients would want. This doesn't mean we could afford to subsidize everything—only what made medical sense. Of course, there is no way to know how long the costs could be kept under control. The initial savings and operational efficiencies of a reformed system might ultimately be eroded by continued expensive technological developments and an insatiable public demand for more medical services. But healthier lifestyles, improved social conditions, and scientific advances in prevention and treatment could reduce the future burden of disease sufficiently to keep the health-care costs of a reformed system under control indefinitely. I am optimistic about our ability to achieve that goal, but only if we institute major reform now.

An efficient, equitable, and universal health-care delivery system, instituted during the next few years, not only would solve our present problems but would give us the resources and ensure the public support that long-term solutions will require. Without major reform now, our health-care system can only go from bad to worse, and the present crisis will turn to chaos.

27
POSTSCRIPT

Richard Titmuss

Richard Titmuss was one of the founders of the field of medical sociology and an inspiring sociological thinker. In his research and writing on the sociology of blood donation systems in the United Kingdom and elsewhere, he viewed blood collection as a social system of giving and receiving among strangers. In *The Gift Relationship* he presented an effective argument for voluntarism and cooperation rather than competition and profit in vital medical systems like blood collection. He also predicted the problems that would eventually arise in the more market-based U.S. system with the advent of the AIDS epidemic. As the United States moved away from reliance on voluntary donation and more of its blood supply was purchased from donors, it seemed likely to Titmuss that problems of security and possible contamination would increase. His larger theoretical point, however, was that the market is not the best institution for regulating supply and demand when questions of the health of the entire society are involved.

In this short postscript to his book *Social Policy,* in which he analyzed and defended the British Health Service, Titmuss describes the period just before his own death. Despite his impending decline, he was gratified to find evidence of social growth in the treatment he and his fellow patients received. By that he meant the evidence of care and compassion in a public social system. Of course, the system is flawed, the phones are antiquated, the attendants can be officious. But the care is dispensed with professional and human concern for the individual, and there are no evident inequalities of race or class, or at least not such blatant ones as are often encountered in other societies, including our own.

I was sitting on a bench with five other people in the outpatient visiting space of the Radiotherapy Department of the Westminster Hospital in London. We were all booked in by appointment at 10 o'clock daily week after week to go into a room called the Theratron Room. I'll explain what that means a bit later on. Next to me on the bench there was a harassed middle-aged woman, married to a postman, who had two children and who lived somewhere near a ghastly part of London called Tooting Broadway. She, like the others, had been brought to the Westminster Hospital by ambulance. She was suffering from cancer of the pelvis.

We talked, as we talked every morning, amongst ourselves and about ourselves and she suddenly said to me, 'You know, the doctors say I should rest as much as I can but I really can't do so.' I said to her, 'Why not?' And she said, 'Well, you see I haven't dared tell the neighbours that I've got cancer. They think it's infectious. Anyway, it's not very respectable, is it, to have cancer?' And then she said, 'You wouldn't tell your students would you?' By then, of course, she knew me and she knew I came from a strange, peculiar place called the London School of Economics where she thought a lot of strange, peculiar students had a lovely time at the tax-payers' expense. My answer to her was, 'Of course. Of course I would tell them; why shouldn't I use six-letter words? They can use four-letter words. Don't you know cancer is not infectious? And it is respectable. Even professors get cancer.' So you see I had to keep a promise I gave her before Christmas.

For many months last year I had experienced an acute, frustrating and annoying pain in my right shoulder and my right arm. This prevented me from doing a lot of things I wanted to do. And, incidentally, it made it difficult for me to concentrate. It began long before the examination period and you know there is one rule that I think students might think about which is that no professor or any teacher at the university who is suffering from any kind of pain (perhaps stress is a better word) should be allowed to mark examination scripts. Anyway, apart from all that, through my local National Health Service general practitioner and my local hospital I went through a series of X-rays, tests of various kinds and they all came out with the answer that my trouble was muscular skeletal—something which the doctors in their shorthand called a 'frozen shoulder.' Later I learned that there is considerable doubt about the causes or cures or reasons for 'frozen shoulders', just as there is about a condition known as 'low back pain' among the working classes. However, with this diagnosis I was fed into the physiotherapy department of our local hospital where I did exercises. I underwent very painful treatment of various kinds and in spite of all this and doing what I was told the pain got worse and it wouldn't go away.

Eventually, and to cut a long story short, I found myself being admitted as a National Health Service patient at 3 o'clock on Saturday, the 30th of September 1972, as an inpatient at the Westminster Hospital. Admission on a Saturday afternoon seemed to me to be very odd but I did as I was told and I was informed that if I came in on a Saturday afternoon a lot of tests and X-rays could be done on me and all would be ready for the arrival of the great men—the consultants—on Monday morning. On the Sunday, the following day, I didn't have any visitors. My wife had had to put up with a lot from me for weeks and months beforehand and so I wouldn't let her come and see me on the Sunday. By about 8 o'clock on the Sunday evening I decided that I would like to talk to her on the telephone. By then I had learned from the nursing staff that there was such a thing as a mobile telephone which could be dragged round the ward, plugged in and then you could have a private conversation. So I got hold of the mobile telephone and tried to get through. But every time I tried I found myself on a crossed line with another man talking to somebody else on the same line. After about ten to fifteen minutes a door opened from a side room near me where I was in the ward, a side room which was used on occasion for amenity patients or private patients. The door opened and out of it came a human being about three feet five inches high in the shape of a question mark. He couldn't raise his head but in a quiet voice he said to me, 'Can I help you? You're having trouble with the telephone.' So I said, 'Yes, I can't get through; I want to talk to my wife.' And he said, 'But don't you know, there are three telephones on the third floor of this ward with the same number so you are probably talking to a patient at the other end of the corridor who is probably also talking to his wife.' Well, that cleared that one up.

The man who came to help me—let's call him Bill—I got to know very well. He was aged 53. In 1939, at the age of 19, he was an apprentice engineer in Portsmouth and he was called up for the Army at the outbreak of war. In 1942 Bill got married. In 1943 he and his wife had a son, their only child. In 1944 Bill was blown up in the desert by Rommel and his back was broken in about six places. Somehow or other in 1944 in a military hospital they put him together again and he eventually came under the responsibility of a war pensioners' hospital attached to the Westminster. Since the National Health Service came into operation in 1948 Bill has spent varying periods from two to four or five weeks every year at the Westminster Hospital receiving the latest micro developments for the care and rehabilitation of people like Bill. He has never worked.

Bill and I one night worked out roughly what he had cost the National Health Service since 1948. When he was due for treatment, they sent for him by ambulance from Portsmouth where he lived in a council house and they took him back. The amount was something like a quarter of a million pounds. Now Bill was a passionate gardener—that was one of his great interests in life. While I was at the Westminster a book was published by a friend of mine, Pat Hamilton [Lady Hamilton of the Disabled Living Foundation]. This book called *Gardening for the Disabled* is a great help to seriously disabled people in carrying on a hobby like gardening. Within two days of the book's publication the mobile voluntarily-staffed library at the Westminster Hospital, remembering Bill's interest in gardening, sent up to him the book to read. Bill in his side room was equipped with a small television set. I joined him because while I was in the Westminster the Labour Party Conference was being held in Blackpool and I attended it, at least in spirit, most of the time. It wasn't easy to concentrate. A hospital ward between the hours of about 8 o'clock in the morning and 6 o'clock in the evening is as busy with traffic as Piccadilly Circus.

There is always somebody coming in to do something. There's the mobile shop that turns up twice a day; there is the mobile library that turns up once a day; there are the people who come in to take your temperature, the student nurse who brings you the menu card for the next twenty-four hours and comes to collect it after you've decided between roast beef and chicken *vol-au-vent* for supper tomorrow; the people who come in to give you clean water; there is the lady from Brixton, homesick for Trinidad, who brings in a very noisy vacuum cleaner. And when I said to her, 'Please, take it away, Bill and I are really very clean, we haven't got any dust under the bed and the Common Market debate is going on. It's the Labour Party Conference in Blackpool,' she said, 'What's the Common Market anyway—never heard of it—I've got my job to do.' Eventually I persuaded her to leave us alone in peace to follow the infighting going on in Blackpool.

After the hospital had taken about eighteen pictures from various angles of my shoulder and I had gone through a lot of other tests, I was told that what was causing all the trouble was what looked like dry rot in the top of my ribs. So they had to operate. They operated and then they had to have a conference to obtain the right histological classification of cancer. Before the operation and after the operation I had a seminar (with official permission of course) with the nursing students and I had a seminar with the medical students of one of the consultants. Somehow or other it had become known in the ward that I had written a book about blood and that I came from this strange place at LSE where many of my students became social workers. Inevitably, I was asked: What do social workers actually do? What *is* a social administrator? Two days after my operation I was allowed by the medical staff, by the house officers and the registrars, by the hierarchy in general to go down to the 'Paviour's Arms' with some of the old-age pensioners where they had a pint of beer at 7 o'clock in the evening and I had a whisky. And I was also allowed to go out to a little restaurant in Ebury Street for dinner with friends and members of the staff of the Social Administration Department. So you see hospitals are flexible and this is an area where the middle classes can often get the best out of the social services. I am, I suppose, middle class. I am, I suppose, articulate whereas many of the patients are not.

After my discharge as an inpatient from the Westminster Hospital it was rather a moving experience because some of the staff of the Supplementary Benefits Commission had sent me a sort of miniature Rochford rockery and, in a little ceremony in the ward, I handed over the rockery to Bill and the staff were arranging for it to go home with him to Portsmouth and I also handed over copies of my book, *The Gift Relationship,* to the Nurses' Library and the Medical Students' Library. I think one of the best compliments I was paid as an inpatient was when I was helping two of the student nurses to make my bed one morning. They knew where I came from—they thought I was an authority on matters of this kind—and they said to me, 'We've been having an argument in the hostel about the right age to get married. What do you think, Professor? When do you think young people should get married?' Well, I really had no answer—all I could say was 'Not too soon and please not too late.'

After my discharge, I and other cancer patients had to attend every day for five to six weeks for radium treatment from a Cobalt 60 theratron machine. Capital expenditure cost was about half a million pounds and there are not many of these machines in London and the South-East. I began with an exposure of eight minutes which gradually mounted to about twenty-five minutes. I can only describe this machine by saying that as you went into the theratron room you walked past a control panel which looked like what I imagine might resemble the control panel of the Concorde cockpit. After that, you lie almost naked on a machine and you are raised and lowered and this machine beams at you from various angles radium at a cost, so I am told, of about £10 per minute. I had in all about seventeen hours. In addition, while one was on the machine, the National Health Service kindly supplied piped music free of charge in order to help patients relax.

Now, as you will have gathered from what I have said, I was extraordinarily lucky. It was a marvellous ward, staffed by some very interesting people looking after an extraordinary interesting and diverse cross-section of the British public drawn from south-east London—south-east England in fact. If all wards in all the hospitals all over the country were anywhere near the standard of this ward at the Westminster we should have very little to complain about in evaluating standards of performance of the National Health Service. But you know, as well as I know, that not all wards are like the ward that I was in.

When I went in on that Saturday afternoon I took with me John Rawls' book, *A Theory of Justice,* which I think is one of the most important books published in the field of social philosophy for the last twenty-five years. I took that with me and I took with me an advance copy of the present Government's Green Paper on Tax Credits, and I also took a bottle of whisky. Anyway, I can tell you that while I was there I didn't get very far with *A Theory of Justice;* there wasn't time, there was too much to do, there were too many people to talk to; one had to help—one liked to help—with the tea trolley at 6 o'clock in the morning, when all the mobile patients served the immobile patients, and one shuffled around not caring what one looked like and learning a great deal about other human beings and their predicaments. But I did read the Green Paper on Tax Credits and, I don't suppose it happens very often, I did write a letter to the Editor of *The Times* from the Westminster Hospital—he didn't know it came from the hospital because I signed it from my home— about the Green Paper because I thought then, indeed I still think, that the proposals, rough as they are, have considerable potentialities for extending some of the benefits of the welfare state from the middle classes downwards to the poor.

In some of the things that I have said and in some of the things that I have written in some of my books, I have talked about what I have called 'social growth'. I believe that my experience at the Westminster provides some of the unquantifiable indicators of social growth. These are indicators that cannot be measured, cannot be quantified, but relate to the texture of relationships between human beings. These indicators cannot be calculated. They are not, as my friends the economists tell me, counted in all the Blue Books and in all the publications of the Central Statistical Office. For example, nowhere will you find any explanation or any statement about the expenditures by the National Health Service on my friend Bill and all the other expenditures—public housing, a constant attendance allowance, a daily home help and meals-on-wheels (his wife, aged 52, went blind last year), an invalid chair, special ramps, an adapted lavatory and kitchen, lowered sinks and raised garden beds (provided by the local Parks Department). He was an example, in practice, of what a compassionate society can achieve when a philosophy of social justice and public accountability is translated into a hundred and one detailed acts of imagination and tolerance.

Among all the other experiences I had, another which stands out is that of a young West Indian from Trinidad, aged 25, with cancer of the rectum. His appointment was the same as mine for radium treatment—10 o'clock every day. Sometimes he went into the Theratron Room first; sometimes I did. What determined waiting was quite simply the vagaries of London traffic—not race, religion, colour or class.

INDEX